Dear Readers,

In October 2002, the Institute of Classical Architecture published *A Decade of Art and Architecture 1992–2002* in celebration of the organization's tenth anniversary. It was a milestone celebrating the considerable classical and traditional work that had been created (without much encouragement from the media or the mainstream tastemakers of the period) during the ten years since our first summer school in 1992. That book was also a tribute to those within the organization—our board of directors, the Fellows and their countless volunteer hours, the small but determined staff —who, against all odds, and not without a few bumps, managed to fuel the growth and existence of what had become a singular resource for those interested in contemporary classicism in the United States and abroad.

Since that landmark year, the Institute has been on an even more vigorous course, meeting and even challenging the vivid imaginations of all those who had a vision and passion for the place from the beginning. First, in late 2002, the conglomeration with the venerable Classical America was forged, growing the board of directors, and combining the best of both organizations. A new conjoined name resulted as well, and depending on which camp you stood, was either amusing or irritating or both. Over time, however, it has found its distinctive place. The new board of The Institute of Classical Architecture & Classical America (ICA&CA) wisely and courageously determined that it was time at long last to have a full-time chief executive with, among other management talents, considerable fund-raising experience; in April 2003 Paul Gunther arrived to take the helm. Prior to his arrival, the ICA&CA had just moved to a temporary location at the American Institute of Graphic Arts building and was conducting classes and preparing for the twenty-first Arthur Ross Awards. Since Paul's arrival programming exploded, the formalization of chapters nationwide was codified, and the staff grew and became ever more professional. A permanent new headquarters was created at the General Society building at 20 West 44th Street, providing classroom space and allowing there the advent of the Historic Plaster Casts Collection; and the Arthur Ross Awards burgeoned into an eagerly-anticipated and successful annual event. A semi-annual benefit auction was added to the calendar; the "Classical America Series in Art and Architecture" was galvanized by the energy from the newly reinstated Publications Committee (eight new books published in five years and eight more underway); the Arthur Ross Director of Education position was established and with it, the arrival of Victor Deupi, who with his colleagues at Georgia Tech and Associate Director Michael Gormley, has created a Master of Science in Architecture with a concentration in Classical Design. The Grand Central Academy of Art, the Institute's allied arts educational arm, was realized in September 2007, propelled by the vision of board member and artist Jacob Collins. In its first year, the GCA has surpassed all expectations and serves as an inspiration for all ongoing initiatives.

On the development front, membership has quadrupled since 2002, which means that our readership has grown and that there are an awful lot of you out there, sponsors and readers alike, who have patiently waited for *The Classicist No. 7*. Fortunately for me, it seems that nearly everyone in the world is perpetually running in a 100-yard dash and perhaps hasn't noticed how many years have passed since *The Decade* book was published, but believe me, this publication is long overdue and no one is happier to see it gloriously completed than I. As with all issues of *The Classicist*, our volunteer editorial staff and contributing writers played a vital part and together we cast a wide net to connect with like-minded practitioners, students, educators, and enthusiasts. It is a privilege for me to work so many remarkable, talented, passionate people and to serve as the hub along the classical tradition information highway. The ICA&CA members and supporters are both our readers and the source of our material, and as a benefit of membership, this publication is for you. Our focus for this issue was primarily on the civic realm, and although by no means a comprehensive chronicle, *The Classicist No. 7* brings you a sampling of professional and student work since 2003. I hope it is worth the wait. I can also assent that these important volumes will be created on a more regular basis and I know that along with the ICA&CA's recent growth across all boards, *The Classicist* will remain a central priority.

We urge all readers to follow and encourage this determination in the auspicious year ahead.

In closing, we dedicate this volume to Arthur Ross, champion of excellence and steward of classicism without parallel.

Sincerely,

Henrika Taylor
Managing Director/Managing Editor

THE INSTITUTE OF CLASSICAL ARCHITECTURE & CLASSICAL AMERICA
20 West 44th Street New York, NY 10036
telephone (212) 730-9646 facsimile (212) 730-9649
institute@classicist.org

WWW.CLASSICIST.ORG

EDITORIAL COMMITTEE
Managing Editor:
Henrika Dyck Taylor

Copy Editors:
Laura Fleder
Vani Kannan
Henrika Dyck Taylor

The Rotunda:
Nora Martin
Doug Wright

Professional Portfolio:
Thomas J. McManus
Justin Ford
M. Damian Samora
Laura Shea

Sketchbooks:
Elisa Cuaron

Academic Portfolio:
Elisa Cuaron

Competitions:
Silvia Neri with
Christopher Liberatos

Good Practice:
Peter J. Talty

Allied Arts:
Daron Builta
John Woodrow Kelley

Sponsorship Managers:
Brendan Connelly
Melodie Torres

*Art Director Emeritus
(and all-around resource)*
Seth Joseph Weine

DESIGN BY:
Dyad Communications *design office*
Philadelphia, Pennsylvania

INDEX BY:
Robert Elwood
Bushwood, Maryland

PRINTED BY:
Meridian Printing
East Greenwich, Rhode Island

© 2007 The Institute of Classical
Architecture & Classical America
All rights reserved

ISBN 0-9642601-1-5
ISSN 1076-2922

FRONT COVER: "WILGUS' DREAM" BY ANDRÉ JUNGET. PEN AND INK ON WHITE SCRATCH BOARD.
The artist wishes to acknowledge Kurt Schlichting for his book *Grand Central Terminal: Railroads, Engineering & Architecture in New York City* (Johns Hopkins University Press, 2001) and the introduction to the work of engineer William Wilgus, who was the genius behind the underground terminal at Grand Central Station as well as the vision for the above ground "Terminal City." Thanks also to Richard Cameron for his friendship and the introduction to the ICA&CA; and to Mark Ferguson, Oscar Shamamian, and Jim Tinson for the opportunity of a lifetime; and lastly to Beth Allen and MK. The illustration is dedicated to the memory of Ann M. and Frederick Valentine Junget.

FRONTISPIECE: "ROCKEFELLER CENTER" BY JAMES BLEECKER
Photographer and ICA&CA member James Bleecker is inspired by the visionary charcoal rendering of Hugh Ferris. Although Mr. Bleecker's style evokes the 1930s, his professional niche is in the tradition of the 1920s estate portfolio in which his handmade albums depict houses, gardens, and the lives of the inhabitants. Mr. Bleecker's fine art photographs are represented in New York City by June Bateman Gallery.

BACK COVER:
Proposed cover for *Classical America V* (late 1970s), by Pierce Rice (1916–2003). This painting on Bristol board was to have been the cover for an issue of *Classical America* devoted to the civic architecture of Washington, D.C. *From the collection of Seth Joseph Weine.*

THE CLASSICIST

№ 7: 2005-2007

Essays

Portfolios

Good Practice

The Allied Arts

The Classicist No. 7 is dedicated to
Co-Founder and Honorary Chairman,
Arthur Ross, whose leadership support
and vigilant counsel have set a guiding
standard for The Institute and all those
who together sustain and inform its
educational mission.

———————

1910–2007

Essays

Of Our Time

By Francis Morrone

In the last half-century we have witnessed a revolution in environmental thinking. I do not refer to our increased concern with natural ecosystems, important as that has been. Rather, I speak of what, in a strange piece of language, we call "historic preservation." This movement to preserve grew from many sources. The most fundamental has been a general increase in historical consciousness that is evident across the broad spectrum of thought. Another factor has been the public disillusionment with the unlovely productions of modernist architecture. (Nowadays, of course, many preservationists devote their energies to preserving modernist buildings. But that's a subject for another day.)

Preservation gave rise to a very serious issue. This was not so much the issue of what to preserve. People do argue about that, but consensuses have emerged regarding standards for designation. Rather, the contentious issue concerns what we should do when the occasion arises, as it frequently does, of building additions onto historic buildings, or of building new buildings within "historic districts."

Do we seek to preserve historic buildings as discrete "texts" like books on a library shelf? Or do we seek to preserve the aesthetics of a traditional urbanism that many of our historic buildings were erected in the first place to serve?

The pendulum of standards swings back and forth. At times, the prevailing standard, as administered by preservation boards, has sought the one, then the other. Today, preservation boards tend, as they have at times in the past, to insist that new construction in historic settings differ in appearance from its surroundings, so that the new construction be evidently "of our own time." Sometimes this takes a subtle form based on recondite notions of archaeological authenticity. Take the case of Grand Central Terminal. In the 1990s, the terminal underwent massive renovation and restoration. The architects in charge, Beyer Blinder Belle of New York, learned in the course of their studies of the building that the original architects, Warren & Wetmore, had wished to balance the east and west ends of the Main Concourse with matching monumental stairways. Original drawings attest to this desire. For reasons we can only guess at, the west stairway was built, but not the one on the east. Beyer Blinder Belle felt that the renovation occasioned the final implementation of Warren & Wetmore's plans, rather as Cologne Cathedral had been completed, according to a sense of original intentions, more than three hundred years after work had been suspended on the unfinished building.

Beyer Blinder Belle needed the approval of New York City's Landmarks Preservation Commission in order to add the new stairway. The commission pondered, then rendered a verdict: A new stairway was OK. But it had to be clearly differentiated from the existing stairway. Thus, while the two stairways are compatible in scale and materials (luscious Bottocino marble), the new stairway lacks the elaborate railings and hand-carved stone rail terminations of the original. It is more "contemporary" in the sense of being simpler, thus "of our own time"—our own time being one that is putatively not given to elaborate stone handwork.

Now, this is odd on several counts. First, we are in our time quite capable of the handwork. Yet a defining feature "of our time" seems to be to keep up the pretense that such work is no longer practical or possible. Beyond that, and even more perplexing, is the notion that there is some *archaeological* value in making the new stairway different. In other words, the Landmarks Preservation Commission does not want any viewer of the stairway to be "fooled" by what one writer calls "faked historic material." That's perplexing for at least two reasons. First, it begs the question: How can any "historic material" be "faked"? Any material, no matter how it is worked, is "historic," in the sense that it is something done in a specific time and specific place for a specific purpose, even if that purpose is to "fool" people into thinking that something made in 1998 had been made in 1913. I will in a moment examine the basic misapprehension of history that informs this way of thinking. But for now we may ask, simply, why the dating must be made apparent in the thing itself, as opposed to being explained in, say, *words*. Those who are in any measure concerned about such things will likely seek out verbal information, whether it be a book, an article, a landmarks report, or a railroad brochure, any or all of which might explain the history, such as a European guidebook or tour guide will tell us which parts of a cathedral were built in which century.[1]

This is par for the course, and may be not worth manning the barricades over. Much more disconcerting things lurk out there. Like "parabuildings."

Take Soldier Field—please! Designed by the estimable Holabird & Roche and built in 1922, this was our noblest football stadium. *Was.* The City of Chicago felt pressured to expand and upgrade the stadium, lest the city's beloved Bears make good on their threat to move to the suburbs. The city hired the firm of Wood & Zapata to undertake the expansion job. The architects responded, not with what we ordinarily think of as an expansion, but with that *très chic* thing called a "parabuilding." What's a parabuilding? It is an addition to an old building that

essentially creates a new building that may engulf the old, an addition not appended to but rather that covers or otherwise sticks out like a sore thumb from the original. The ethos is one of disjuncture, premised on the value presumed inherent in making a radical break with the past. But the break is made more expressive than if the old structure were to be altogether replaced. It is, in fact a deliberate defacement.

Once, the prevailing ethos in preservation was that of continuity with the past. In 1966, New York's mayor, Robert F. Wagner, got tired of the ceremonial intrusions upon his family's quarters in the then official mayor's residence, Gracie Mansion, a turn-of-the-nineteenth-century country house on the Upper East Side of Manhattan. So the city built a new wing onto Gracie Mansion. The architect entrusted with the tricky job was Mott B. Schmidt, whose career went back to the teens of the last century. It was an inspired choice, for Schmidt could be counted upon to understand and respect the Federal-period architecture of the house. Schmidt added a neo-Federal wing that did not ape the original but was thoroughly compatible with it—that, indeed, excelled the original, considered solely from the standpoint of architectural quality. It worked. But because it is hard for most to tell that the new wing might not have been built around the same time as the original, Schmidt's work would likely not pass muster with many preservationists or architecture critics today. Today, preservation boards approve such stuff as, in New York, the Polshek Partnership's new front on the Brooklyn Museum, or Sir Norman Foster's tower atop the Hearst Magazine Building, or Davis Brody Bond's western addition to McKim, Mead & White's Harvard Club. Or, in Chicago, Wood & Zapata's parabuilding over Soldier Field.

The parabuilding has so utterly overwhelmed, without dismantling, the stately colonnades of the old stadium that one may reasonably infer that the only reason the original wasn't dismantled was so that it may be more thoroughly and aggressively disrespected.

GRACIE MANSION, SUSAN B. WAGNER WING (*top*): The Archibald Gracie house is the last of the surviving East River country houses from the eighteenth and early-nineteenth centuries in Manhattan. From Fiorello La Guardia in the 1940s to Rudolph Giuliani in the 1990s, it served as New York's official mayoral residence, and is still used for important civic functions. In 1965–66, Mayor Robert F. Wagner and his family got tired of the ceremonial intrusions upon their private space, and had a new wing built to serve such functions. The city retained the architect Mott B. Schmidt, who worked with John Barrington Bayley in crafting a magnificent solution. The addition is in a New England Federal style that in no way apes the original building yet is perfectly harmonious with it. It may serve as a model for all additions to historic structures. *Photograph courtesy of Gracie Mansion.*

THE JEWISH MUSEUM (*bottom*): The former Felix Warburg mansion, designed by C.P.H. Gilbert and built in 1907–09, is located at Fifth Avenue and 92nd Street in Manhattan. The châteauesque building is one of the great Gilded Age private houses still standing in New York, and is a designated New York City landmark. Now the home of the Jewish Museum, it was expanded to the north in 1990–93 by the well-known modernist firm of Kevin Roche John Dinkeloo & Associates. In an uncharacteristic turn for this firm, they chose to replicate as exactly as possible the original mansion. We may question whether this was precisely the way to go—after all, if C.P.H. Gilbert had been asked to design a house twice as large, would he not have come up with a substantially different design? Nonetheless, the exacting replication marked the perhaps most extreme case in New York of additions designed in the manner of the original. *Photograph © Peter Aaron/Esto. All rights reserved.*

But even where parabuildings aren't the case, and changes are more subtle, as at Grand Central Terminal, we see that the prevailing ethos consists in the promotion of additions—or, in archi-speak, "interventions"—that are "of our own time." And this is an issue that bedevils all practitioners of traditional architecture.

As I said earlier, anything that *is* done in our time is, ipso facto, *of* our time. It cannot be otherwise. To maintain otherwise involves a grave error. The error is that of regarding history as something that exists outside of human agency. In the nineteenth century, the Romantic movement, the increase of democracy and nationalism, and biological theories of evolution all contributed to the rise of a historical consciousness quite different from anything that had existed before. Hegel, for example, made history central to his systematic philosophy, while some post-Hegelian philosophers suggested that historical consciousness obviated systematic philosophy. For many people, Darwin's and other biological ideas inspired a tendency to study all phenomena genetically. Thus, Geoffrey Scott, in *The Architecture of Humanism*, which remains for me the best philosophical discussion of architecture, enumerated several fallacies in the conventional thinking about architecture in his time. One of these he labeled the "biological fallacy."[2] According to those who adopt this fallacy, architecture evolves. I prefer the term "historicist fallacy," by which we mean that architecture "progresses." "Historicism" is the belief that each period or age of history has an essence all its own and that the artist and architect must seek or tease out that essence in works that are markedly distinct from those of all other periods or ages. (Please note that this philosophically correct use of *historicism* differs from the term's common misuse to mean architecture that derives from "period styles."[3])

All of this made of history a putatively objective entity. The scientific tendency ascribed immutable "laws" to history, which thus was seen to function according to its own imperatives and exigencies. History became something not that results from people's actions, but that exists according to its own purposes that may or may not be

SOLDIER FIELD *(top):* Chicago once boasted of America's noblest football stadium, Soldier Field, designed by Holabird & Roche and built in 1922–26. Its magnificent colonnade was once one of the most visible sights along that city's glorious lakefront. When the city felt forced to expand the stadium so as to include more "luxury boxes" and the like, the architects Wood & Zapata responded with a "parabuilding" that arrogantly obscures, indeed defiles, the original so as to make us think it would have been preferable to demolish the original rather than to disrespect it in this way. *Photograph courtesy of Francis Morrone.*

THE HARVARD CLUB *(bottom):* On Manhattan's West 44th Street (directly across the street from ICA&CA headquarters, as it happens) stands the Harvard Club, one of Charles Follen McKim's excellent essays in the neo-Georgian. The clubhouse was built in 1894, then twice expanded by McKim, Mead & White, in the same style, in 1905 and 1915. Recently, the clubhouse was expanded again, to the west, by the architects Davis Brody Bond, a prominent New York modernist firm. This addition is an aggressively disjunctive modernist appendage to the neo-Georgian complex. The addition was designed as such in part on the presumption that only such a disjunctive design would pass muster with the Landmarks Preservation Commission. From the Jewish Museum to the Harvard Club we see a remarkable, and deeply sad, sea change in the philosophy of adding to historic buildings. *Photograph courtesy of Richard Cameron.*

acknowledged by individuals. Those who fail to acknowledge the historical imperative "opt out of history." This is a view that we see in politics, as when Spain's Prime Minister Zapatero recently attacked the Catholic Church for not being "on the side of history." And we often speak this way in our everyday lives when we say that someone is "behind the times"—a locution that I cannot imagine anyone used before the 19th century.

Few classical architects of today seek to recreate buildings from the past. The architects I know and admire seek to create new, sometimes even novel, works in an idiom continuous with that of the past. But what if an architect *did* seek to make an exact copy of a building from the past? We may justly criticize such a thing, perhaps on the grounds that we don't *need* another Parthenon or Pantheon, or that the particular situation may warrant a novel design, and so on. But these criticisms concern such matters as conserving resources, or adapting to environmental conditions. The criticisms do not suggest that the copyist has "opted out of history." For the urge to copy in itself may help to define a moment in history. This is so self-evidently the case that one wonders that establishment thought holds otherwise.[4]

Most of us would agree that progress is an enormously useful concept in many areas of human endeavor. I think even those of a conservative temperament, who believe that most improvements in the conditions of life are paid for with corresponding deteriorations, nonetheless would not deny that the isolation of insulin, or the invention of means of fireproofing iron, or the discovery that drinking sewage-contaminated water causes cholera, have in fundamental ways marked movements forward from old ways of thinking. But is it then incumbent upon us that we analogize from this and presume that in human endeavors in which material forward movement does not exist that there must nonetheless be forward movement of a sort? Such an endeavor is art. We hear architecture critics all the time bemoaning the lack of "progressive architecture" in our cities. A recent architecture critic for *The New York Times* even said, amid the patriotic swirl of the weeks following 9/11, that our American patriotism would have more resonance and meaning if our urban environments were more "progressive." In the fall of 2004, another architecture critic, one whom I greatly respect, said that though our politics may be drifting rightward, she was pleased to report that the new architecture in her city's downtown was "progressive."

History, in such views of progressive architecture, does not flow from human agency, but rather is something that human agency must seek to divine in the impersonal forces of the time. But how do we know what history mandates? The answer is that we do not know, and cannot know. The belief that we can is a reliable blueprint for despotism.

In the 1980s, many architects, dismayed by modernist architecture, sought to broaden, under the rubric of "post-modernism," the vocabulary with which buildings could be designed. One strand of post-modernism was deeply affected by notions of traditional urbanism, and decided that new buildings should fit in with their historic contexts. Preservation boards agreed. When the Jewish Museum on Fifth Avenue in New York decided to expand its building, they hired the classic

modernist firm of Kevin Roche John Dinkeloo & Associates, most famous for their Miesian Ford Foundation on 42nd Street. The museum was housed in the former mansion of the financier Felix Warburg, which had been designed by the École des Beaux-Arts-trained C.P.H. Gilbert, who gave us several of the outstanding private houses of New York's Gilded Age. The Roche firm chose—as it would not have done ten years earlier or ten years later—to replicate the original's façade in their addition. We may argue about the wisdom of doing this. After all, if Gilbert had had to design a much larger house, he probably would have come up with a very different design. Responses today are mixed. Recently, I heard one of New York's landmarks commissioners assert that the addition should have included some elements to establish that it had not been built at the same time as the original.

I agree. The date should be incised in the cornerstone. ✦

Francis Morrone is an architecture critic, literary historian, lecturer, and teacher. His five books include An Architectural Guidebook to Brooklyn, *and his column "Abroad in New York" appears every Friday in the* New York Sun. *He is a Fellow of the ICA&CA, serves as the Advocacy Committee Chairman, edits the Institute's blog, and somehow finds time to teach the Institute's Architectural Literacy course. He can be contacted at fm27@nyu.edu.*

Endnotes

1. It may be worth pointing out in this context that Warren & Wetmore sought in their original design to "fool" the spectator. The principal interior wall-covering of Grand Central Terminal is molded plaster that aids the "deception" that the vaulted ceiling of the Main Concourse is supported by massive stone piers rather than by the internal steel supports that actually do the work.

2. Geoffrey Scott, *The Architecture of Humanism: A Study in the History of Taste.* (1914; New York: W.W. Norton & Company, 1999), See ch. 6.

3. Karl Raimund Popper, *The Poverty of Historicism* (1957; New York: Harper & Row, 1964).

4. In 1897, the city of Nashville, Tennessee, held a Centennial Exposition, the centerpiece of which was a temporary replica of the Parthenon. When the exposition ended, many Tennesseans did not want to let go of the replica. As a result, the city of Nashville chose, in 1920, to reconstruct the building in permanent materials, and reopened it to the public, as a museum, in 1931. One may criticize this reproduction on several grounds. But does not a desire for the reproduction of an ancient monument tell us as much about the Tennessean *zeitgeist* as if they had chosen to build in the style of Walter Gropius's Bauhaus?

Urban Echoes: Listening to the Lessons of Rome

Written and Illustrated by David Mayernik

PRELUDE

raditional urban design today has focused almost solely on recovering the formal and functional patterns of the traditional town. As valuable as this approach is for re-establishing a humane civic realm where *res publica* and *res privata* interact in a balanced, harmonious urban fabric, it is insufficient to create a true renaissance of the complex intellectual and cultural fabric of the great Western cities. Only by addressing the City as a complete work of art, one invested not only with classical form but with humanistic meaning, can we credibly claim to be engaged in the building of an urban legacy as rich as our urban heritage. Two major intellectual impediments stand in the way of recovering this meaningful approach to urban form-making: one, a rarely-questioned supposition on the part of most architects that meaning is grafted onto form in the design process, post-dating the architectural idea, and two, the notion that any consensus on meaning in the public realm is well nigh impossible today, given the diversity of our urban populations. I hope to show, first, that meaning in the work of the greatest architects and urbanists of the past was literally fundamental to their conceptual process, and second, that the strategies outlined here are possible anywhere that civic and cultural institutions operate with some degree of consensus.[1]

Rome, and the two churches (Saint Peter's and San Giovanni in Laterano) that anchored her most important civic procession (known as the *Possesso*), will serve as metaphors for the layers of thought that informed the creation of the humanistic urban architecture of the Renaissance. The danger in using Rome as an example is, of course, its exceptional quality. But as Edgar Wind said about the study of Renaissance emblems, "[I]t seems to be a lesson of history that the commonplace may be understood as a reduction of the exceptional, but that the exceptional cannot be understood by amplifying the commonplace."[2] Engaging Rome as architects, therefore, is proof that we mean to embark on a true renaissance, and I will answer the historical Renaissance themes presented here with responses that address contemporary urban problems.

REVERBERATIONS

Rome's seven great pilgrimage churches are scattered inside and outside the Aurelianic walls; the circumstances which gave birth to them, and which influenced their physical relationship to the city, are varied.[3] The twin foci of this essay, the Vatican and the Lateran, are at opposite ends of the city; and the reasons for their importance and position are crucial for understanding their impact on the physical structure of Rome. But their distance from each other did not preclude the development of a complex formal and symbolic relationship between them, and indeed their echoes across the city are metaphors for the ways in which humanist culture understood the connections that a reasonably informed spectator would make.[4]

St. Peter's was founded by Constantine on the presumed site of the apostle's tomb; that the site is a credible one is attested by recent excavations, which show a tomb below the crossing, venerated at least since the early second century. The fourth century basilica, which survived until Bramante's rebuilding in the early sixteenth century, was oriented toward Rome's center, with its façade to the east. The Renaissance rebuilding of the basilica respected both the orientation and crossing location of the earlier structure;[5] and while the project changed over the course of the sixteenth century as architects came and went (from centrally planned to basilican to centrally planned to basilican again),[6] the fundamentals of its position and *raison d'être* mostly did not.[7] So, when Carlo Maderno came to design the nave and the eventual façade in the early seventeenth century, he must have recognized the return, in plan at least, to something like the ancient basilican form that the new church had replaced. And he would have understood that a connection had been re-established thereby with the cathedral of San Giovanni in Laterano across the city, which still retained much of its ancient form. The Lateran basilica was one of two founded by Constantine within the city walls. (The Vatican, we should remember, was outside the walls.) Much medieval lore had grown up around the basilica and the name of its location,[8] but Renaissance humanists had a fairly solid idea that the roots of the building were on land controlled by Constantine—thus the Emperor's deliberateness in building here and at nearby S. Croce in Gerusalemme, and his reluctance to build other churches elsewhere within the walls.

San Giovanni in Laterano, as the cathedral of Rome, is the home of the bishop who is the pope, and it functioned as such until the popes returned definitively from Avignon in the fifteenth century to their current home at St. Peter's. Like the Vatican basilica, the orientation of the front entrance here is eastward, ignoring in this case the direction of the city both in antiquity and in the Renaissance. However, the position of the baptistery, the pilgrims' hospital, and the bishop's palace on the western, city side of the building, indicates a tacit acknowledgment of the direction from which the crowds came. San Giovanni had, therefore, from its inception a complex double orientation, and if anything it is the approach from the west toward the north transept doors that counted most in people's minds for centuries.

These two poles of papal authority—the Lateran basilica given to the Church by Constantine as home for the bishop of Rome and the Vatican basilica set over the tomb of the first pope—gave rise to an intricate, dynamic relationship across the city, one exploited most explicitly by the procession known as the *Possesso*, which marked the election of every pope since Leo III in 795.[9] The *Possesso*, literally the pope's taking possession of the Lateran after his election (and of his simultaneously secular and sacred authorities), stitched a city back together that had become dramatically shrunken and fragmented with the Roman empire's wane [FIGURE 1]. By the fifteenth century San Giovanni was found in the hinterlands within the Aurelianic walls, with St. Peter's ostensibly outside the walls but adjacent to the

Figure 1: POSSESSO ROUTE. Based on G. B. Nolli's map of 1748, pen and ink drawing, 1994. The spine of the Renaissance processional route extends from the Vatican across the Tiber River, through the *abitato* to the Capitoline and the Forum, onto the Colosseum and finally to the Lateran. Significant projects that heralded the Renaissance began to be built along the route starting in the fifteenth century.

SAN PIETRO IN VATICANO

A.

B.

C.

D.

E.

F.

G.

H.

SAN GIOVANNI IN LATERANO

remaining inhabited urban area known as the *abitato*. The structure of the city fabric along the *Possesso* route is an important topic, but our concern here is the way in which the route's beginning (St. Peter's) and end (San Giovanni in Laterano) continually referenced each other architecturally and urbanistically, establishing powerful mnemonic connections for regular pilgrims in lieu of the exceptional event that was the *Possesso*. The processional route serves for our purposes therefore as an ephemeral and yet explicit linking up of these two important landmarks: it is a bridge across the intervening Roman landscape.

Pope Paul V Borghese resolved to complete the nave and façade of St. Peter's in 1606. Maderno, his architect, was no doubt aware of the challenges the façade presented as he began designing the nave. The issues he had to confront included the imposing width of the basilica, the unusually high side aisles, and the fact that the view of the dome would be irretrievably lost because of the length and height of the nave.

Maderno's first solution, which consisted of seven bays and corresponded to the width of the nave and side aisles, was expanded under papal pressure to include two additional bays that would support bell towers;[10] thus the façade not only spanned the width of the basilica itself but also the passage to the south side of the church and was linked to the northern stair (later to be Bernini's Scala Regia) to the Vatican palace. The papal solution therefore exacerbated the problems of width. Without a central crowning focus (in deference to what was left of the view of the dome), Maderno had to be content with some sort of flanking tower arrangement: not only would this have given the long façade compositional termini, but it would have recalled the two towers that crowned the Lateran's northern transept entrance. An echo would have been established, then, back to the venerable cathedral, still the home of

Figure 2: SAN GIOVANNI IN LATERANO AND ST. PETER'S. Composite Veduta, based on Piranesi, watercolor wash, 2004. The primary image is based on Piranesi's view of the approach to the Lateran complex from the Colosseum along the via San Giovanni; the two framed images in the foreground, also based on Piranesi, show the east façades of San Giovanni (left) and St. Peter's (right).

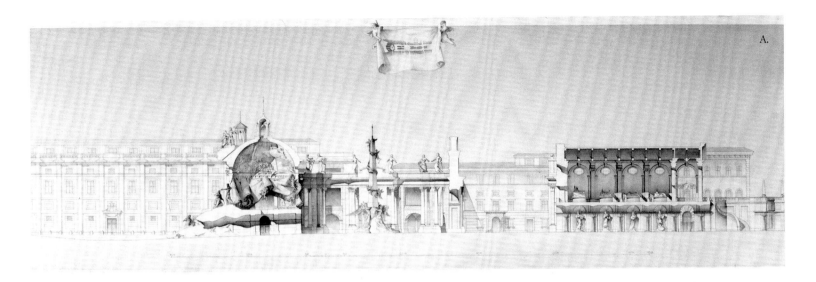

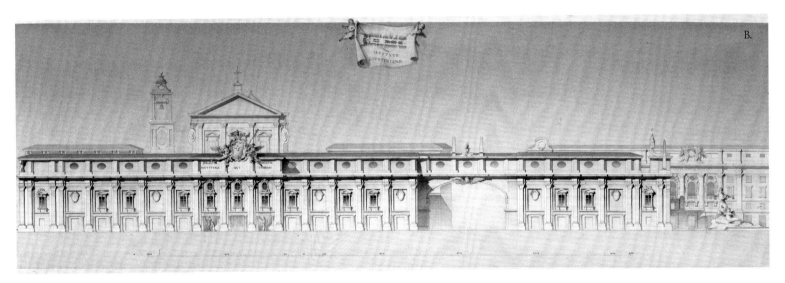

the bishop's chair, and would have reinforced the connection across the city in the mind and memory of pilgrims. It is notable, therefore, that this problematically wide façade, and its towers (built over unstable ground that would ultimately prevent their realization), were imposed on Maderno by the Pope. The motivation was more symbolic than practical[11] and the fact that there is a history of tower designs for St. Peter's that extends back to the project of Antonio da Sangallo and beyond,[12] and forward to Bernini's ultimately disastrous designs, indicates a long-standing interest in the towers' symbolic value in the face of overwhelming practical obstacles.

A redesign of San Giovanni's north transept façade was part of the radical re-structuring of the whole Lateran complex under Pope Sixtus V. Sixtus is best known for the radiating system of streets linking the seven pilgrimage churches (with obelisks as termini), that transformed the map of Rome for pilgrims and residents alike. His energies were just as much directed to architecture as urbanism and, although his work in the two fields was rigorously coordinated, a policy which seems to us

radical and innovative urbanistically was often conservative architecturally insofar as questions of style are concerned. This is not to imply, however, that he was timid. Sixtus' interventions at the Lateran were nothing short of ruthless and perhaps even made sense when that part of the city was still a remote region of the *disabitato* (the uninhabited area within the walls). But by the late nineteenth century, when block after block of apartments were filling in the whole *disabitato* and beyond, the vast open spaces around San Giovanni became loosely-defined voids

Figures 3 and 4: VIA DELLA CONCILIAZIONE. Partial Elevations, A and B (read right to left), watercolor wash, 1989. The project's urban intent is a simple infill of the current over-wide boulevard created by Mussolini's planners. The more important intent of the project is its allegorical function, articulating a transition from an earthly civitas (the Justice Institute in A) toward a celestial one (the Piazza of St. Peter's) by way of a new Audience Hall and gateway (and the Monastic Institute, both in B). The "mixed" façade articulation of the Justice Institute (whose major and minor orders recall the Campidoglio) eventually gives way to the simpler, yet more monumental, colossal order of the gateway.

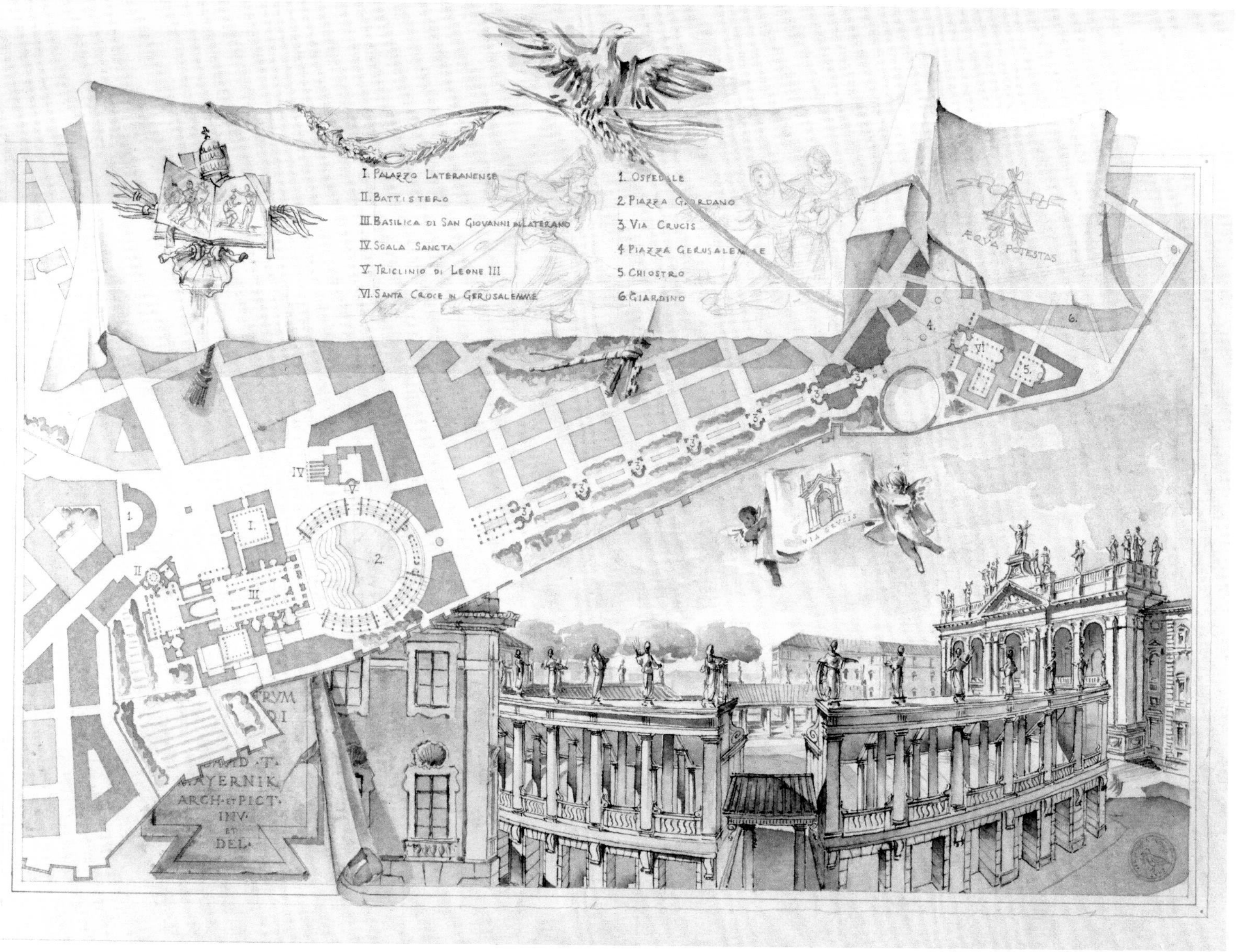

I. PALAZZO LATERANENSE
II. BATTISTERO
III. BASILICA DI SAN GIOVANNI IN LATERANO
IV. SCALA SANCTA
V. TRICLINIO DI LEONE III
VI. SANTA CROCE IN GERUSALEMME

1. OSPEDALE
2. PIAZZA GIORDANO
3. VIA CRUCIS
4. PIAZZA GERUSALEMME
5. CHIOSTRO
6. GIARDINO

in the new fabric, to be filled later (unsurprisingly) by roaring traffic.

Admittedly, the Lateran complex before Sixtus' reign was a sprawl-ing, somewhat dishevelled collection of buildings on uneven terrain that betrayed its "rural" setting. The Pope's Lateran interventions were numerous, and varied: the old fortified Torre degli Anibaldi, already in ruins, was torn down to make room for the obelisk that terminated both the via San Giovanni coming from the Colosseum, and the via Merulana, which connected San Giovanni with S. Maria Maggiore; the large, loosely-organized papal palace that linked the basilica to the Scala Sancta and to the chapel of San Lorenzo was eradicated to make room for Sixtus' architect Domenico Fontana's formidable, compact palazzo block. (The space between the new Papal Palace and the now free-standing Scala Sancta was left undefined.) At the north transept, Sixtus and Fontana left the medieval twin towers visible and added a lower two-story loggia in front, with the upper story used for papal benedic-

tions (as its frieze permanently proclaims). Like the door to the right aisle at St. Peter's, San Giovanni's rightmost door behind the loggia was a Porta Santa, reserved for Holy Years. With the large scale of the piazza, the combined view of towers and loggia was always available to those approaching the church from the north and west. The Lateran

Figure 5: SAN GIOVANNI IN LATERANO. Analytique, ink and watercolor wash, 2000. The project addresses both the urban and symbolic aspects of the site, requiring again an urban and an architectural solution. At the Piazza di San Giovanni (at the basilica's northwest end), the urban space is reshaped and reduced with an extension to the ancient hospital, and the transition from the piazza to the basilica's east front is rede-fined by new fabric buildings. The east piazza (Piazza Giordano) is formed by a lon-gitudinal, oval amphitheater, with urban poche that embeds it in a fabric continuous with the wider context. Between the Lateran and the nearby Constantinian basilica of S. Croce is a series of seven via crucis pavilions in a garden, terminating in a new gateway to a new Piazza S. Croce.

Palace no doubt recalled the earlier Vatican Palace begun by Bramante; but while the Vatican palace's courtyard remained open and "incomplete" in impression, Sixtus' pile was nothing if not complete, an evident improvement on its model. It is worth noting, then, that Sixtus' building efforts presented to visitors a vastly more coherent image than that presented by St. Peter's at the same period in time.

Old St. Peter's, unlike San Giovanni, had been built with an atrium between it and the city. At its inception, church and atrium must have presented visitors with a measured, coherent sequence of impressions. Over time, with accretions to both atrium and basilica, that coherence was lost, exacerbated by the final, century-long rebuilding. Maderno's façade at the very least presented a consistent image of the basilica toward the piazza, counterbalanced by the roughly contemporary clock tower added to the north by Martino Ferrabosco. As for the piazza that replaced the atrium, it had no particular axial relationship to the basilica's façade, despite Fontana having moved the venerable obelisk on axis with it.[13] Annual processions like the Corpus Domini attempted to give structure to the space with temporary canopies that lined the route (beginning at Ferrabosco's tower and returning to the main door of the basilica), but again, they could not permanently resolve the spatial asymmetries. When Bernini was commissioned to design a new piazza for St. Peter's, his design process took into account a complex range of issues, from the aforementioned formal problems with Maderno's façade, to the tradition of a papal blessing from the pope's apartment window in the Palace, the memory of Constantine's atrium, the ephemeral structures of the Corpus Domini procession, and the symbolic baggage attendant upon the ancient structures (like the Colosseum) that provided models for the colonnades. In a single, efficient architectural gesture, Bernini found in the oval plan a *parti* that simultaneously resolved the formal and iconographic challenges, which meant that the final architectural elaboration (the Order of the colonnade, the statues crowning the balustrade, etc.) would only enhance the space's meaning.

An amphitheater is, literally, a double theater.[14] Turning a building type inside out, Bernini employed both the oval plan and the lower external order of the Colosseum to shape the Piazza, a deliberate inversion of that notorious site of early Christian martyrdom. Like Bramante and his design for St. Peter's,[15] Bernini uses the remains of the past as raw material, concurrently absorbing and transforming their significance in the process. The Piazza's pilgrims thus become actors on this urban stage, dynamic participants rather than passive spectators, in a great Theater of the World that links modern and ancient Rome into a continuous web of references.

Bernini was never called upon to similarly re-design the urban space around San Giovanni in Laterano. While the great impresario extended the narrative meaning of his Piazza San Pietro with his ecstatic Cathedra Petri in the basilica's apse, and later wrote its prequel with his redesign of the Ponte Sant' Angelo, the work at San Giovanni

in the late seventeenth and early eighteenth centuries focused on Francesco Borromini's redesign of the nave, and the introduction of monumental sculpted Apostles in his dynamic aedicules. It was Pope Clement XII Corsini,[16] from Florence, who re-engaged an urban aspect of the Lateran basilica by initiating a competition for its ostensibly "front" façade to the east. Filled with intrigue, the competition settled on Clement's fellow Tuscan Alessandro Galilei, whom the pope also commissioned to design his burial chapel just inside the basilica to the left. The brilliance of Galilei's design lay in the way it simultaneously echoed and varied Maderno's façade of St. Peter's [FIGURE 2]. In both façades major and minor orders address the scale of the whole and the scale of the intermediate story; but at San Giovanni the space between the major orders is excavated as a series of powerful voids, giving the work a strong sense of *chiaroscuro*. Maderno's façade instead is an exercise in the plastic articulation of the wall and achieves its effect with a carefully calibrated building up of elements toward the center.

Both façades have attic stories, but Galilei's is a simple (if gargantuan) balustrade, whereas Maderno extends Michelangelo's attic story and introduces windows that cleverly light the corridors behind. San Giovanni's façade is crowned by sculpted figures, including the twin dedicatees of the basilica, Johns the Baptist and the Evangelist, and culminates in a central pedestal sweeping upwards to support a commanding figure of Christ and the cross. Both façades have pediments, but Galilei's is compositionally more pronounced.

All of Galilei's references back to Maderno's precedent at St. Peter's were not esoteric or merely formalist: we are all meant to understand the connections, so that we can understand how and why the two basilicas are connected. Architecture for Renaissance humanist culture had a mnemonic function, and deliberate formal references were rarely made without the intention that those references would be recognized, comprehended, and remembered by more than just connoisseurs. Post-modern strategies of "precedents" and "contextualism" pale by comparison. The meaningful references made by St. Peter's and San Giovanni, and by many other buildings in Rome to each other, build intellectual and iconographic bridges across the city.[17] They transcend the efforts of urbanists because the links make the city a "whole" place in the mind, where many narratives are woven into a dense meta-narrative about the City as the place where we speak most profoundly about ourselves and our highest aspirations.

San Giovanni remains a work in progress, the urban implications of its east front left unresolved, its west front accessible at great peril from Roman traffic; and although Clement XII had begun the process of having an obelisk erected in front of his new façade, the pope's death, followed soon after by the architect's, allowed the project to languish.[18] If the powerful artistic relationships between the two great basilicas' façades are evident to anyone with the stamina to walk from one to the other in the span of a day, and if those relationships were set

David Mayernik · Veduta verso S. Croce in Gerusalemme · Inv. et Del. MMIV

RESONANCES

Historians remain undecided as to Bernini's intentions for the streets leading to St. Peter's, but Mussolini's excavation of the vast via della Conciliazione out of the dense fabric that had been the Borgo Leonino was certainly not what the great artist had in mind. The project to infill the current street not only re-establishes the scale of the two streets that once had led into the Piazza San Pietro; it takes the opportunity to create a string of new buildings to develop an iconographic and functional program that articulates a transition from the earthly city to a terrestrial paradise [FIGURES 3 and 4]. This measured approach to the basilica, which begins in fact at the Ponte Sant' Angelo, also incorporates a dramatic gateway to the Piazza, heightening the effect of moving from dark, urban streets into the light-filled "amphitheater," while investing that threshold moment with allegorical significance. (The gate, under a new audience hall, is not unlike a passage through the rock ledges of the Trevi fountain, recalling Christ's charge to Peter, "Tu es Petrus," literally "you are rock.")

At the other end of the *Possesso* route, the project for the Lateran neighborhood addresses both practical problems and iconographic opportunities [FIGURE 5]. Managing vehicular traffic is the most obvious problem, which is accomplished by channeling cars through a better-defined network of streets and *piazze* that both calms and reduces traffic. Re-calibrating the scale of Piazza San Giovanni at the basilica's northwest end, by extending the ancient hospital to the west with a semi-circular wing, not only humanizes the space; it also redefines the boundaries of the piazza, giving it greater coherence. All of this is to improve an already rich assemblage of elements, but at the east front it is an absence of any urban form at all that poses the real challenge. Here, an oval piazza echoes St. Peter's while transforming Bernini's space in several ways: at San Giovanni, the oval is rotated 90° to extend the basilica's axis toward nearby S. Croce; the colonnade that surrounds the piazza is raised above amphitheater seating, making the ancient source more overt and the modern space useful; and the piazza is filled with a shallow pool, alluding to John's baptisms in the Jordan. The "amphitheater" and the nearby Scala Santa are embedded in new urban fabric. From this new Piazza Giordano, a *via crucis* makes the connection to the ancient basilica of S. Croce in Gerusalemme (whose name suggests we are anagogically transported to Jerusalem by means of the relic of the cross and actual soil from the Holy Land kept in the basilica), which also gets a redefined piazza [FIGURE 6]. S. Croce was redesigned not long after Galilei's project for San Giovanni, and the former's convex façade wrapped around an oval atrium fuses aspects of both the Lateran and the Vatican to a dynamic late-Baroque composition, providing an energetic coda to the connections we have made across Rome.

in motion by a desire for reverberations of meaning that would in fact induce the walk, we find ourselves left with an incomplete urban condition at the Lateran, echoed by one at St. Peter's ravaged by modern planning.[19] As exercises, then, in extending the humanistic tradition of the Renaissance, proposing designs for those two sites is a challenge to engage the minds of Maderno, Bernini, and Galilei in a dialogue, as they had done among themselves. That kind of exercise is, perhaps inevitably, destined to remain on paper. But, while much good classical work is being built today, we are certainly not yet afforded the public building opportunities of a Bernini or a Galilei. Paper architecture, therefore, may still be the greatest legacy we leave our successors, at least for a time.

Figure 6: CROCE IN GERUSALEMME. Veduta, watercolor wash, 2004. The view of the basilica (based on Piranesi's) is framed from within the terminal gateway of the via crucis sequence. The gateway is embellished with mosaic copies of Piero della Francesca's Invention of the True Cross frescoes in Arezzo and a mosaic floor map of the Holy Land, reinforcing the anagogical reading of the basilica as being in Jerusalem.

CONCLUSION

With the words of Edgar Wind still echoing in our minds, we should address the problem implied by the religious iconography developed in these two projects. It is certainly not as if those are the only narratives left to us, and that they are left uniquely to Rome. Rather, similar connections have been made elsewhere (in Florence and Venice, of course, but not only in Italy: think of Henry IV's projects throughout Paris, which combine ideal plan geometries with a coherent architectonic style that began to stitch the city together centuries before Haussman's boulevards), and they can still be made between significant urban events in any sphere of human activity—wherever there is a consensus on principles and purpose. Libraries and law courts, town halls and history centers, museums and art academies can make meaningful connections that reinforce not only the fabric of the city but the fabric of our culture. The formal strategies of traditional urbanism are not enough to achieve this; an articulate architecture is essential to creating an articulate urban landscape. As long as we recognize that the classical language of architecture is a rhetorical means, not an aesthetic end, we have the chance to project an urban legacy as rich as our cultural inheritance. ❧

David Mayernik is an Associate Professor at Notre Dame's School of Architecture. While he is sometimes a paper architect, his firm David Mayernik Ltd. also builds bricks and mortar projects, like those for the TASIS schools in Switzerland and England, which articulate his interest in a meaningful classicism. He is, at the same time, a painter working in oil, watercolor, and buon fresco, and a writer whose book Timeless Cities: An Architect's Reflections on Renaissance Italy *(Westview Press, Icon Editions, 2003) extends the themes of this essay. He is a fellow of the American Academy in Rome and is a 2005 recipient of Traditional Building's Palladio Award for his Library at TASIS.*

Endnotes

1. On the second point, my contention is that civic and cultural institutions must, *per force*, assume a degree of consensus if they are to function at all—but the consensus need not be the same as, nor look exactly like those of seventeenth-century Rome.
2. Edgar Wind, *Pagan Mysteries in the Renaissance*, New York, W. W. Norton & Co., 1968, p. 238.
3. It is a curious accident of history that none of the basilicas within the walls are oriented canonically with their altars toward the east, a fact that gives liturgists fodder for debates even today (not to mention that, at St. Peter's, the altar has always been at the crossing and oriented toward the congregation).
4. Regarding those connections in the arts, see John Shearman, *Only Connect . . . : Art and the Spectator in the Italian Renaissance*, Princeton, 1992. In this case, a "reasonably informed specatator" would include most pilgrims.
5. No doubt the sixteenth-century builders came across the tomb around which so many others were clustered and carefully built over it.
6. Christoph Luitpold Frommel, "St. Peter's: The Early History," in Henry A. Millon, ed. *The Renaissance, From Brunelleschi to Michelangelo*, Rizzoli, 1994, pp. 399–423.
7. Apart from Bramante's short-lived proposal to reorient the church toward the south, where the obelisk then stood; Charles L. Stinger, *The Renaissance in Rome*, Indiana University Press, 1985, p. 185.
8. "The ancients conceived their cities in the shape of wild beasts, each according to the peculiar significance of its attributes. Wherefore Rome has the form of a lion, because it prevails over other animals like a king. Its head is the city constructed by Romulus and its flanks the buildings placed on either side. Whence it is also called the Lateran . . ." From the early twelfth century *Imago Mundi*, transl. Philip Jacks, *The Antiquarian and the Myth of Antiquity: The Origins of Rome in Renaissance Thought*, Cambridge University Press, 1993, p. 54.
9. It is the same Leo's *Triclinium* (built as a meeting and banqueting hall), the remaining apse of which provides one of the most significant landmarks at the Lateran.
10. Sarah McPhee, *Bernini and the Bell Towers: Architecture and Politics at the Vatican*, Yale University Press, 2002, pp. 5–35.
11. Ibid, pp. 205–206.
12. Ibid, pp. 191–193.
13. Tod Marder, *Bernini's Scala Regia at the Vatican Palace*, Cambridge University Press, 1997, pp. 59–63.
14. Bernini staged a famous play that had an audience in a seating circle watch an actor who revealed backstage a mirror-image theater populated by another audience watching another actor. The conceit of blurring actor and audience implicit in an amphitheater breaks down the boundary between art and spectator and is exploited, with many layers of additional meaning, at St. Peter's, where the columns adopt figurative meaning from the "audience" of sculpted saints and martyrs that crown them.
15. David Mayernik, *Timeless Cities: An Architect's Reflections on Renaissance Italy*, Westview Press (Icon Editions), 2003, pp. 47–51.
16. Reigned 1730–40.
17. The formal similarities between the Lateran's east façade and the south façade added by Ferdinando Fuga to Santa Maria Maggiore must have been intentional, conditioned by the fact that these two churches were linked by the via Merulana; Piranesi includes St. Peter's, S. Maria Maggiore, and Santa Croce in Gerusalemme in his views that frame the bottom of G. B. Nolli's so-called small map of Rome.
18. The obelisk was eventually erected at the top of the Spanish Steps in front of the church of SS. Trinità dei Monti; Malcolm Campbell, ed. *Piranesi: Rome Recorded*, American Academy in Rome, 1990, p. 46; see also John Pinto, "Architecture and Urbanism," in E. P. Bowron and J. J. Rishel, eds., *Art in Rome in the Eighteenth Century*, 2000, p. 115.
19. Following the treaty (*conciliazione*) that finally, and "formally," separated the Vatican state from the city of Rome (at the edge of the Piazza of St. Peter's) Mussolini's planners began demolishing the *Spina*, or blocks of buildings between the two venerable streets that led through the Borgo Leonino toward St. Peter's, in order to create the current via della Conciliazione.

The Classicism of the Transect

By D.V. Marcantonio

After coming to the realization about a quarter century ago that the current system of zoning codes could not simply be tweaked to allow for classical urbanism, Andrés Duany and Elizabeth Plater-Zyberk went in search of a way to replace the system entirely. They finally found inspiration in a nineteenth-century invention called a "Transect," a drawing used to analyze the ecology of a place. It depicts a cross-section of a large geographic region and its component sequence of relatively discrete environments, each a complex of mutually dependent plant and animal species [FIGURE 1]. Duany and Plater-Zyberk had the insight to add the human habitat onto this diagram. Thus, the Urban Transect was born, and it has already proven useful for the design and coding of towns which are more civilly laid out than the mono-functionally zoned pseudo-cities that currently dominate the landscape. Even though much progress has been made through the use of the Urban Transect, it has yet to realize its full potential in aiding a recovery of the classical city, one more deeply rooted in the Western intellectual tradition.

The Urban Transect describes a continuum from untouched wilderness to the densest urban condition, and it divides that continuum into a manageable number of categories [FIGURE 2]. The city, according to this model, is no longer carved up into mono-functional zones as it is with modernist codes in place today. Instead, each Transect zone is comprised of a complex of uses that all depend on one another to flourish, just as in nature.

Toward T6 in the Urban Transect (everything from the marketplace to the courthouse) the interdependence is generally between human beings, whereas toward the rural T2 zone, plants and animals obviously figure more prominently. Each zone, from T6 to T2, contains a range of activities appropriate to its place in the Transect. Additionally, each Transect zone comprises what Duany calls an "immersive environment," that is, it prescribes a certain coherence with respect to density and massing.

This model gets us closer to the design of beautiful cities than is currently possible. With the help of "build-to lines," which require building façades to meet a prescribed edge, the Transect can bring together a number of buildings on a variety of plots to form larger, more public rooms, i.e., streets and squares. For example, the kind of city depicted in the Nolli plan of Rome [FIGURE 3]—which defines the city as a coherent complex of rooms, be they interiors, streets, or squares—is now theoretically obtainable. Modernist codes on the other hand, which assign an entire zone to a particular activity and enforce set-back lines, do not allow for the public room.

On a more abstract level, the Urban Transect describes a continuum from center to edge. This may seem like an obvious point; however, it is an important one. Thanks to the center/edge distinction, a building's placement in the Transect continuum actually becomes meaningful. Placing a building at the conceptual center of a place (not necessarily the geometric center) quite naturally symbolizes the relative importance of the building, and by extension the institution it houses, to the people who live there.

By nesting a hierarchy of urban types—city, town, village, and hamlet—the diagram also suggests that within the overall center-edge range of a city are a number of smaller center-edge ranges. For example, the Transect zone Urban Core (T6) may describe the conceptual center of a fairly large city. But surrounding T6 are likely to be a number of quarters, each of which has its own center, perhaps at T5 density. And further out might be even more neighborhoods with their own centers at T4 density. Thus, a hamlet is like a neighborhood set in a larger urban context, and a town is like a freestanding urban quarter. The diagram suggests a coherence among a number of urban types of varying size, which are presumably bonded politically (as otherwise there would be little reason for such coherence). The center of a hamlet is relatively less dense than the center of a village, which is also less dense than that of a town, and so on.

A city, then, which is large enough to contain a number of quarters and neighborhoods, will have a principal center and a number of minor centers. At each center the tendency will be to place institutions of importance: major institutions at major centers and minor institutions at minor centers. For example, a courthouse, an institution of major importance, is not likely to be placed in the center of a mere hamlet or neighborhood but rather in the center of a town or city. Likewise, a small public library would make an appropriate civic feature at the center of a hamlet but would be insufficient at the center of a city.

The Urban Transect diagram, with its steady gradation from zero to maximum density, is so seductive that it can obscure the fact that the city has a definite edge. Although we no longer wall our cities to protect ourselves from enemies, we have prescribed boundaries within which other protections such as police protection, fire protection, sanitation, etc., are afforded to citizens. The city that is designed compactly is simply more practical than one that spreads out—it requires less energy, both human and artificial, to build, to maintain, and to inhabit. Surely this energy efficiency is the principal explanation for the compactness of those ancient cities without perimeter walls. And today, with sustainability such a concern, it seems politically feasible to make an argument for building compact cities.

This is not to argue against the existence of the suburb. The argument does imply, however, that the suburb is by definition an edge condition; it cannot be a center. Léon Krier's interpretation of the Transect already suggests the clear edge [FIGURE 4]. Note the sharp distinction between T3 and T4.

So, one might tweak the Urban Transect diagram to reflect these ideas. First we have the nesting property of urban types of varying sizes, each with its own center. Second, we have the idea of boundaries such that the urban fabric communicates the distinction between that which belongs to the city proper, the urban, and that which is outside, the sub-urban and the rural. Finally, all categories of urban type ought to have a transect zone at their centers that can be described as urban. The hamlet, although small by definition, is nevertheless an urban place rather than a free-standing suburb (almost a contradiction in terms). Therefore, one might shift the categories of urban types up a notch, and the modified Urban Transect [FIGURE 5] is the result.

In summary, this Urban Transect diagram contains three distinct yet related principles underpinning Western architecture as it has developed over the past several millennia: the idea of inside and outside, or jurisdiction; the idea of center and edge, or hierarchy; and the idea of the coherence of the various members of a body, whether that

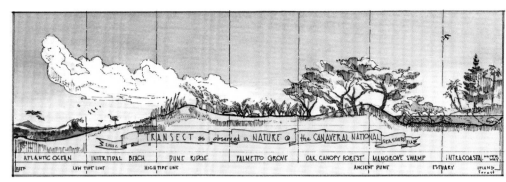

Figure 1: A Natural Transect by James Wassell.

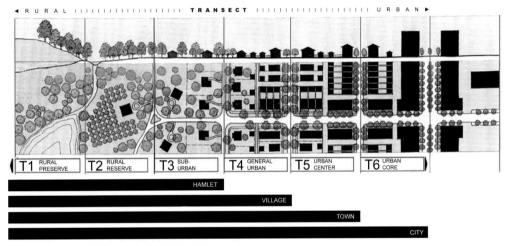

Figure 2: Duany and Plater-Zyberk's Urban Transect diagram.

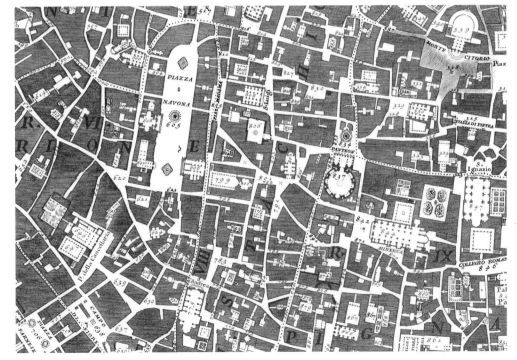

Figure 3: Part of Nolli's Plan of Rome, 1748.

body be a city and its component parts, or a larger political entity (a province, a state, a country, a kingdom, a civilization, etc.), which bonds together a variety of urban types. These three principles can also be taken down in scale to help us understand individual buildings as well. The fifteenth-century scholar Leon Battista Alberti brought the whole canon of Western thought to bear on the subject of architecture in his *Ten Books on Architecture*. His scholarship proved to be vital for laying the groundwork for the Renaissance. Book I, Chapter 9 of his *Ten Books* reiterates:

> *... for if a City, according to the*
> *Opinion of philosophers, be no more than*
> *a great House, and on the other Hand,*
> *a House be a little City ...*

Palladio's Palazzo da Porto Festa in Vicenza is a case in point. First, the inside/outside idea is fairly obvious. Step beyond the threshold of the front portal and you enter the jurisdiction of the head of the house. Second, the center/edge continuum is clear in the plan [FIGURE 6]. One can identify two continua nested one within the other, a public continuum and a private continuum. The more public continuum has at its conceptual center the entrance atrium. Surrounding it are secondary and tertiary rooms that are off the entrance axis and decline in scale, signaling their lesser importance. The spatial sequence eventually leads us to what is the center of the private sphere,

the circular domed room on the piano nobile [FIGURE 7]. And surrounding it are private rooms of secondary and tertiary importance. None of this would be legible, of course, without the presence of the third principle, the coherence of the parts to one another as well as to the whole.

Still more is happening in the palazzo if we look closely—there is another continuum at work in the elevations. If we line up the building's door surround types, we arrive roughly at FIGURE 8. Thus, the architectural details of the palazzo can be analyzed using the same technique used by the Urban Transect because they also exist in a continuum. The diagram shows several things happening at the same time. First, as one proceeds from left to right, from the less important doors to the more important, the architectural ornament becomes more elaborate—from no surround, to a simple architrave, to an architrave with frieze and cornice, to a shouldered architrave, and finally to a pedimented door supported by consoles. Second, sculptural ornament appears at the upper end of the spectrum. And third, there is an increase in scale.

Since these three aspects—amount of architectural ornament, sculptural ornament, and scale—are related, changing as they do in concert with one another to signify relative status, one might group them all together under the general term iconography. The term "iconography" means the representation of something, and in this case, the relative status of the doors is represented.

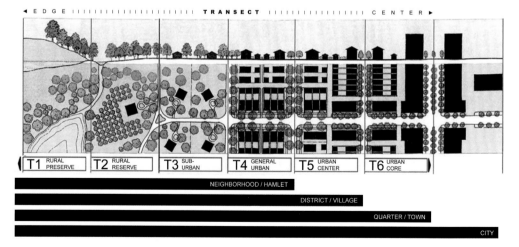

Figure 4: Transect by Léon Krier.

Figure 5: The Urban Transect modified.

Turning back to the city, one can find the same thing happening writ large. If one were to line up all the buildings of a place and select a few representative examples, one might end up with a diagram like FIGURE 9— the more important the building, the grander the architectural scale, the more profuse the architectural ornament, and the more profuse and specific the non-architectural ornament. By "specific" I mean that in high-status buildings the sculpture and painting will represent quite particular things—past governors in a government house, for example, or deities in a pagan temple. In low-status buildings at the level of the Rustic or Vernacular, on the other hand, it would be inappropriate to represent much at all. Other features also have symbolic value, such as quality of construction, rarity of finish materials, and formality.

Clearly, a city is a more complex affair than a house and cannot aim for the degree of coherence that one expects of a house. First, the city is composed of a variety of institutions which will each naturally assert a distinct identity to some degree. Second, the city is built by many different hands over a long period of time. Each architect will contribute to the architectural tradition in his own way; he will have his own ideas regarding the most beautiful forms to employ, and he will be more or less skilled at designing and executing a building than the architects who have preceded him. And third, due to practical and historical considerations, some buildings are not executed as they were intended to be. If buildings that fall short of the ideal stay around long enough, they enter the common vocabulary as they are. Thus, it may be that some less-than-ideal forms are consciously imitated, perhaps by institutions that wish to associate themselves with those institutions that happen to be housed in less-than-ideal buildings. Hence, the Iconographic Transect of a city must speak in terms of an ideal that will always be mitigated by the particular anomalies of a place.

However, the built fabric of the city has as its first priority some sort of coherence. In Book IV of his Ten Books, Alberti asks what can explain the great variety of buildings all about him, and he answers: "This great Variety and Difference among them, are owing principally to the Variety there is among Mankind" (p. 64). By variety

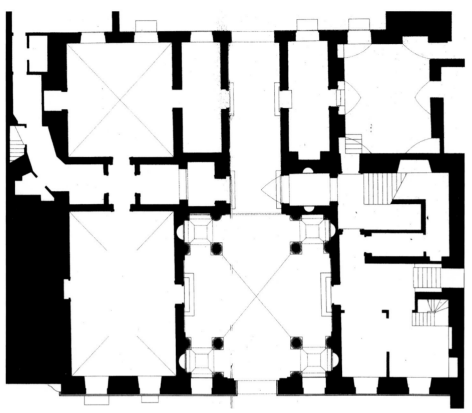

Figure 6: Ground Floor of Palazzo Porto Festa.

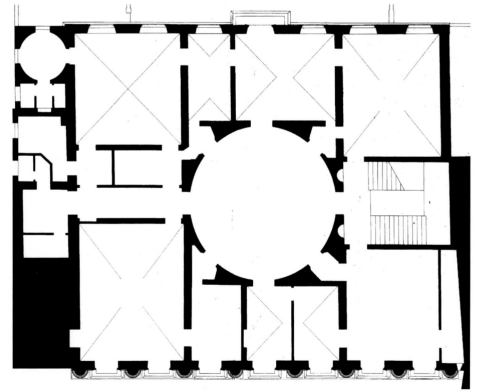

Figure 7: Piano Nobile of Palazzo Porta Festa.

he does not mean a variety of temperments or personalities but rather the offices and institutions that comprise a body politic. He breaks down to a very fine grain the hierarchy of the polity, from the leaders and leading institutions at the top to the commonality at the bottom. If this variety is to be legible architecturally, there must be some means by which the buildings can bear rational comparison.

Alberti returns regularly in his treatise to these two themes: center/edge and high status/low status. In Book V, Chapter 2, regarding center and edge, he states:

> ... Vestibules, Halls, and the like Places of publick reception in Houses, ought to be like Squares and other open Places in Cities; not in a remote private Corner, but in the Center and the most publick Place, where all the other members may readily meet ...

And in Book V, Chapter 6, he writes:

> Of Temples, some are principal, as is that wherein the chief Priest upon stated Seasons celebrates some solemn Rites and Sacrifices: others are under the Guardianship of inferior Priests, as all the Chapels in Town, and

Oratories in the Country. Perhaps the most convenient Situation for the principal Temple may be in the Middle of the City ...

Regarding status, he states in Book I, Chapter 9:

> ... as the Members of the Body are correspondent to each other, so it is fit that one Part should answer to another in a Building; whence we say, that great Edifices require great Members.

And toward the end he offers a summary in Book IX, Chapter 1:

> I think that a sacred Edifice should be adorned in such a Manner, that it should be impossible to add any Thing that can conduce either to Majesty, Beauty, or Wonder: Whereas a private Structure should be so contrived, that it shall be impossible to take any Thing from it, without lessening its Dignity. Other Buildings, that is to say, the Profane of a publick Nature, should observe the Medium between these two Extremes.

Although centrality signifies status by itself (certain important building types, such as the cathedral and the courthouse, naturally demand a central position), both center and edge conditions in a city are comprised of a complex of uses that can be arranged hierarchically. Thus the center/edge continuum (the Urban Transect), and the high status/low status continuum (the Iconographic Transect), operate independently and can be charted together on X and Y axes to produce FIGURE 10.

At the center of a large city, a whole range of institutions may be found, from monuments, courthouses and cathedrals, to schools and townhouses, to humble market stalls. At the center of a small hamlet or neighborhood, one finds a more limited number of high status institutions, perhaps only a small parish church and a high status house. On the edges and outside, one also finds a range, from the historic battle monument to the industrial warehouse.

The city thus conceived—the classical city—is essentially an image of the values held in common by the people who live there.

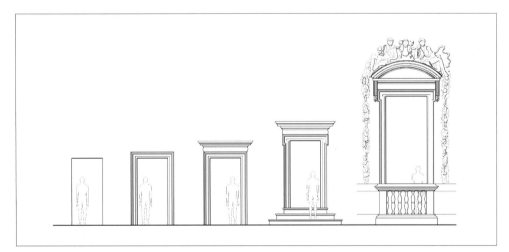

Figure 8: Analysis of Palazzo Porta Festa.

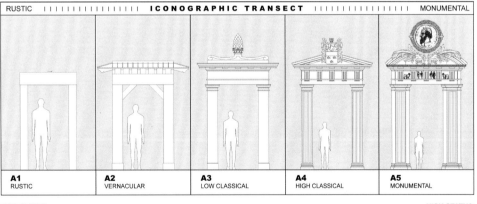

Figure 9: The Iconographic Transect.

As values change the city changes. For example, as the confessional state fell out of favor in the West, church buildings ceased to occupy central sites, and were no longer the most majestic buildings in the city. They were displaced by the courthouse and the legislature. Washington, D.C., whose most important buildings are the Capitol, the White House, and the Supreme Court (in that order), is a case in point.

Because the Urban Transect bears more directly on issues of practical consequence (density of the urban fabric, assignment of uses, etc.) it is better adapted to coding legislation than is the Iconographic Transect. It would be difficult to legislate all matters of scale, amount of iconography, and specificity of iconography. Even if one could code a significant number of iconographic issues, it would be imprudent to do so because one would weaken the constant critique that keeps a tradition healthy: every new building is both a restatement and a critique of the pre-existing canon.

Nevertheless, it must be recognized that the appearance of buildings is already being legislated to some degree. As it stands now, however, that legislation typically uses the language of style. An architectural review board, for example, will ensure that a new building be minimally faithful to the particular forms of a historical style, be it Gothic, Georgian, Federal, etc., but pay little conscious attention to matters of appropriateness and legibility relative to the status and meaning of a building.

Worse, high-status buildings are often treated more leniently for the sake of artistic freedom by the architect. The Transect shows, however, that every building is a part of the larger whole that is the city, and indeed the nation and Western civilization. It makes little sense to code humble middle-class housing strictly for the sake of the coherence of a place, while granting museums license to destroy that coherence.

Even though the Iconographic Transect is in large measure a thing that we must carry around in our heads rather than in law books, a polity may justifiably legislate a few key elements. It may legislate that private buildings may not have a pedimented façade, for example, as was done in Annapolis, Maryland. Or it may require that building

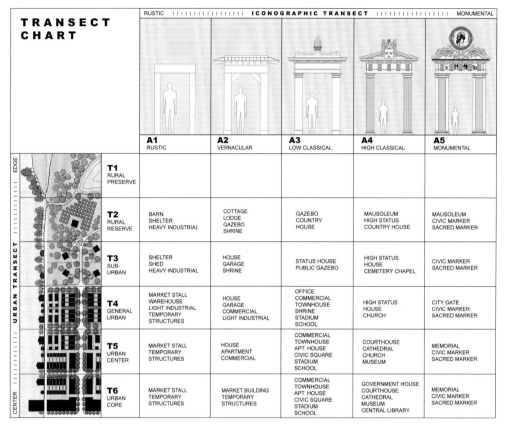

Figure 10: The two Transects charted.

façades that form part of public squares contain certain monumental window types, as was done in Siena's Campo. These types of laws help the architectural intelligibility of a place and give it character; they provide a datum which makes artistic freedom meaningful.

The issue of the social meaningfulness of architecture is at the heart of the Iconographic Transect. Ovid was perhaps the first to put it into words when he described in his *Metamorphoses* (Book 8) how Jupiter and Mercury rewarded the only hospitable people they could find in Phrygia, the poor couple Baucis and Philemon, by transforming their little hut into a temple:

> ... [*Baucis and Philemon*] *saw their home,*
> *so old and little for their simple need—*
> *put on new splendor, and as it increased*
> *it changed into a temple of the gods.*
> *Where first the frame was fashioned of rude*
> *stakes columns of marble glistened, and the*
> *thatch gleamed golden in the sun, and legends*
> *carved, adorned the doors.*

Does this not describe perfectly a transformation from the Rustic to the Monumental?

The Urban Transect and Iconographic Transect have always been a feature of the Western tradition. Only now, in this age of unprecedented incoherence, have we needed to bring it out explicitly. We have so emphasized individual expression in our day, that the cities we have built are little more than a cacophony of monologues, our streets a ragtag collection of babbling façades. It is high time for a call to order—not a fascist order enforced by bayonets, but a civilized order founded on the notion that man is a social animal whose speech is meaningful. ❧

Dino Marcantonio studied English Literature and Philosophy at the University of Toronto, and Architecture at the University of Virginia, and has worked in several high profile offices in Washington, D.C. and New York City. He now lives in Manhattan with his wife Paloma Pajares, and teaches at the Yale School of Architecture.

The Rotunda

I f this issue of *The Classicist* has been guided, however loosely, by a theme of sorts, it was the editors' intention to focus on the built world of the public and civic realm both real and imagined. The preceding essays by Francis Morrone, David Mayernik, and Dino Marcantonio were selected to that end, and so was "The Rotunda" question that was posed to our Council of Advisors, a diverse body of professionals who assist the ICA&CA in a variety of ways based on their area of expertise.

The Rotunda continues a tradition begun in *The Classicist No. 6*, which offered an opportunity for our readers to become familiar with members of the then ICA Advisory Council. Much has happened in the four years since that issue's publication: the ICA published its tenth anniversary book, *A Decade of Art & Architecture: 1992–2002*; the name of the organization evolved into The Institute of Classical Architecture & Classical America (ICA&CA) through the amalgamation with Classical America and alliance with the Council of New Urbanists; and we invited a number of extraordinary individuals to form a new Council of Advisors that would echo the Institute's growing membership, programming initiatives, and mission.

Nine of our Council members responded to our question: "What five things comprise a great urban building or place you have visited, documented, or designed?" Their varied and colorful replies follow below. — NM, DW

Elizabeth Meredith Dowling, AIA
CITIZENS AND SOUTHERN NATIONAL BANK, HEADQUARTERS BUILDING (1929); ATLANTA, GEORGIA, AT MARIETTA AND BROAD STREETS.

1. A great urban building should enhance the experience of both the users and the pedestrians who enjoy the building as a presence in their civic life. The main banking room of the former Citizens and Southern Bank Building (now Bank of America), designed by Philip Trammell Shutze, was conceived as a Renaissance passageway at mid-block. It was customary for many people without banking business to cut through the space simply to enjoy the beautiful architecture.

2. Stimulation of the intellect is essential to urban life. Shutze created complex layers of design references for the C & S National Bank that provide moments of discovery even after years of familiarity.

3. Symbolic ornament enlivens, delights, and creates readable landmarks. The C & S Bank covers half a city block and has three prominent façades. Each face presents a major entrance of stately grandeur.

4. An important urban building must age gracefully and exude the aura of permanence, like a trusted friend. Fortunately, this bank is still in constant use and very much appreciated.

5. A noteworthy building must be made of fine materials that clearly demonstrate that it will stand the test of time. The patina of years only increases the degree to which we admire this fine piece of architecture.

Top: View of the renovation of the first floor of the Citizens and Southern National Bank looking south towards Marietta Street, c. 1930. *Used by permission of Tebbs and Knell, New York, Shutze Collection, Atlanta History Center.*

Bottom: Aerial view of Windsor. *Photograph courtesy of Duany Plater-Zyberk and Co.*

Andrés Duany
THE URBAN TRIAD

From time to time there appears a concept of exceptional longevity. In the field of architecture the pre-eminent instance is Vitruvius' triad of *Firmitas, Utilitas, Venustas.* This Roman epigram was propelled into immortality by Sir Henry Wotton's felicitous translation as Commodity, Firmness, and Delight fifteen centuries later.

Commodity: that a building must be suitable to its intended use. Firmness: that it must creatively engage the natural elements, among them gravity. Delight: that it must satisfy the senses. To architects, with the exception of a tiny, aberrant avant-garde, this formulation remains authoritative.

Urbanism has not been fortified by a conceptual statement of equal power, one having the combination of technique and mystique that supports the Vitruvian Triad: technique, in the sense that the proposition is undoubtedly useful, essential, and supportive of the Law of Parsimony, which states that the best scientific explanation is the simplest one that fits the data. And its mystique is tangible, as Sir Henry's translation retains the superb tripartite equipoise while exchanging the Latin gravitas for English grace.

As I have said, urbanism has not benefited from an equivalent statement. Toward the reinforcement of this bedraggled field, I would propose a comparable paradigm. Consider then, the triad of Function, Disposition, and Configuration as categories that would both describe and test the urban performance of a building or building type.

Function describes the use that the building induces. A first cut may include five subcategories: exclusively residential, primarily residential, primarily commercial, exclusively commercial, and civic. An elaboration would differentiate the functions at the all-important sidewalk level from those above. The ideal of a mixed-use urban building may require no further parsing.

The second element of the triad, Disposition, describes the location of the building relative to its site. This may range from a building placed straight across the frontage of a lot—the streetwall that spatially defines urbanity—to the relatively rural condition of a building freestanding in the center of its lot. Perhaps the easiest way to categorize the Disposition of a building is by describing it through its residual open space: a Rearyard building has the building along the street frontage; a Courtyard building internalizes the space; a Sideyard building is the "zero-lot line"; an Edgeyard building is the freestanding one. This is simple enough and perhaps all we need to know about the urban disposition of buildings.

The third element is Configuration. This describes the height and massing of a building and, if visual harmony is considered a tool of urbanism, then architectural expression too would be included. Buildings could be judged to be contextual in massing and suitable in syntax, with exceptions differentiating the public buildings. Harmony of configuration stealthily enables the diversity essential to urbanism, since the people seem not to mind it so long as the visuals are similar.

How can this triad be useful?

A standardized analytical protocol on the basis of Function, Disposition and Configuration could organize the writing of codes. The intrinsic refinement of this triad could be the means of elevating codes away from the lawyers and bureaucrats that currently coarsen the city. Codes as a field of architectural endeavor should attract the best minds. Perhaps the urban triad will become the common language of codes, simultaneously the most operationally powerful and abstract of the design endeavors.

In the field of criticism, to assess a building based on its architectural expression is of little consequence, as it is ultimately only a matter of personal opinion. But urban criteria, how a building affects a city—and inescapably, the life of its citizens—is a matter of common interest. This simple triad may restore the authority of traditional architecture by inserting it into a rational political discourse.

Miguel Flores-Vianna
Monasterium De Wijngaard Begijnhof
Bruges, Belgium

1. A Sense of Timelessness
The complex of the Monasterium De Wijngaard Begijnhof, comprised of a church, convent, retreat house, and buildings for public housing, creates an atmosphere that is universal and timeless.

2. A Sense of Belonging
Although self-contained and inward looking, the *begijnhof* (walled enclave) buildings form an irregular circumference, managing to blend with and extend the Bruges cityscape.

3. A Sense of History
The begijnhof's organic growth allows for the mutual contrast and enhancement of its gothic, baroque, and neoclassical architectural components.

4. A Sense of Environment
The buildings surround a green, where trees provide natural beauty and recall an ancient forest.

5. A Sense of Beauty
The begijnhof is situated next to a canal populated by swans. There is a constant rustle of trees, and the ever-changing northern sky makes the whole complex a place of serenity, contemplation, and otherworldliness.

Top: Grassy square in Beguinage (Begijnhof). Bruges, Belgium. *Photograph courtesy of Terra Galleria Photography.*

Bottom: Peacock-pattern ironwork graces a soaring tiled arcade-turned-hotel-lobby on the Gresham Palace's ground floor. *Photograph courtesy of the Gresham Palace.*

Eve Kahn
FOUR SEASONS GRESHAM PALACE
BUDAPEST, HUNGARY

1. A SPECTACULAR, CITY-DEFINING LOCATION
The Gresham Palace is located fabulously at the base of the Chain Bridge, the oldest Danube crossing in town.

2. INTERNATIONALIST ORIGINS
Originally built in 1906 as a mixed-use building by the Gresham Life Insurance Company of London, The Gresham hails from Budapest's most cosmopolitan era before the current post-communist spring.

3. INSPIRING, INDIVIDUALISTIC DETAILS
A fine example of Art Nouveau/Secessionist design, the building is enhanced by some of Hungary's finest decorative artistry of the period, which includes glass mosaics on the exterior, a soaring Zsolnay-tiled arcade at the ground floor level, and stained glass portraits of Hungarian heroes in the stairwells.

4. GREAT BONES FOR ADAPTIVE REUSE
Zsigmond Quittner's design features high ceilings and expansive courtyards.

5. STRONG EXISTING PERSONALITY AND HISTORY
Now remodeled and restored with art nouveau revival decor, the Four Seasons Gresham Palace opened in the summer of 2004.

Michael Lykoudis
MEMORIAL TO SUN YAT SEN, NANJING CHINA

1. This memorial, designed by Lu Yanzhi and built 1926–31, fits the criteria of *Firmitas, Utilitas, and Venustas*.

2. It relates to both Chinese and American precedents—traditional Chinese temple architecture, Ming tomb site planning, and the Pan American Building by Paul Cret—making it a building that, while rooted in local culture, aspires to the universality of the human condition.

3. It is symbolic of a culture's quest for a modern national identity.

4. It is a fine example of how a non-western building can be defined by classical character: precision of form and assembly, ornament, proportional relationship of parts, and rhythm of elements.

5. It meshes landscape, architecture, symbolism, and cultural lore into a seamless composition.

Right: Memorial to Sun Yat Sen, Nanjing, China. *Photograph by Michael Lykoudis.*

Witold Rybczynski
THIRTIETH STREET STATION, PHILADELPHIA
GRAHAM, ANDERSON, PROBST & WHITE, ARCHITECTS (1929–33)

1. MONUMENTALITY
A great urban building like Thirtieth Street Station (originally called Pennsylvania Station) should have a commensurate monumental scale. The two porches, supported by colossal columns with stylized Corinthian capitals, act as huge gateways to and from the city. The main concourse, with its 95-foot ceiling, comfortably accommodates the urban mass. It turns travelers and commuters into citizens.

2. WELCOMING THE BUSTLING CROWD
An urban building should integrate the complexity of urban life. The original station included a dining room, a lunchroom, a cafeteria, a barbershop, a women's rest area, a waiting room, and a chapel, as well as office space.

3. ECONOMY
Density is the urban condition, and while this building is large and generous, it is also compressed and hard at the edges. It fills the site and does not waste space.

4. SOBRIETY
Urban buildings should exhibit a high degree of seriousness, the architectural equivalent of a business suit. This also has to do with showing respect for one's neighbors—another urban trait.

5. SOPHISTICATION
The city is no place for rustic charms. This urbane building, with its stripped classicism and Art-Deco details, always makes me hear Fred Astaire tap dancing over its Tennessee marble floor.

Thomas Gordon Smith
CATHEDRAL CITY CIVIC CENTER, CATHEDRAL CITY, CALIFORNIA (1998)

1. ONE MUST RESPOND TO THE POWER OF NATURE BY ORIENTING THE BUILDING TO THE TOPOGRAPHY, THE CLIMATE, AND THE SOLAR CONDITIONS OF THE BUILDING SITE. A large civic plaza suitable for festivities and informal gatherings was designed for the southern half of the site. I stretched the Civic Center along the east-west axis to gain maximum southern exposure while protecting these windows with deep overhangs and pergolas. The windows to the east and west were minimized in the offices and the large windows in the third floor Council Chamber recessed in deep vaults. I developed a central block with a high, vaulted *paseo*. This open passage provides breezy comfort from the desert sun. The balconies that open from four sides of the chamber provide spectacular views of Cathedral Mountain.

2. ONE MUST DISPOSE THE BUILDING IN A FUNCTIONAL AND HIERARCHICAL MANNER. The Civic Center's civic purpose grants it the right to a position of authority, a place of hierarchy within the city. In establishing its civic authority, how one approaches the Civic Center and views it from the square outside is as important as how one moves through and within it. The hierarchy is reinforced on each of these levels. The *paseo* through the central block provides circulation by separating the functions of the city offices from the police headquarters located on the east and west sides. The City Council Chamber surmounts the vault, crowning the structure and symbolizing the chamber's hierarchical importance. It is visible from a great distance and has become a symbol for Cathedral City.

3. ONE MUST EXPRESS IDEAS THROUGH THE RANGE OF ARCHITECTURAL LANGUAGE TO ACHIEVE A HIGH PLANE OF ARCHITECTURAL SYMBOLISM. To the untrained eye, the elements of classical architecture may be mute, but when the traditional associations of character are studied, rich meaning can be decoded. These ideas may capture significant aspects of a culture, place, and history. In addition, iconography can delineate ideas more vividly. Sculptural reliefs depicting the heads of mountain rams, for example, enliven the parapets of the main block and refer to the mountain beyond, the city's namesake.

4. ONE MUST USE THE CONCEPT VITRUVIUS CALLED *SYMMETRIA* TO CALIBRATE ALL OF THE ELEMENTS TO CREATE A SENSE OF BEAUTY THROUGH PROPORTIONAL RELATIONSHIPS. Just as I worked to balance the aspirations of the citizens with the budget at hand, the architecture must balance the proportions of the whole with the details of the parts. On a larger scale, the building must be complete in itself and in relationship with the structures and spaces that adjoin it. This concept does not rigorously command the end design of the project; rather, it is an invaluable tool with which to begin.

5. THE BUILDING AND ITS SURROUNDINGS MUST CONVEY A SENSE OF WHOLENESS. This is achieved by evaluating how well the plans meet the requirements of strength, function, and beauty throughout the process

Opposite Top: Thirtieth Street Station, Philadelphia. *Photo courtesy of Berry&Homer, Philadelphia.*

Top: Cathedral City Civic Center. Thomas Gordon Smith, South Bend, Indiana with MWM Architects, Oakland, California. *Photograph by Simon Wolfgang.*

Bottom: The paving stones at Pompeii. *Photograph by GettyOne.*

of design. Each detail must contribute to the whole. The civic center design uses a simplified Tuscan architecture in the pediments above the pavilions that terminate the east and west wings. The dry winds of the region make the use of exposed wood impractical, so decorative brackets are incised in the ends of the structural I-beams. A new civic building and plaza must meet the highest standard possible to be able to attract civic participation and stimulate adjacent construction. We created a monument that has improved the quality of local development.

Simon Verity
PAVINGS OF POMPEII

The ancient roads of Pompeii tell more of human habitation than anything built on the ground, and from our archaeological digging, the painful losses of visual material show that in stone time nothing will remain but traces of feet. A concrete road or paving, replaced every ten years, has none of this. Marks of our passage, and of the people who walked there, are obliterated, and part of the soul of the city is wiped away as trash.

Our built environment must outlive us and give us reassurance from the past. Pavings are even more potent than buildings to give this testimony.

Carroll William Westfall
WILLIAMSBURG, VIRGINIA

A great urban place must satisfy five criteria—not four, not six, but these five. Not every place can be great in the grandest sense, but even lesser places must embody these characteristics to the extent that it is appropriate for them to do so. A paradigmatic example embodying all five, one that is easily accessible and pervasive in innumerable versions throughout the country, is Williamsburg, Virginia.

For an urban place to be great:
1. IT MUST BE BUILT TO SERVE AN IMPORTANT PUBLIC PURPOSE, AND SERVE IT WELL. This criterion stands on the maxim that more important than architecture is politics, that is, the political life lived by people seeking justice and nobility through their governing of themselves according to the principal of majority rule with protection of minority rights. Architecture is always in the service of an urban realm that facilitates the activities of people engaged in that life.

That life is exemplified in the experience of those who initially built and continuously rebuilt Williamsburg. The people who first moved from England to the virgin land of the New World in 1607 quickly learned that the most certain way to secure their ends required them to put their affairs in their own hands. They therefore reorganized their form of governance in 1619 to institute a representative government, the first in the New World. Their success, after numerous trials in Jamestown, led in 1699 to the founding of a new capital which they sited inland to serve the expanded settlement pattern.

For the next three quarters of a century, Williamsburg hosted the government that nurtured in Virginia's citizens the love of self-government which, when thwarted, erupted in Revolution. Ever since its earliest days, the capital's original plan had been altered and filled in with an ever richer urbanism, formed and served by public and private buildings, each new one usually an improvement over its predecessors. As the capital of the largest and most prosperous of the rebellious colonies, it was an obvious target of the army seeking to maintain England's hegemony.

Our most thorough, and enticing, knowledge of Williamsburg as a war city is the map made by a skillful but unknown mapmaker among the French army allied with the Continental Army. This so-called Frenchman's Map portrays the city (for a city it was in the legal structure of the Commonwealth) at its most important moment, a moment when the Commonwealth and the city were at war, an undertaking that always causes a polity to define what ends it most values, and forces its citizens to take a stand relative to the polity's purposes.

2. It Must Establish a Reciprocity Between Landscape, Private and Public Buildings, and Private and Public Places.

3. It Must Make Clear the Distinction Between Public and Private, have a Gradation from One to the Other, and Present the Graded Importance of the Several Buildings as They Serve the Purpose of Facilitating the Political Life. Reciprocity between landscape and buildings is a distinctive mark of American urbanism, one that sets it apart from European (or at least Continental) precedents. Equally important, and unique, is the synthesis of the double geometric structure that organizes the public order and the private holdings that this structure coordinates and protects, a synthesis that also incorporates the landscape it inhabits.

This synthesis is evident even in the map. We find that the principal buildings, the public ones, are fenced in by low brick walls and arranged within an easily grasped geometric order, one of the two ordering the plan. This order exploits the topographic features that can serve the urban order, and it gives way to the topographic features that can serve the urban structure. The Capitol (the seat of the lower and upper houses and the council with authority for final adjudication) and the College, two centers where reason is to prevail, define an axis running along a ridgeline. The Church that embodies the transcendental ends of the citizens marks the junction with the right-angled cross axis leading to the Governor's Mansion. Here a greensward facing out toward the countryside runs from the Governor's Mansion across the axis and into the landscape where the government's jurisdiction lies and where more of the citizens who authorize its acts reside.

The other geometric order provides the ground against which that geometry can be read. This second geometric uses streets and alleys to order the holdings of the citizens to whom the public institutions minister. These are the private parcels that the new American constitutional order will include among the properties whose protection from the intrusion of government is a basic human right (Amendments I and V). Neither the public realm nor the private precincts can exist without the other. And neither can the rights of the governed exist without the protection of those rights by the government. The two sides, private and public, and their counterpart of rights and authority, are always in a dynamic relationship, a relationship that the urban realm must portray and an interaction that the urban realm must facilitate.

The fences, required by law to surround the private holdings, make visible and enhance the right of privacy and security of ownership by hemming in the buildings and gardens required to sustain the families resident within the defined precincts. The conspicuous position given to the private commercial structures, which are strung along the Capitol-College axis within the grid, reveals the central role of prosperity in promoting liberty. This gridded order of streets, which edges out into the landscape that deforms the grid, is opened up by the regular open square crossed by the Capitol-College axis, a void focused on the courthouse, the seat of adjudication for local affairs, and the powder magazine and militia armory (see Amendment II). These buildings are clearly embraced by the municipal realm that surrounds them. They are set apart from the geometry of the public buildings, which serve the larger polity composed of this and other municipalities. To govern well the governors must be readily accountable to those they govern. Here in the municipal center fellow citizens known to one another seek justice and fulfill the fundamental obligation of a polity to its free citizens, namely, to "provide for the common defense," as the Preamble of the Constitution would put it.

More than the buildings' locations fulfill this purpose. Throughout the city, the buildings' formal properties display the polity's civil structure. The public buildings clearly portray their greater importance by being lodged within the larger geometry, being larger and better built, and being based on the familiar conventional forms given to buildings serving the public purposes these serve. So too the private buildings: some of them are brick, as are the public buildings, but many are wooden. The private buildings are not primarily individualistic but instead are built to portray their service to the polity. The commercial buildings stand near to the main street and front it. The more important residences are more distinguished in appearance than their ancillary structures, which are smaller, of lesser material and formal quality, and further away from the public streets and market square.

4. It Must Encourage a Variety of Individual Interpretations by Different Individuals Working Within a Common Range of Conventions Embodying the Traditions Appropriate to the Purpose and the Place. Williamsburg's buildings are familiar examples of buildings common to the purposes they serve within conventions long in use in both the colony and its mother country; but no two are alike, and not one of them is dramatically discordant with any other. And so too, the activities of the citizens whom the buildings serve. A person filling a civil office, be it voter, tax payer, army private, father, or governor, will acquit himself in the office in a unique way, a way that no matter how unique nonetheless enlarges the understanding of the office without distorting the role it plays in the civil life.

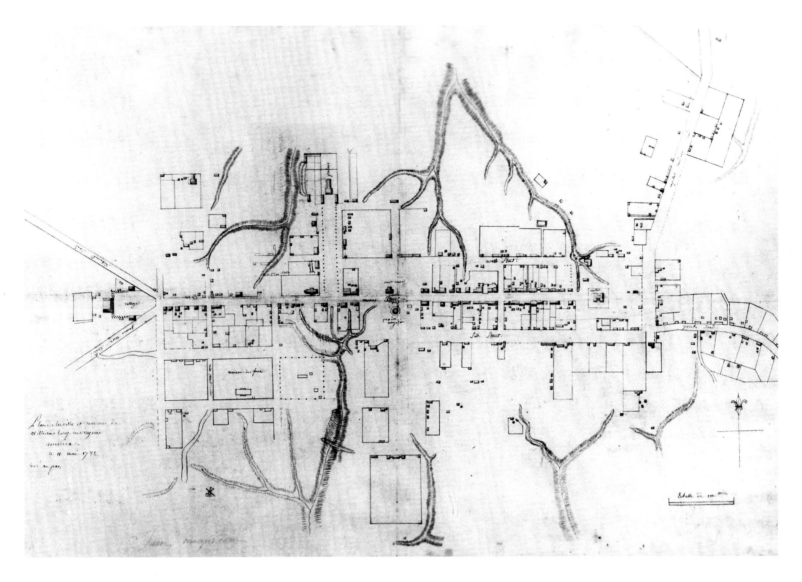

5.   It Must Contain Within It the Potential for Variations That Are Exploited by Others Who Draw on It for Their Work, Thereby Extending Tradition on Whose Edges the Constantly Building City and its Buildings Innovate. Jaquelin Robertson has said that Williamsburg is the best new town built in America in the twentieth century. The product of restoration, rehabilitation, and new construction that began after World War I and continues today, Williamsburg presents at the same time an image of what we imagine this important city looked like at the nation's birth and what our cities might look like now. From the beginning of the nation's history it has provided paradigmatic guidance for those imagining what form American urbanism ought to have. Enlarged, it became L'Enfant's Washington (surely Williamsburg was a more important model than the gardens of Versailles). Distilled to its barest essentials, it is replicated in innumerable courthouse towns in the lands of the Northwest Ordinance and beyond. And ever since its recovery in the last century, it has instructed the sensibilities of homebuilders and builders of public buildings.

Those drawing on it have been increasingly insensitive to the way a building, whether public or private, occupies an important private and public place in a town, choosing instead to be preoccupied with capturing for their private life that which they take to be the more gracious life of a simpler America. That the model can be so abused does not invalidate its use in giving body to a uniquely American urban type capable of being imitated fruitfully wherever regional traditions are appropriate.

The map also reminds us of an important right that our government is charged to guarantee. The Frenchman most likely made the map to show where soldiers fighting for independence might be billeted. Amendment III would remove this power from military authority and place it in the hands of a government that is answerable to the governed. Williamsburg continues to remind us how important the rights of citizens are in the face of overweening government. ✦

Above: Anonymous, Frenchman's Map of Williamsburg, Virginia, 1782. *Used by permission of Swem Library, Special Collections, College of William and Mary.*

Portfolios

From the Offices

Professional Portfolios

The editors of the Professional Portfolio section of *The Classicist No. 7* were exceptionally pleased by the volume of work submitted for consideration. In contrast to years past when editors of this section toiled to collect appropriate work, we found ourselves painfully editing out beautiful work that we hope to present in future editions of this publication.

Even more exciting than the quantity of work, was the diversity and quality of the projects—nicely addressing, in our view, the banal argument that classical architecture is only suitable for houses of wealthy patrons. Instead, this year's selection of professional projects specifically aims to show that the ideas of firmness, commodity, and delight prevail in architectural typologies ranging throughout the spectrum of the New Urbanist transect.

Just as Dino Marcantonio identifies and maps out architectural character across a transect in his essay, "The Classicism of the Transect," at the beginning of this journal (see pages 18–23), so too did the editors of this section wish to illustrate a similar range of current architectural work, which of course also includes houses. The projects on the following pages represent an uplifting fact for practitioners of classical architecture: The ideas behind classical and traditional design work aesthetically and functionally, and increasingly, clients are as likely to ask for traditionally built work as they are for the parabuildings that Francis Morrone speaks of in "The Classicist at Large" (pages 6–9).

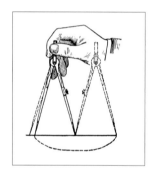

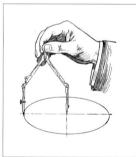
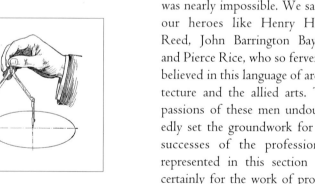

In other words, the nature of classical architecture is appropriate at all levels—from the house in the rural environment to the large pubic projects in an urban setting. New Urbanist principles are being implemented to reestablish the character of existing neighborhoods in disrepair, as well as to create new neighborhoods and cities with a sense of place.

As the success of the traditional language is expressed by the breadth of new traditional projects, so too is it illustrated by the range of professionals highlighted in this section. From single practitioners and small firms to large, established architectural offices, the ideas of history, beauty, and context are taking hold in new projects across the country—even in firms perhaps most noted for past projects of an entirely different ilk.

Fifty years ago the study and practice of classical architecture was nearly impossible. We salute our heroes like Henry Hope Reed, John Barrington Bayley, and Pierce Rice, who so fervently believed in this language of architecture and the allied arts. The passions of these men undoubtedly set the groundwork for the successes of the professionals represented in this section and certainly for the work of professionals in years to come.

The editors of this section would like to thank all those firms who submitted material for publication in this year's journal. Thanks also to those firm representatives with whom we worked closely to organize images and materials that accurately describe the work that was selected. —TM, JF, MDS, LS

Franck & Lohsen Architects, Inc.

Washington, D.C.

FRANCK & LOHSEN ARCHITECTS is dedicated to producing the highest quality work for its clients through a thoughtful and sophisticated combination of classical approaches and modern sensibilities. As great architects throughout history have done before, the firm researches ways other architect-craftsmen have responded to their clients' needs, which creates a baseline of innovation for almost any project. The firm also regularly proposes designs in the public arena. From Pennsylvania Avenue to Lincoln Center to the World Trade Center and sites in between, Franck & Lohsen seeks to enhance the way civic architecture in America is experienced and represented.

Principals: Michael M. Franck and Arthur C. Lohsen

CHAPEL OF THE SACRED HEART OF JESUS, CATHEDRAL OF ST. JOSEPH
Sioux Falls, South Dakota

CLIENT
Bishop Robert J. Carlson

PROJECT TEAM
Design Architect: Franck & Lohsen, Architects, Inc.
Architect of Record: Team TSP, Sioux Falls, SD

CONSULTANTS
Mural Painting: Leonard Porter, New York, NY
Series of Nine Icons: Feodor Streltsov, Moscow, Russia
Metalwork: Patrick Cardine Studios, Chantilly, VA
Sacred Heart Medallion Sculpture: George Kelly, New York, NY
Chadsworth's 1.800.Columns, Wilmington, NC

CHAPEL FLOORPLAN *(right)*
Built within an existing series of disused sacristies at the Cathedral of St. Joseph in Sioux Falls, this project, completed in October of 2004, is a new daily mass chapel, which is occupied around the clock by a group of cloistered nuns in Perpetual Adoration of the Blessed Sacrament. Working with the sole requirement that several existing stained-glass windows needed to remain in place, Franck & Lohsen joined several rooms to create a larger space and modified the underside of the roof structure, which allowed for a barrel-vaulted ceiling to run the length of the new chapel.

VIEW OF THE CHAPEL INTERIOR FACING THE MURAL OF CHRIST ENTHRONED *(left, top)*
The chapel features an extensive artistic program, which included a mural by Leonard Porter, icons by Feodor Streltsov, and sculpture by George Kelly. The creation of this chapel is a unique synthesis of the arts, and it demonstrates the effects achieved when art and architecture are conceived interdependently.

DETAIL, CORINTHIAN COLUMN:
VIEW OF CORNER OF BALDACCHINO *(left, bottom)*

All images prepared by Franck & Lohsen, Architects, Inc.

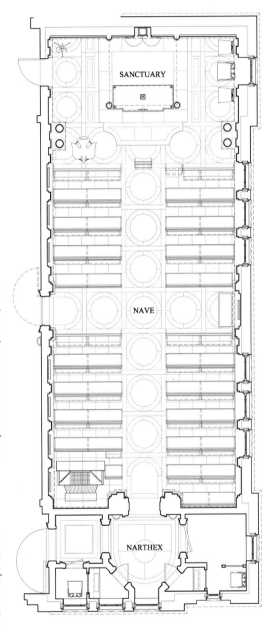

Kallmann McKinnell & Wood Architects, Inc.

Boston, Massachusetts

IN FORTY-TWO YEARS OF PRACTICE, designing many different building types, Kallmann McKinnell & Wood (KMW) has deliberately pursued architecture of diversity, resisting the limitations of an office style. Instead of maintaining a rigid ideological stance, KMW welcomes differences in program, clients, site and context.

Yet beyond such a pragmatic attitude, Kallmann McKinnell & Wood maintains certain continuity in their work, a preoccupation with themes that recur as generating influences. These may be described as deriving from a marked interest in an urbanistic architecture that regards the building and its link with the urban fabric surrounding it as equally important. The firm's designs have covered a range from totemistic, autonomous building to the fabric building; from the landmark Boston City Hall to the campus insertions at Harvard, Yale, Princeton, and Washington University in St. Louis.

Principals: N. Michael McKinnell, FAIA, Design Director; S. Fiske Crowell, Jr., FAIA, Managing Principal; Theodore Szostkowski, AIA, Principal; Bruce A. Wood, AIA, Principal; Bruno Pfister, RA, Principal; Rayford W. Law, AIA, Principal

CHARLES F. KNIGHT EXECUTIVE EDUCATION CENTER, WASHINGTON UNIVERSITY
St. Louis, Missouri

PROJECT TEAM
Design Director: N. Michael McKinnell, FAIA
Managing Principal: S. Fiske Crowell, Jr., FAIA
Project Architect: Bruno Pfister, RA
Senior Associates and Project Managers: Anne Tansantisuk, AIA; Timothy Scarlett, AIA

CONSULTANTS
On site Architect: Paradigm Architects, St. Louis, MO
Contractor/Construction Manager: Tarlton Corporation, St. Louis, MO
Mechanical/Electrical/Plumbing/Fire: William Tao & Associates, Inc, St. Louis, MO
Structural: Alper Audi, Inc., St, Louis, MO
Kitchen Design: Dennis G. Glore Inc., St. Louis, MO
Interior Design: Kallmann McKinnell & Wood Architects, Inc., Boston, MA
Photographer: Robert Benson Photography, Hartford, CT

SITE PLAN FOR CHARLES F. KNIGHT EXECUTIVE EDUCATION CENTER *(below)*

VIEW OF SOUTH ELEVATION *(top)*

VIEW OF NORTH ELEVATION *(above)*
The new Charles F. Knight Executive Education Center has become an integral part of the Hilltop Campus of Washington University in St. Louis. The new building is located on the northern edge of the great lawn "quadrangle" that forms the heart of the campus. The building is located directly across the lawn from Simon Hall (also designed by KMW), which houses the full complement of the programs for the Olin School of Business.

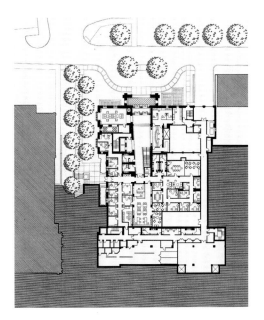

VIEW OF EAST ELEVATION AND STAIR *(above)*
As a center for executive education and campus conferences, one of the primary objectives of the Charles F. Knight Executive Education Center is to integrate executive students and conference attendees into the physical and social environment of the university. Toward this end KMW designed the new facility to spatially reintroduce the executives to an academic environment.

Upon passing through the double height lobby, one discovers a monumental stair, which fosters the student's progression through the program as well as through the building. This stair ascends through a three-storied atrium space, which gently navigates the dramatic change in grade from the initial point of entry to the Hilltop Campus. Flanking this stair is the reception desk and the main bank of elevators. To the west, off the lobby, is the first of three well-appointed student lounges.

DETAIL VIEW OF COURTYARD *(top)*

VIEW OF ENTRANCE *(above)*

FIRST FLOOR PLAN *(above)*
The entrance floor offers an introduction to both the academic and business functions of the school. Beyond the reception desk for the hotel and conference functions is the Student Resource Center. This facility provides a broad range of student support and placement functions for both the undergraduate and graduate programs of the School of Business. It contains a resource library, study rooms, placement offices and 24 individual interview rooms. There are significant recruitment programs for the school, and this facility supports all related activities.

At the second floor level, accessed by the monumental stair, flooded with natural light from the courtyard windows of the level above, the atrium serves to organize the main instructional level. Here, three state-of-the-art tiered classrooms and a traditional classroom are supported by ample breakout rooms, a classroom lounge, and the student Business Center, which form the instructional core of The Charles F. Knight Executive Education Center. Finally, on the upper two floors of the building are 63 hotel rooms, fitness center, seminar rooms, and Pub Lounge for the executive programs.

Léon Krier

Claviers, France

LÉON KRIER is an architect/theorist who has taught at the Architectural Association and Royal College in London, Princeton University, Yale University, and Harvard Design School. His New Urbanism theories are widely applied by the Organization for Economic Cooperation and Development (OECD) and the European Union as well as in the rest of Europe and in the United States. He is the author of numerous articles and chapters and his books include the following titles: *Rational - Architecture - Rationnelle,* (Archives d'Architecture Moderne, Brussels, 1978); *Léon Krier: Drawings,* (Archives d'Architecture Moderne, Brussels, 1980); *Houses, Palaces, Cities,* Demetri Porphyrios, editor, (Academy Publications, London, 1984); *Albert Speer: Architecture 1932–1942,* (Archives d'Architecture Moderne, Brussels, 1985); *Architecture and Urban Design 1967–1992,* Richard Economakis, editor, (Academy Publications, London, 1992); *Architecture: Choice or Fate,* (Andreas Papadakis Publisher, Windsor, England, 1998). Mr. Krier is the also the recipient of several awards including the Berlin Prize for Architecture, the Driehaus Prize, and the Jefferson Memorial Medal.

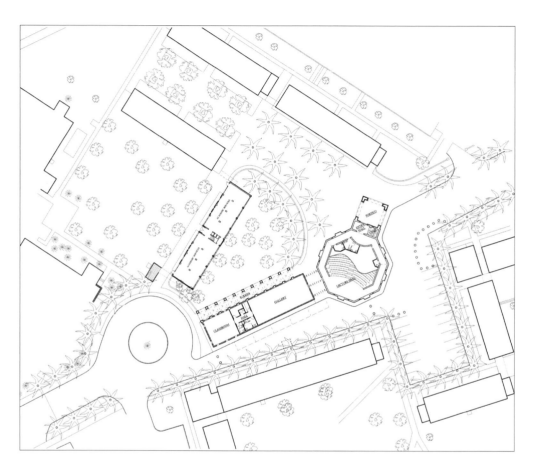

JORGE M. PEREZ ARCHITECTURE CENTER, UNIVERSITY OF MIAMI
Coral Gables, Florida

CLIENT
Elizabeth Plater-Zyberk, Dean, University of Miami School of Architecture

DESIGN TEAM
Designer: Léon Krier
Architectural Consultants: Merrill, Pastor and Colgan Architects, Vero Beach, FL
Architect of Record: Ferguson, Glasgow, Schuster, and Soto, Coral Gables, FL

SITE PLAN OF THE JORGE M. PEREZ ARCHITECTURE CENTER *(above)*
The Jorge M. Perez Architecture Center at the University of Miami School of Architecture was completed in the summer of 2005 and dedicated in the fall of that year. The $6 million, 8,600 square foot building is the centerpiece of the five-building architectural complex located in the heart of the University's Coral Gables campus. It complements the other buildings designed in the 1940s by Marion Manley, the first woman to become a registered architect in Florida.

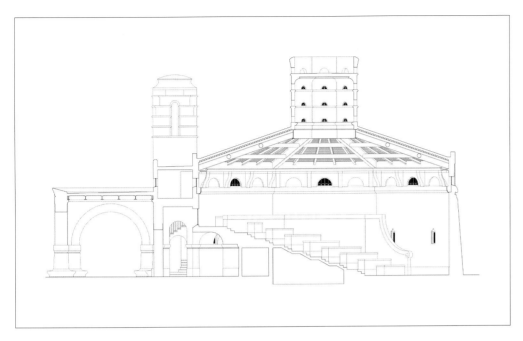

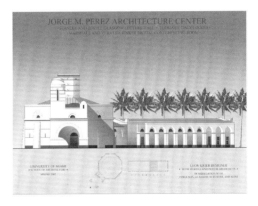

RENDERING OF NORTHEAST ELEVATION OF
THE PEREZ ARCHITECTURE CENTER *(above)*

SECTION THROUGH THE LECTURE HALL AT
THE PEREZ ARCHITECTURE CENTER *(top left)*
The new building houses a 145-seat hall, a
gallery, and a classroom that provide venues
for a variety of public events. It is a one-story
structure tall enough for theatre seating, and
the whitewashed stucco of the exterior reflects
the surrounding international style.

RENDERING OF THE WEST ELEVATION OF THE
PEREZ ARCHITECTURE CENTER *(bottom left)*
There are over 300 students enrolled in the
five-year undergraduate program and two
graduate programs at The University of
Miami School of Architecture, which is noted
for its pedagogical involvement with the New
Urbanism. The new Architecture Center
engages with the existing freestanding modernist buildings to define a series of public
squares, and will serve as the hub of the
school's activities for students as well as the
local community.

*All computer and hand-rendered images courtesy of
Léon Krier, Scott Merrill, David Colgan, Chris Janson,
and Cory Padesky.*

Mark P. Finlay Architects, AIA

Southport, Connecticut

MARK P. FINLAY ARCHITECTS, AIA is dedicated to designing distinctive architecture that combines a keen sense of tradition with contemporary insight and techniques. The result is a range of award-winning architectural projects that range from a streetscape for Fairfield, Connecticut, to a historic renovation of a diner, to a 100-unit colonial village that sets a standard for new suburban development.

The commitment to quality and contextual expression is governed by the ability to interpret a client's needs, whether the project is residential, multi-family, corporate, commercial, or a historic renovation. Pride in craftsmanship also enables the firm to provide a design product that elevates the business of building to the fine art of architecture.

Principals: Mark P. Finlay, President; Rob DeVore, Senior Partner; Joseph Mulligan, Partner; Jay Valade, Partner

GLEN ARBOR GOLF CLUB
Bedford Hills, New York

PROJECT TEAM
Mark P. Finlay, Joseph Mulligan

CONSULTANTS
Structural: DeStafano Associates, Fairfield, CT
Mechanical & Electrical: Perillo Associates, Pleasantville, NY

SITE PLAN FOR THE GLEN ARBOR GOLF CLUB *(top)*
This project is a master-planned private golf club in Bedford, New York, that includes a clubhouse and eleven golf-related outbuildings situated around an existing Gary Palmer-designed golf course.

Drawing courtesy of Mark P. Finlay Architects, AIA.

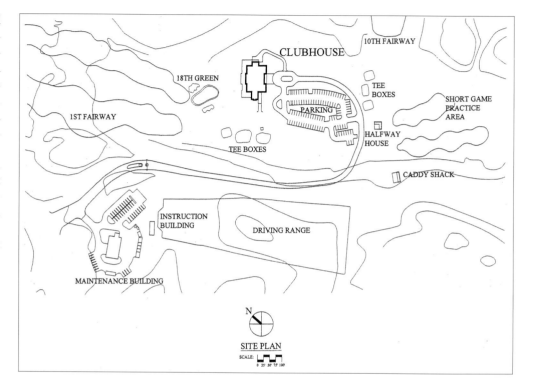

PALLADIAN WINDOW ON EAST ELEVATION
(FRONT OF CLUBHOUSE) *(above)*
Photograph by Mark P. Finlay.

DETAIL OF WEST ELEVATION
(REAR OF CLUBHOUSE) *(left)*
The goal for the clubhouse was to re-create
the quintessential Bedford homestead, making
it appear that the golf course was planned
around it. The scale and form of the clubhouse
was inspired by the Greek revival vernacular
farmhouse architecture from the turn of the
century. *Photograph by Larry Lambrecht.*

DRAWING OF THE GLEN ARBOR GOLF CLUB
EAST ELEVATION *(opposite, bottom)*
One of the many challenges of the project was
to design a new building that looked old.
Additionally the club members wanted to feel
comfortable and relaxed, which required a
design that would feel like a home but operate as a commercial building. As a solution to
the numerous commercial requirements of the
14,000-square-foot clubhouse, the golf cart
facilities were situated under the building;
deliveries are received in a satellite delivery
building and then brought discreetly to the
clubhouse as needed. *Drawing courtesy of Mark
P. Finlay Architects, AIA.*

WEST ELEVATION OF GLEN ARBOR
CLUBHOUSE (above)
In keeping with the hierarchy of traditional farm estates, the clubhouse stands on the summit of the property adjacent to the first tee and eighteenth green, an ideal location for the activity pattern of golfers. Sited throughout the property, the outbuildings are simpler in detail and reminiscent of older farm buildings. *Photograph by Larry Lambrecht.*

GLEN ARBOR CLUBHOUSE LIVING ROOM
FIREPLACE (*left*)
The member spaces include a living room, dining room, bar/grill room, pro-shop, and locker rooms, all of which are detailed with moldings, coffered ceilings, and paneling in keeping with the old house theme. *Photograph by Nancy Hill.*

Michael G. Imber Architects

San Antonio, Texas

BASED IN SAN ANTONIO, TEXAS, Michael G. Imber Architects is a classical design firm of individuals well-versed in traditional architecture, preservation, and landscape architecture. Rough and varied landscapes, cultural diversity, and a rich history of craftsmanship have contributed to a body of work that has utilized modern building methods of concrete and steel as well as more traditional materials of stone, timber frame, adobe, and straw bale. The firm has projects which are primarily located in Texas, Florida, and Colorado. Their early works have been recognized with awards and in print, and have been exhibited in New York City, Chicago, Seaside, Rome, Mykonos, and Versailles. Most recently, Michael G. Imber Architects was the 2007 recipient of the Arthur Ross Award for Architecture.

KINGHART RANCH
Lipscomb County, Texas

PROJECT TEAM
Michael G. Imber, Julie Valadez, David Holland

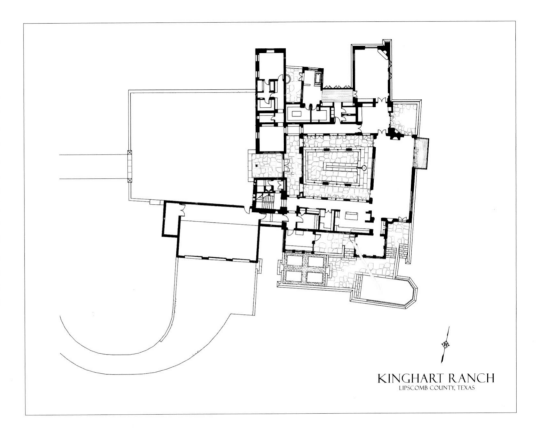

KINGHART RANCH
LIPSCOMB COUNTY, TEXAS

KINGHART RANCH FLOOR PLAN *(upper right)*
Situated on a grassy rise above First Creek, the KingHart Ranch is located in a part of Texas known as the *Llano Estacado*. The Spanish explorer Coronado called this area a landscape of "buffalo and sky." Arranged as a compound, the floor plan composes the structure of the house in a defensive position common for western outposts of earlier times. Today this traditional layout guards against the severe weather of the plain and the intrusion of prairie wildlife and cattle. Exterior spaces, protected from exposure to the summer sun and winter winds, are positioned for dramatic views as well as for capturing cooling breezes in the summer. *Autocad drawing.*

WATERCOLOR STUDY OF TOWER AT MOTOR COURT *(right)*
The house draws its form and materials from the Andalusia region of Spain and the frontier forts of Texas. Arrival to the compound is from the west into a motor court flanked on two sides by the west wing of the house and garage wing. The entry is marked by a viewing tower that gives the ranch a vertical landmark in the vast horizontal world of the Great Plains. *Watercolor and ink by Michael G. Imber.*

PALAZZO SAN ANTONIO
Bexar County, Texas

PROJECT TEAM
Michael G. Imber, Mac White, Armando Juarez, Clayton Fry

MODEL OF PALAZZO SAN ANTONIO *(above)*
Situated in Texas Hill Country in northern San Antonio, Palazzo San Antonio is a large estate occupying a private hilltop. Designed after the villas of Italy, the three-story residence is a modern structure of concrete, steel, and aerated autoclave concrete block, which is clad in Texas Leuders limestone and ochre plaster. *Bass wood model by Mac White, David Holland, Orlando Juarez, and Clayton Fry.*

STUDY FOR PALAZZO SAN ANTONIO MAIN ENTRY *(opposite, top left)* Watercolor by Stefan Molina.

DETAIL OF CUT STONE BALCONIES AT WEST ELEVATION *(opposite, top middle)*
The west elevation is scaled to the landscape and serves as a backdrop to the gardens. It features a large pillowed limestone base and broad overhangs which shelter the windows and central mass. Flanking loggias rise full height to foil the sun. *Photograph by Michael G. Imber.*

MAIN ENTRY SECTION ANALYTIQUE *(opposite, bottom left)*
Approached by a long drive, the entry court provides a formal presentation of the two-story baroque south façade. The east side of the court is flanked by a tall stone wall and fountain, and the west side is open to a distant view of the Hill Country and the gardens below. A drive under the bridge connecting to the service wing leads to the motor court, which provides an informal entrance to the house along the secondary east-west axis. *Autocad drawing by Mac White.*

WEST ELEVATION OF KINGHART RANCH *(top)*
The west wing is built of native stone with deep-set windows and is two stories in height in order to shade the inner courtyard from western exposure.

The space between the west wing and the tower is bridged by a timber balcony and offers a deeply shaded entry to the house from the motor court. *Watercolor rendering by Michael G. Imber.*

EAST ELEVATION OF KINGHART RANCH *(above)*
The east side of the compound contains the principal room, master chambers, and breakfast room. These spaces all have an unfettered view of First Creek and the natural landscape beyond. The white plaster walls of the structure offer a sharp contrast to the soft grassland, as the ochre color of the Spanish barrel tile roof reconciles the house to its prairie environment. *Watercolor rendering by Michael C. Imber.*

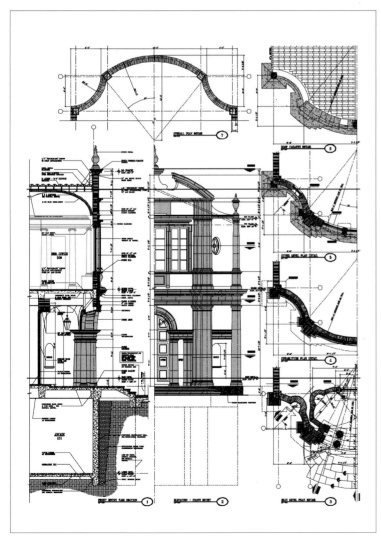

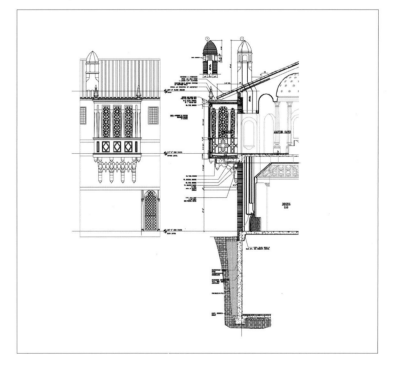

SHOWER ORIEL *(top right)*
The north façade remains austere, broken only by the composition of the north stair tower and the wooden Mudajar shower structure that expresses the interior spaces within.
Photograph by Michael G. Imber.

WALL SECTION AT MASTER SHOWER
(above)
Autocad drawing by Mac White.

The S/L/A/M Collective

Glastonbury, Connecticut, Atlanta, Georgia, and Boston, Massachusetts

THE S/L/A/M COLLECTIVE is a 150-member architecture, engineering, and planning firm with offices in Glastonbury, Connecticut, Atlanta, Georgia, and Boston, Massachusetts. A studio-based, award-winning practice, S/L/A/M specializes in master planning and design of healthcare, educational, science and technology, and corporate facilities. The firm offers master planning, architectural design, landscape architecture, interior design, structural engineering, and construction management services.

Principals: Steven Ansel, Bruce Arneill, Richard Connell, Don Crowe, Terri Frink, Glenn Gollenberg, Rick Herzer, William Karanian, Peggy LaVin, Joseph League, John McDonald, James McManus, Peter Nuelson, Mary Jo Olenick, Robert Palaia, Robert Pulito, John Rivers, Kyle Slocum, Christopher Williams

THE ROXBURY LATIN SCHOOL
West Roxbury, Massachusetts

CLIENT
The Roxbury Latin School

PROJECT TEAM
William D. Buckingham, RA; Dennis Keefe, AIA; Gerald J. Sullivan, AIA

CONSULTANTS
Structural: Wayne Weaver; Odeh Engineers
HVAC: TMP; Michael Zimmerman; Fitzemeyer & Tocci; Crowley Engineering
Plumbing & FP: R.W. Sullivan
Electrical: Lottero & Mason; Vincent A Dilorio; Anthony D'Ambrosino; Prior Engineering
Civil: GEOD; SMMA
Theatre: Hugh Fortmiller and Alan Symonds

The S/L/A/M Collective, Inc. strives to be a self-perpetuating collaborative practice. It is one of the few New England architectural firms to specialize in the design of traditional buildings for educational institutions. One such project is the Roxbury Latin School, an independent day school with an enrollment of 275 boys in Grades 7 through 12. The school was founded by British charter in 1645, making it the oldest school in continuous existence in North America.

BIRD'S-EYE VIEW OF THE ROXBURY LATIN SCHOOL *(top)*
Over the years the design goal has been to meet the school's current educational needs while ensuring that all added components blend seamlessly with the original building to form a cohesive campus plan. The buildings shown in this article are the Mary Rousmaniere Gordon Wing, the Robert P. Smith Arts Center, the Charles T. Bauer Science Center, the Albert H. Gordon Field House, and the Jarvis Refectory Building. *Photograph by Dognik Lee.*

COURTYARD OF THE NEW SCHOOLHOUSE AS COMPLETED IN 1927 *(above)*
When the school moved to its present campus in the 1920s, the firm of Perry, Shaw & Hepburn (later famed for the restoration of Colonial Williamsburg) designed its New Schoolhouse, using an interpretive blend of traditional English vernacular and high style themes. Since 1985, the school has undergone a series of additions and renovations by S/L/A/M, nearly tripling the square footage of its educational facilities. *Photograph by Vernon L. Small.*

ROBERT P. SMITH ARTS CENTER (1992)
(above)
The central element of the new Robert P. Smith Arts Center is a 300-seat theatre distinguished on the exterior by bold Doric pilasters and a high hip roof. A long entrance lobby with vaulted plaster ceiling, quarry-tile floor, and numerous windows overlooking the courtyard, stretches across the entire width of the Arts Center. The lower, flat-roofed sections at either side of the theatre are devoted to a music room and art studio. The art studio has two copper-clad roof monitors to bring in northern light. An open loggia with cast-stone columns, exposed wood rafters, and a copper roof links the Arts Center to the rest of the school. *Photograph by Douglas Gilbert.*

SCIENCE CENTER VIEWED FROM THE PLAYING FIELDS *(above)*
The two-story portion of the Bauer Science Center houses four classroom/laboratory units, each of which includes a preparation room and a faculty office. All four laboratories open off a double-height, sky-lit entrance lobby. The one-story wing contains a lecture hall and connects the science facilities to the adjacent Arts Center. *Photograph by Aaron Usher.*

MARY ROUSMANIERE GORDON WING (1987)
(top left)
Each floor of the Mary Rousmaniere Gordon Wing consists of one major room and its ancillary spaces. The three main rooms—Refectory, Library, and Great Hall—are identical in floor area, but distinctly different in proportion, detail, and atmosphere.

Externally, the Gordon Wing repeats the water-struck brick walls, slate roof, and cast-stone trim of the school's 1926 building by Perry, Shaw, & Hepburn. The addition also echoes their idiosyncratic blend of Georgian and Jacobean motifs, a mixture appropriate for a school that traces its origins to the seventeenth century. *Photograph by Richard Mandelkorn.*

CHARLES T. BAUER SCIENCE CENTER (1997)
VIEWED FROM THE COURTYARD *(top right)*
The new Charles T. Bauer Science Center extends along one side of the school's forecourt and resembles the other school buildings in style and detail. The most striking features of the exterior are the many-windowed stair towers facing the courtyard and the two-story polygonal bay windows looking toward the sports fields. *Photograph by Aaron Usher.*

F. Washington Jarvis Refectory (2003)
(directly above)
The new 18,000-square-foot Jarvis Refectory Building houses a dining hall seating 216 with servery, kitchens, and storage; a 20-seat faculty dining room; three classrooms; and Alumni and Development offices. It plays a pivotal role on the school campus, completing the enclosure of a pedestrian courtyard conceived in the early 1990s, around which all the school's academic facilities are grouped, including the New Schoolhouse of Perry, Shaw, & Hepburn (1926), a classroom wing (1964), the Smith Arts Center (1992), and the Bauer Science Center (1999). *Photograph by Aaron Usher.*

Reception Room in the Field House
(top left)
The Gordon Field House provides the Roxbury Latin School with state-of-the-art facilities for interscholastic and intramural sports, fitness training, and post-game receptions. The project comprises 34,000 square feet of new construction, including a 20,000-square-foot double-court gymnasium, new locker rooms, and an elegant timber-trussed reception hall with adjacent terrace, catering kitchen, and storage. *Photograph by Aaron Usher.*

Albert H. Gordon Field House,
Enlarged in 2000 (directly above)
The 1950s gymnasium, locker rooms, and other portions of the complex were renovated. A significant grade change across the site encouraged the design of a grand sky-lit stair between the reception hall and the main gymnasium, which can be viewed from above through glass balcony doors. In addition, a deep red brick and stone arcade faces the varsity football field, giving spectators protection from the hot sun or a sudden shower. *Photograph by Aaron Usher.*

Torti Gallas and Partners, Inc.

Silver Spring, Maryland

TORTI GALLAS'S DESIGN PHILOSOPHY is based on the inextricable link between urban design and architectural issues. As a firm, they are dedicated to the design of the built environment which includes both the responsible development of greenfield sites at the edges of metropolitan areas and the revitalization and redevelopment of inner cities and suburbs.

As architects, Torti Gallas designs residential, commercial, and institutional buildings to be in context with their environment and to be functionally and aesthetically innovative, economically sensible, and a visual delight to the user.

As master planners and urban designers, the firm creates neighborhoods that integrate architecture and the public realm; they try to ensure that their buildings, neighborhoods, and campuses contribute physically, socially, and economically to the cities and towns of which they are a part.

Principals: John Francis Torti, FAIA; Thomas M. Gallas, CPA; Tunca Iskir; Luis H. Bernardo; Robert S. Wallach, RA; Sylvia S. Munero; Cheryl A. O'Neill; Charles G. Coleman III, RA; Michael R. Nicolaus, AIA; Maurice Walters, AIA; Daniel Ashtary, AIA; Bruce D. Kennett, AIA; Sherief Elfar, AIA; Robert S. Goodill; Neal I. Payton, AIA; Chaiwat Pilanun; Thomas E. Danco, AIA; Lawrence V. Antoine Jr., AIA, AICP; Mark David Drake, RA; Raymond M. Jenkins, AIA; Patrice E. McGinn; Paul R. Mortensen, RA

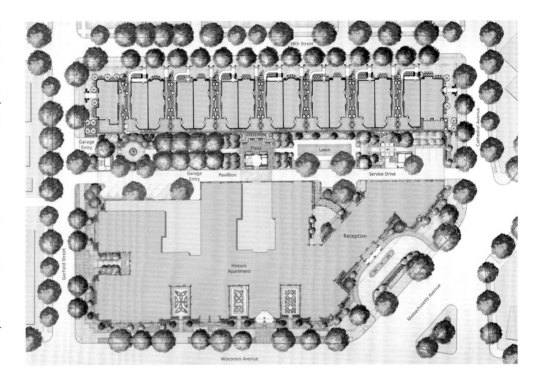

ALBAN TOWERS AND THE RESIDENCES AT ALBAN ROW
Washington, D.C.

CLIENT
Charles E. Smith Residential (Alban Towers);
Encore Development (The Residences at Alban Row)

PROJECT TEAM
Architect: Torti Gallas and Partners, Inc.
Preservation Architect (Towers): Martinez and Johnson Architects
General Contractor (Towers): Foulger Pratt Companies
Civil Engineer: VIKA, Inc.
Landscape Architect: Lee & Liu Associates
Landscape Architect: Parker Rodriguez, Inc.
Interior Designer: Phyllis Hartman Design Group

ILLUSTRATIVE SITE PLAN OF ALBAN TOWERS *(above)*
When it opened in 1929, the Alban Towers six-story historic structure was Washington, D.C.'s largest apartment building. It was designed to complement the National Cathedral and St. Alban's School across the street. Over time, however, the lack of nearby public transit, deteriorating interior and exterior architectural features, and most critically, insufficient off-street parking, had relegated the property to nothing more than an average housing asset. Faced with these issues, Torti Gallas was charged with the rehabilitation of the building and site, stitching Alban Towers back into the surrounding neighborhood.

THE RENOVATED HISTORIC ALBAN TOWERS APARTMENTS *(top)*

Torti Gallas's work was extensive. In addition to repairing the exterior brick and limestone façade, replacing all 1,700 windows, and unobtrusively modernizing the 350,000-square-foot building with new life/safety equipment, the firm added an additional tower and replicated the building's original architectural details to complete the design. To improve parking and site conditions, Torti Gallas designed a partially below-grade parking structure and a new row of duplex homes.

THE NEW DUPLEX UNITS OF THE RESIDENCES AT ALBAN ROW *(bottom)*

Juxtaposed against stately single-family residences, the western side of the site posed an awkward relationship between two greatly differing urban densities. To create a gentle transition between the historic structure and the surrounding residential fabric, fifteen luxury, duplex villas were added to the western portion of the site atop the original underground parking. Reminiscent of District of Columbia homes built in the late-nineteenth and early-twentieth centuries, the villas present individuality and a classic urban look.

Today, Alban Towers is one of Washington's most desired addresses, and the building was listed on The National Register of Historic Places in 1994 for its historic main lobby and residential corridors. The wide- ranging preservation effort returned a long-vacant apartment building to its former prominence as a neighborhood icon while also improving the surrounding neighborhood's urban character.

Photography by Steve Hall © Hedrich-Blessing; Drawings by Torti Gallas and Partners, Inc.

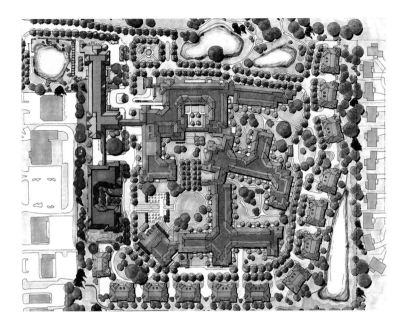

THE GARLANDS OF BARRINGTON
Barrington, Illinois

CLIENT
Barrington Venture, LLC

PROJECT TEAM
Architect: Torti Gallas and Partners, Inc.
General Contractor: Pepper Construction Company
Civil Engineer: Gewalt Hamilton Associates, Inc.
Structural Engineer: Smislova Kehnemui & Associates
Mechanical/Electrical Engineer: Environmental Systems
   Design, Inc.
Landscape Architects: Joe Karr & Associates and
   Harry Weese Associates
Geotechnical Engineer: STS Consultants
Interior Designer: Kenneth E. Hurd & Associates
Consultant: Life Care Services Corporation

ILLUSTRATIVE SITE PLAN OF THE GARLANDS
OF BARRINGTON *(top left)*
The Garlands of Barrington is a mixed use "village within a village," serving as a campus open to the surrounding community instead of a gated enclave of senior housing. Landscaped public spaces, traditional architectural forms, mixed uses, and a variety of housing types contribute to its character. The 31½-acre project site, 40 miles northwest of Chicago, is within walking distance of the existing Barrington village center and its businesses and services.

A sequence of landscaped courtyards organize the site, defined by three-and-a-half story buildings, which provide a variety of public and semi-public spaces. To enhance these spaces, parking was moved underground and existing trees were preserved wherever possible. The two-and-a-half story villas at the perimeter of the site relate to the scale of the adjacent single-family neighborhoods.

CHIMNEY DETAIL AT GARLANDS OF
BARRINGTON *(right)*
Picturesque massing, a variety of bays, and steep roofs with dormers and chimneys modulate and enrich the building façades. The architectural forms and details are based on traditional suburban Chicago precedents, which combined with materials of brick, stone, stucco and slate, create a traditional village character.

Mixed uses in the program bring Barrington citizens into this new neighborhood to eat, exercise, shop, meet and have casual interaction with the senior residents. These facilities include restaurants, shops, salons, meeting rooms, doctors' offices, a theater, party rooms, a health club, and a pool. This concept, developed during a public ten-day design charrette on site, helps to knit the existing village and the new campus together and creates an interdependent, intergenerational neighborhood.

VIEW OF INDEPENDENT LIVING UNITS FROM
ENTRANCE *(top right)*
Housing choices allow residents to "age in place" as their needs and lifestyles change. The 310 units include lavish duplex villas, independent living apartments, assisted-living units, skilled nursing units, and units for residents with dementia. There is also a successful bed and breakfast that operates on the site.

The independent living building and villas were completed during Phase I. Phase II, which includes the spa and fitness center and the health center, is under construction. Future phases include additional independent living units.

*Photographs by Steve Hall © Hedrich-Blessing;
Drawings by Torti Gallas and Partners, Inc.*

Urban Design Associates

Pittsburgh, Pennsylvania

URBAN DESIGN ASSOCIATES (UDA) is an architectural firm that designs cities, towns, and neighborhoods with the goal of creating beautiful places with lasting value for the communities they serve. A typical team working together in the creative process includes citizens, economists, engineers, architects, developers, policy makers, government officials, and builders. The goal is always to construct humane and appropriate visions for the future by building on the unique character and positive qualities of each place. By working at many levels, UDA tries to find ways of coordinating the design of individual buildings, public spaces, and neighborhoods, towns, and cities into a viable and vital urban tapestry.

Principals: Raymond L. Gindroz, FAIA; Donald K. Carter, FAIA, AICP; Paul B. Ostergaard, AIA; Rob Robinson, AIA; Barry Long, AIA

A PATTERN BOOK FOR NORFOLK NEIGHBORHOODS
Norfolk, Virginia

CLIENT
City of Norfolk

PROJECT TEAM
Raymond L. Gindroz, FAIA; Rob Robinson, AIA; Debbie Blattistone

The City of Norfolk, Virginia, determined that enhancing the quality and character of its neighborhoods is not only critical for the quality of life for its citizens, but also a key factor in attracting new businesses and investment to the city. Norfolk has a rich architectural heritage and a collection of neighborhoods remarkable for their diversity and unique character. In recent years, however, the distinct quality of the traditional architectural styles has been affected by generic, mass-produced housing.

NEIGHBORHOOD PATTERNS *(above)*
The Norfolk Pattern Book is organized into four sections: The Overview, Neighborhood Patterns, Architectural Patterns, and Landscape Patterns. The Neighborhood Patterns section provides a description of the various Norfolk neighborhoods by era. Building setbacks, the character of the streets, landscaping, and architectural diversity are described for each era.

A NORFOLK NEIGHBORHOOD PATTERN *(left)*
The city of Norfolk produced *The Pattern Book for Neighborhoods,* a resource for homeowners, builders, and communities as they repair, rebuild, and expand houses and preserve neighborhoods in ways that are consistent with traditional Norfolk architecture and compatible with neighborhood character. *The Pattern Book* sets standards for street design and for the way in which houses relate to streets and public spaces, and provides specific architectural guidelines for ensuring harmony with existing buildings.

CHIMNEY AND PORCH DETAILS FROM THE ARCHITECTURAL PATTERNS SECTION *(opposite left)*
The Architectural Patterns section provides detailed examples of massing types; key character elements; common architectural details such as eaves, windows and doors, porch details; and compositional guidelines based on style or vocabulary. The Landscape Patterns section offers a variety of planting and landscaping strategies that reinforce the overall character of the neighborhood.

NORFOLK ARCHITECTURAL STYLES *(opposite right)*
Six distinct architectural styles give Norfolk neighborhoods their character: Classical Revival, Colonial Revival, European Romantic, Arts & Crafts, Victorian, and Coastal Cottage.

ASSEMBLING THE ELEMENTS OF A NORFOLK HOUSE *(opposite bottom)*

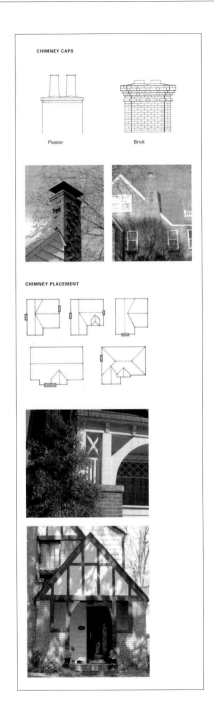

CHIMNEY CAPS

Plaster   Brick

CHIMNEY PLACEMENT

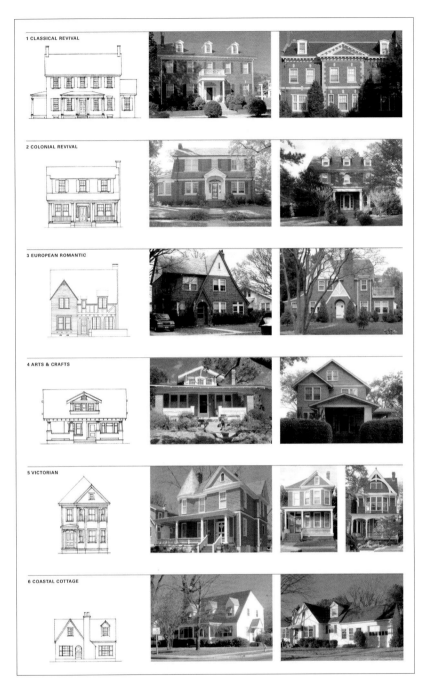

1 CLASSICAL REVIVAL

2 COLONIAL REVIVAL

3 EUROPEAN ROMANTIC

4 ARTS & CRAFTS

5 VICTORIAN

6 COASTAL COTTAGE

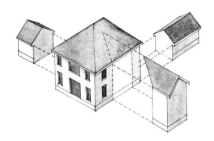

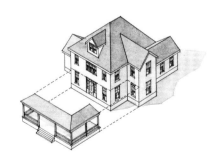

EAST BEACH PATTERN BOOK FOR NORFOLK, VIRGINIA

CLIENT
Norfolk Redevelopment and Housing Authority in association with East Beach Company, LLC

PROJECT TEAM
Raymond L. Gindroz, FAIA; Rob Robinson, AIA; Paul B. Ostergaard, AIA; Maggie Connor

CONSULTANTS
Master Planning Consultant: Duany Plater-Zyberk & Company, Miami, FL
Landscape Consultant: CMSS Architects, Hampton Roads, VA

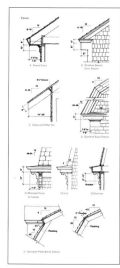

PERSPECTIVE OF THE EAST BEACH BAYFRONT AREA *(above left)*

East Beach is a new neighborhood on Norfolk's Chesapeake Bay that draws upon southeastern building types and town planning practices to create a unique waterfront village rooted in the traditions of the region. It is intentionally and distinctly Tidewater in character, from the overall layout and landscape design to the details of the buildings, pathways, and parks.

The plan of East Beach is a response to the historic pattern of neighborhood forms, specific natural features, and contrasting qualities of the site. Pedestrian-scaled streets, hidden gardens, shuttered porches, narrow alleys, and overhanging roofs have been brought together to provide a sense of familiarity, stimulation and ease.

East Beach has a mix of unit types, including: small garden houses, cottages, neighborhood houses, attached houses, and flats over retail in the marina area. The Townscape of East Beach is broken down into four parts: The Neighborhood Parks, The Pretty Lake Marinas, The Bay Front, and Shore Drive. The Neighborhood Parks are designed around a series of organic parks along the streets that take advantage of existing landscape and mature trees.

PRETTY LAKE DISTRICT *(above)*

The Pretty Lake Marinas are a precinct alive with a mix of residential and commercial uses in mixed-use buildings that add contrast and character to the inland residential neighborhoods. This precinct will have a continuous series of public spaces and thoroughfares that provide access to the waterfront for residents, slip owners, and visitors.

The Bay Front shore will have a continuous public beach with access points at the ends of streets or through public greens and paths. Shore Drive includes stately housing designed in the tradition of an "Admiral's Row" and a neighborhood shopping precinct at the entrance of Pleasant Avenue.

DETAILS FOR A TIDEWATER SHINGLE STYLE HOUSE *(above right)*

The East Beach Pattern Book defines the elements of vernacular architecture that evolved in the coastal regions of the mid-Atlantic settlements. Houses are simple, low-key, and refer to one another and to the indigenous qualities of the landscape. The architectural goal is a simple elegance derived from well-proportioned massing and fenestration, a rich color palette, and details that are derived from the building traditions throughout the region.

The East Beach Pattern Book is divided into four sections: an Introduction, which gives an overview of the proposed community; Community Patterns, which sets the relationship between housing types and their lots as well as setting the character for the different places within the new development; Architectural Patterns, which illustrates key elements for four different vernacular housing vocabularies that are appropriate for this region; and Landscape Patterns, which gives guidelines for appropriate native plant materials, paving elements and ancillary site structures.

All images courtesy of Urban Design Associates.

Wadia Associates

New Canaan, Connecticut

FOR OVER TWENTY-FIVE YEARS, Wadia Associates has been designing homes with the philosophy that a house should be traditional but not complacent, with its delights not all revealed at once. Emphasis is on the practical needs of the client, and houses are designed for all of life's events. Inspired by the site and by historical precedent, importance is placed on detailing, proportion, sunlight, and strong relationships between the interior and exterior spaces. The intention is that craftsmanship and quality of materials complement the land on which a house is built as well as the surrounding neighborhood.

PRIVATE RESIDENCE
New Canaan, Connecticut

PROJECT TEAM
Principal: Dinyar Wadia
Project Architect: David Barham
Project Managers: Tony Castor and Peter Ferraro

EXTERIOR VIEW OF THE GREAT ROOM
FROM THE GARDENS *(top left)*
The design for this house, which was completed in 2002, is based upon Jacobean and Elizabethan details, which are most evident in the building's form, the window details, and the decorative brick and stonework. The house has brick laid in a Flemish bond and features prominent gable ends. Cut stonework is used as a unifying element in the gable ends and the Gothic-arched doorways, as well as around the windows.

INTERIOR VIEW OF THE GREAT ROOM *(top right)*
The metal windows are housed in stone surrounds and mullions that carry through from the exterior to the interior. The interior spaces are richly decorated with "Jacobethan" elements throughout.

All images courtesy of Wadia Associates.

CLOISTER LEADING TO THE GREAT ROOM

SITTING AREA IN THE GREAT ROOM

PRIVATE RESIDENCE
Greenwich, Connecticut

PROJECT TEAM
Principal: Dinyar Wadia
Project Architect: David Dunn
Project Managers: Tony Castor, David Barham,
    and Hossein Kazemi

ENTRANCE ELEVATION *(top)*
This Georgian-inspired residence, completed
in the fall of 2003, is situated on a large piece
of property in the mid-country of Greenwich,
Connecticut. Classical detailing is employed
throughout the exterior and interior of the
home. Exterior materials include handmade
brick laid in a Flemish bond, cut limestone,
and a slate roof with white painted dormers
and cupola.

VIEW OF DINING ROOM *(bottom right)*
The dining room features an intricately
designed decorative plaster ceiling inspired
by the work of Robert Adam. Although the
dining table seats twelve, an intimate semi-
circular bay was created off the dining room
with a table for four.

GARDEN FAÇADE *(below)*
The façade features a double-height loggia,
with 21-foot-tall limestone columns, overlooking terraces and lawns that are framed by
mature beech trees.

POOL HOUSE *(top)*
The property also includes a tennis court, swimming pool, and a pool house featuring a trabeated loggia.

PANELED LIBRARY *(bottom left)*
The paneled library was made in England out of English burl oak. The lower level of the house includes entertainment for the children: a game room for billiards and table tennis, a playroom for pinball machines and video games, a model train room, a home theater, and a batting cage.

DETAIL AT STAIRCASE *(bottom right)*

All images courtesy of Wadia Associates.

The Grand Tradition, Faith, and Mentorship:
A Visit with Quinlan Terry

By Stephen Wiseman

y journey from the architecture of the classroom in the early 1980s (it seems that Deconstruction was in vogue that season) into the grand tradition of authentic classical architecture began with the correspondence between myself and two extraordinary men: Henry Hope Reed and Quinlan Terry. This article concerns the latter, whom I discovered in Clive Aslet's book, *Quinlan Terry: The Revival of Architecture* (Viking Press, 1986). This treasure of a book stood out from the typical collection of architectural monographs at the public library, which I frequented while I was an intern for a local architectural firm in Lexington, Kentucky. The book, the man, and his work made a prophetic impact on my view of architecture.

Within the above-referenced book I found note of Quinlan Terry's only U.S. project at the time, which was then underway. It turned out to be a thoroughbred horse farm just outside Lexington which was called Pine Oak Farm [FIGURE 1]. The owner, Mrs. Josephine Abercrombie, was very generous and allowed me to visit the house, by then completed, and even gave me permission to conduct a Central Kentucky Chapter AIA tour. I also found out that Mrs. Abercrombie donated Mr. Terry's drawings of her house to the University of Kentucky's College of Architecture, where I found them tattered, dusty, and unprotected on top of a file cabinet (while of course Le Corbusier was under lock and key). These drawings proved to be a great resource to me, and I was successful in persuading the library to store them properly.

My first letter to Mr. Terry in 1991 was a letter of desperation more than anything else. I was determined to learn about the classical tradition but was living in Kentucky at the time, with no mentor available. I was fortunate that Mr. Terry kindly agreed to help me through correspondence. This correspondence has spanned more than a decade, providing me with insight and guidance not only about architecture but in matters of faith as well. As many readers may know, Quinlan Terry is an unabashedly, unapologetically devout and spiritual man.

In my initial correspondence, I wrote that I desired to travel to Rome. Chapter Three ("The Roman Sketchbook") of his book made it very clear that studying in Rome was essential to studying the classical.

Unfortunately my circumstances at the time did not allow me this luxury. Encouragement from Mr. Terry came soon in his reply:

> *You don't need to go to Rome. America has many*
> *examples of good classical details and I recommend that*
> *you measure there and draw your measurements*
> *full size in a sketch book. In this way you will understand*
> *how things are put together in the proper manner.*

Happily, I have since traveled to Rome with the ICA's travel program on a ten-day sketch tour in the fall of 2000. However, Terry's encouragement, especially during my early development as a classicist, was immeasurably helpful and kept me on the right path. I began filling my sketch book with good classical details of local buildings from the Federal Period to the American Renaissance. More assistance was to follow from across the pond on general theory, materials, and methods. As an example, a signed copy of *Architects Anonymous* (Academy Editions, London, 1994; distribution by St. Martin's Press, New York, NY) arrived from Mr. Terry, which further reinforced the idea that architects can learn so much from looking at and studying good examples in one's own area. Another letter early in our correspondence also emphasized this concept:

> *Your final question is the most difficult to answer because the*
> *'certain rules' are not engraven on tablets of stone. They*
> *become apparent to people working in the classical tradition.*
> *The tragedy today is that so few attempt to work in the tradition.*
> *On the other hand, the few who want to seem somehow unable*
> *to find a suitable mentor or patron. The success of classical*
> *architecture is in understanding and using the traditional skills*
> *and materials in the traditional way; that is why 18th century*
> *work was so good even when practiced by unskilled [unskilled was*
> *marked out in pen and written in as 'unknown'] builders.*
> *Similarly, that is why modern work is so bad, even when*
> *practiced by gifted designers; it is the tradition*
> *that matters not the individual talent of a particular person.*

And in a 1995 letter critiquing some of my sketches Terry wrote:

As for your sketches; it is most important, as I have said before,
that you attempt to draw these to scale. The mental effort
required of drawing mouldings is one thing, but if you can draw
them to scale as you look at them then you will have useful
measurements which will come in handy when you design new work.

The opportunity to meet Mr. Terry came in December 2003, when I was required to visit England for work. It was arranged that I would take the train from Liverpool Station, London, to Colchester (about one hour), and then a taxi to Terry's office in Dedham.

Colchester is like any other mid-size town, with some of the old and a lot of the new, and not especially charming, compared to many of the villages I had previously visited in Northern England and Scotland. Dedham, on the other hand, was idyllic [FIGURE 2]. I arrived in Dedham and settled into a room overlooking Dedham's St. Mary's Church, a fifteenth-century church looked after by Roger Barrell of Mr. Terry's office.

Roger Barrell is currently an Associate Partner and is the son of Hugh Barrell, who is now retired. Hugh Barrell was a long-time Associate Partner of Erith and Terry whose position was highly regarded. Mr. Barrell (the older) was responsible for making sure Mr. Terry's designs were strictly followed and tectonically sound; he basically ran projects as a Project Architect/Manager would here in the States. His knowledge of stone types, building lime, proper flashing details, etc. was encyclopedic. In keeping with the grand tradition in the office, Hugh Barrell has passed the torch to his son, Roger who is now an associate himself.

This lineage is an example of how things are in the Terry office. There are no *prima donnas* or star designers as in so many offices in the States. At the time of my visit, Mr. Terry acknowledged that the firm would be changing its name from Erith and Terry Architects to Quinlan and Francis Terry Architects (Francis is his son). Out of respect for his late partner Raymond Erith, Mr. Terry kept the name Erith and Terry Architects for over thirty years.

Mr. Terry's office in Dedham is in the middle of the village, diagonally opposite the post office, and is strikingly unchanged from a description of it written for *The Guardian* by Martin Pauley in 1985. He wrote of "a radiant bar electric fire, antiquarian drawing boards, a total absence of designer furniture, assistants wearing ties who work six days a week, and work being produced for millions sterling inside this low-ceilinged, Spartan, rabbit-warren of a village house." And yes, sheets of the *Times* from when it was Erith's office in the seventies still remain as a wall covering. I even wondered if Mr. Terry was wearing the same tastefully distressed three-piece suit with a button gone missing [FIGURE 3]. There is one upper room where I had to duck to enter a five-foot-high opening where a lone draftsman, Mr. Clive Dale (who has been with the firm 28 years), was drawing full-scale window sections. In my view the office of Quinlan and Francis Terry Architects is and has always been interested in providing sound architectural services; it is not at all interested in trying to impress in a superficial way. Designing classical buildings is hard work.

After an introduction to Mr. Terry's son Francis and the office staff, Mr. Terry and I were off to the city of Brentwood to deliver a concept design within Brentwood's Cathedral grounds. (We buzzed along in a Volkswagen Beetle that had recently replaced his previous vehicle—a Citroen. According to Mr. Terry, the Beetle gives him the much-needed head room.) At Brentwood, Mr. Terry completely renovated and transformed a banal 1970s structure attached to a Gothic Revival Church into a classical cathedral inspired by the Italian Renaissance and British masters such as Christopher Wren. The connector of existing buildings within the campus, also by Mr. Terry, is a jewel.

We arrived in the late afternoon and were told that the Bishop would like Mr. Terry to wait for him, since he would be arriving soon and would most definitely like to speak with him in person. When the Bishop arrived, he wanted Mr. Terry to hear the new organ pipes—

Figure 1 (top left): Front elevation, Pine Oak Farm, Kentucky, 1986–88. Drawing by Quinlan Terry, based on Roger Morris' design at Marble Hill, Twickenham.

Figure 2 (top right): Village of Dedham from St. Mary's Tower.

Figure 3 (bottom): The author with Quinlan Terry in the Quinlan and Francis Terry offices, December 2003. Note the sheets of *The Times* covering the walls.

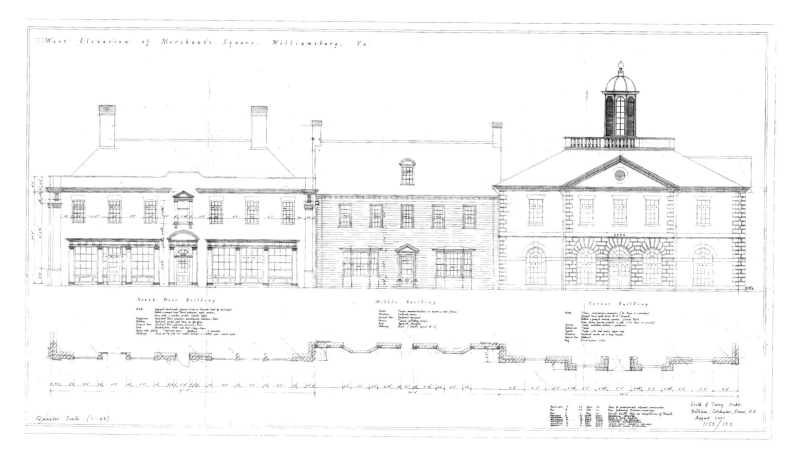

a sound that had to be experienced! We then sat for tea while Mr. Terry presented the drawings to the Bishop and the Father in charge of buildings and grounds. This particular project was a refurbishment of an ancillary building, and I could sense the deep respect and trust that the Bishop had for Mr. Terry.

After this informal presentation and discussion, we headed back to Dedham, checked into the office, and then walked up to the Great House by the late Raymond Erith for a call on Mr. and Mrs. Archer, Mr. Erith's son-in-law and daughter. This house shows a fine contrast between Mr. Erith's bare classicism and Mr. Terry's rich ornamentation. We, of course, discussed architecture, my visit to the Soane Museum the day before, and the upcoming exhibit of Raymond Erith's work at the Museum (which was on display through December 2004). Conversation was enhanced by a glass or two of sherry, continuing a household tradition from when Mr. Erith was alive.

Then we were off again to Higham Hall, just across the border of Essex into Suffolk, for dinner with Mr. and Mrs. Terry, Francis, and a family friend. The Terry home is elegantly designed, yet very lived-in and warm. There were abundant architectural models, rare architectural books, and furniture from Greek to Rococo; a portion of the walls are in trompe l'oeil by Mr. Terry himself. One would assume that the house in which Mr. Terry chose to reside would have a canonically symmetrical façade, but this is not the case! Mr. Terry is not as canonical as you would expect and indeed leans more toward Mannerism.

Although Mr. Terry did not design his residence, he chose it and describes his appreciation for it in *Architects Anonymous*:

> *The familiar pattern of five sash windows in arches has been ingeniously employed to conceal the irregular piers and modillions, only apparent after close measurements. It makes a virtue of an asymmetrical plan with good rooms of 15 feet span. The small study to the left of the front door is ideally arranged with a window placed asymmetrically to allow for the door swing. This thoughtful flexibility incorporated into the design exhibits a skill known to many country builders but often rejected by architects because of their views on symmetry.*

Our conversation that evening focused on architecture and Christianity—but reader, please notice that only the latter is capitalized. Mr. Terry had previously stated to me that he would never confuse the two, for as he put it, "architecture is not salvation!" How others have confused this issue I can only speculate. Mr. Terry has frequently been labeled a fundamental Christian and has been accused too often of mixing the two as equally important (as Pugin did), but Mr. Terry cannot and must not be placed in that coterie. His answer to one of my letters in 1998 concerning my own resistance to the use of CAD in traditional architecture couldn't be clearer. Mr. Terry writes:

I think it is important that your resistance to modernism in the
Christian sphere is not transferred to your day-to-day work without
closely considering the differences. The fact that you are a Christian
is the greatest privilege and will last for eternity. The fact that
you are an architect is a much lesser thing and the normal constraints
of life apply where you have no special privileges.

Concerning technology, what new technologies he accepts or
dispels in his own office are based on a practical analysis rather than
the latest trends. All presentation and construction drawings are still
hand drawn by Quinlan and Francis Terry [FIGURE 4]. However, when
I arrived, the office secretaries, Katrina and Nancy, had just been set
up with new desktops (yes … computers!) [FIGURE 5], and I'm confi-
dent they would not go back to typing specifications with a Selectric
typewriter. In contrast, that afternoon Francis was beautifully hand-
drawing and shading a ceiling ornament plan and profile sheet for
the Hanover Lodge project [FIGURE 14]. *Gibbs' Rules For Drawing the*
Several Points of Architecture was opened nearby for precedent.

Before I left Dedham, I made sure that I visited many of Erith
and Terry's "Little Houses" at Frog Meadow, as well as Dedham's
vintage buildings, which Terry sketched and printed in *Architects*
Anonymous. He borrowed a niche design from Sherman's Hall in
Dedham [FIGURE 6] as well as The Old Grammar School's corner
pilaster [FIGURE 7] and transported them to our shores for Merchant's
Square in Williamsburg, Virginia. [FIGURES 8 AND 9]. For Mr. Terry,
the niche ensemble is the *pièce de résistance*, meant to surprise and
delight in its miniature detail; and it does just that [FIGURE 10].

He seemed very satisfied that such details from an anonymous
architect or builder (unknown, but skilled!) from his tiny village in
England could be so appropriate and beautiful for Williamsburg.
Mr. Terry's appreciation of ordinary, sound work is described in
Architects Anonymous:

> *To focus on an obscure or neglected building and to discover*
> *the hidden subtleties, the wisdom and ingenuity of its often*
> *nameless or forgotten author is the most valuable exercise for a*
> *practicing architect. Inevitably, on closer study, accumulated*
> *knowledge and common sense come through and inspire one's own*
> *efforts at solving similar problems. Neither is this process new to*
> *our times: countless great buildings demonstrate their obvious*
> *provenance from uncelebrated antecedents. The great architecture*
> *of the Renaissance owes its existence to the study of anonymous*
> *architectural remains.*

Measuring and drawing details to scale has been important to Mr.
Terry since his late partner's dream concerning this practice, described
in *Quinlan Terry: The Revival of Architecture*:

> *Shortly before Raymond Erith died he had a dream. He dreamt*
> *that he was in a conclave of architects. They were all there—*
> *Lasdun, Spence, Casson—every celebrity of the profession who was*
> *alive at the time. And a great figure from the past, as it might be*
> *Vitruvius, came down to speak. He went up to Erith and said that,*
> *really, he was not much good, he had got this, this and this wrong*
> *in his work, and he had not spent enough time measuring*
> *Classical buildings—particularly drawing them in a sketchbook*
> *on the spot, to scale. This was the message Erith felt he had to*
> *deliver the next day to Quinlan Terry: measure, measure,*
> *measure Classical buildings, and always draw them to scale.*
> *Not, however, that it had been a wholly depressing dream.*
> *Erith said that he had woken up feeling elated. For while the*
> *Vitruvius figure had told Erith that his architecture was less*
> *than perfect, he had not spoken to the other architects present at all.*

Figure 4 (opposite): West elevation of Merchant's Square, Williamsburg, Virginia.
Drawing by Quinlan Terry, August 2001.

Figure 5 (top left): The secretaries Nancy and Katrina at Quinlan and Francis Terry
Architects after their new computers were installed, December 2003.

Figure 6 (top right): Niche precedent for Merchant's Square in Williamsburg, Virginia,
from Sherman's Hall, Dedham.

Figure 7 (bottom left): Corner pilaster from The Old Grammar School, Dedham,
which served as inspiration for Merchant's Square.

Figure 8 (bottom right): Completed niche of Merchant's Square West Building,
built fall 2004.

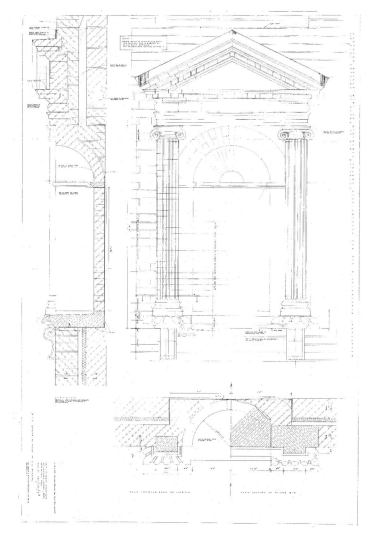

Returning to the Williamsburg Merchant's Square project [FIGURES 11, 12, AND 13], some may wonder why the Colonial Williamsburg Foundation contracted an English architect, but we must remember that we were essentially British at the time of Williamsburg's creation. Terry even specified the same "foreign" materials, such as the red-brown sandstone and the rubbed gauged brick, which are typical to several Williamsburg buildings. The source for Williamsburg was English classicism hundreds of years ago, and the Colonial Williamsburg administrators have returned to that source embodied in a contemporary English architect today.

Similarly, mentorship can be considered a return to source. A mentor's responsibility is not to mold his student in his form but instead to bring out the best that is embodied in his student's own character. It is a very Platonic notion that our search for wisdom is an effort to recall that which is already within us. Hence the act of mentoring is to help the acolyte return to the source that is his essential self. The architecture of Western civilization has oscillated to and from the Grand Tradition of classicism. Now, we too are undergoing a return to source: patrons and clients want traditional designs; classical architectural firms like Terry's have a viable way to practice; and institutions that support this culture, like Notre Dame, the University of Miami, and the Institute of Classical Architecture & Classical America are flourishing.

My gratitude goes to all, but most of all to Mr. Terry. ❧

Stephen Wiseman, AIA is a dedicated classicist and preservationist currently practicing architecture in Petoskey, Michigan and in Lexington, Kentucky.

Quinlan Terry is an internationally recognized architect who was honored with the 2005 Richard H. Driehaus Prize for Classical Architecture. He is the principal of Quinlan and Francis Terry Architects located in Essex, England.

All photographs by Stephen Wiseman.

Figure 9 (top left): Corner pilaster detail of Merchant's Square North West Building.

Figure 10 (bottom): Niche ensemble on Merchant's Square North West Building. *Construction drawing by the office of Quinlan and Francis Terry Architects.*

Figure 11 (top right): The realized North West Building, Merchant's Square, Williamsburg, Virginia.

Figure 12 (middle left): The realized Middle Building, Merchant's Square, Williamsburg, Virginia.

Figure 13 (middle right): The Corner Building of Merchant's Square, Williamsburg, Virginia.

Figure 14 (opposite): Hanover Lodge ceiling detail and design. *Hand-drawn by Francis Terry, 2005.*

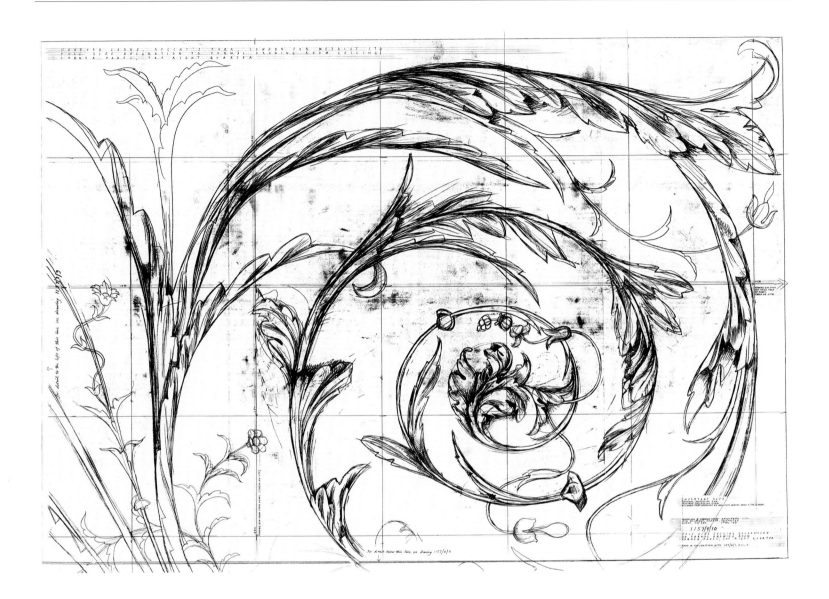

Sketchbooks

From the Sketchbooks
of Thomas A. Spain

The ability to sketch is a fundamental skill in the process of design. It is the means by which an idea first takes visual form on paper. For years, many architects practice to refine and perfect this skill, constantly document-ing buildings and details they encounter, and producing schematic sketches of their designs. Through sketching, the architect begins to understand the three-dimensional building as a two-dimensional projection, dissecting form onto a flattened surface, extracting shapes, shades and shadows; and convert-ing them into pencil, pen or brush strokes.

The University of Miami's School of Architecture treats travel sketching as a crucial element of an architect's education. While many schools have eliminated sketching as a discipline and skill in exchange for speedy computer techniques, the curriculum at U.M. includes sketching, thereby emphasizing the relevance of exploring history and traditional architec-ture forms. From the first semester of study through graduation, the important role of sketching is emphasized through site visits, sketch-ing tours around Florida and abroad, and electives such as watercolor rendering and figure drawing.

A real challenge comes during the fourth year of study, when students spend a semester in Rome. Much of the time is spent walking through the streets and squares, just looking at and recording on paper the beauty of Rome's monuments and spaces. This endeavor has been spearheaded by Professor Thomas A. Spain, who teaches his students drawing techniques in different mediums while in the field. His own habitual sketch-ing and discipline sets an example to students and faculty alike and further stresses the importance of learning through drawing.

The impact of seeing their teacher and colleague at work is undoubtedly one of the most important contributions Professor Spain has made to the School of Architecture. Greatly admired, a catalogue of sketches in pastel, pen, and pencil entitled *Drawings of Rome: 1991–2001*, was published in 2002 by the School of Architecture to accompany an exhibition curated by Professor Carie Penabad. The exhibition featured sketches produced during ten years of Professor Spain's travels to the Italian capital since 1991. The selections reproduced on the following pages are examples of work produced after the book and exhibition and hence, form a sequel to the school's publication.

I welcome you to enjoy *The Classicist's* selection of Spain's work, and leave you with a quote which describes his modest nature and devoted spirit.

— EC

"Drawing more equals seeing and remembering more. But there is also a curious social ingredient. I have drawn with and without students. The former is clearly preferred. I remember who sat alongside me for almost every sketch, for sharing the efforts builds more meaning into the experience. I consider the opportunity that they provided to be one if my life's true highlights and thank them for their work, inspiration, and companionship."

—Thomas A. Spain in
Drawings of Rome: 1991–2001

Piazza Farnese; *Conte Crayon on Patel Paper, 2004.*

Teatro di Marcello; *Conte Crayon on Paper, 2003.*

Piazza Navona; *Pencil on Bristol, 2002.*

Piazza del Popolo; *Pen on Bristol, 2004.*

Trajan's Column; *Pen on Bristol, 2002.*

Santa Maria in Cosmedin; *Pen on Bristol, 2003.*

Palazzo Farnese; *Pen on Bristol, 2004.*

Dome of St. Peter's; *Pen on Bristol, 2002.*

Piazza Navona; *Pen on Bristol, 2004.*

From the Academies

From the Academies

T he curriculum for a project given to Cooper Union students in 2001 made quite an impression on me. The semester's assignment was to study the city plans of Rome, Berlin, and New York. Upon finishing figure ground and massing analysis, students were to propose a master plan for a contemporary civic institution, which should reflect Sigmund Freud's definition of the city as a psychic creature. Part of this definition, taken from Freud's *Civilization and its Discontent*, reads: "Rome was not so much a human inhabitation as psychic substance or creature, with a rich and substantial past in which not only whatever has been in existence has never perished but also, parallel to the last phase of development, all earlier incarnations live on."

I found the problem at hand both compelling and odd. Although it seemed reasonable to ask students to study major civic centers like Rome and New York, the design problem was, and remains, too abstract to visualize. Had the design problem been to create a mixed-use building in Manhattan's Financial District, a design might be a straightforward challenge (see one student's solution shown on pages 86–88). Had someone requested a concept for a villa on Via Julia in Rome, many students could have sketched a solution within a few hours time. But inventing an aesthetic for a twenty-first century civic structure, based on an Austrian neurologist's definition of Rome, was not within my realm of comprehension.

The curriculum that shaped me as an architecture student, admittedly my point of reference, was at the opposite end of the spectrum from Cooper Union's. The design problems were very tangible and did

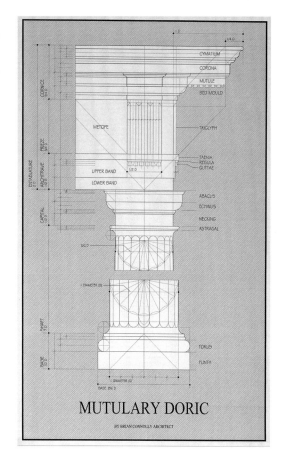

MUTULARY DORIC

BY BRIAN CONNOLLY ARCHITECT

not require a re-invention of the wheel. My very first design problem was an urban bus stop. Our class was given a site near the university, scheduled numerous site visits to document existing conditions, and had a series of lectures about different precedents for bus stops. Fast-forwarding to my fourth year, our class was designing an extensive addition to the Fourth Presbyterian Church, one of Chicago's most historically significant Gothic churches by Ralph Adams Cram. We traveled to Chicago and studied the city's architectural history from Louis Sullivan to Mies van der Rohe, working to understand the city's tectonic identity and influences, which were then used as a basis for our proposals. In all our design courses throughout my five years of education, the final design solution was always driven by site conditions and local character, the goal being to create a building that was appropriate within the existing urban fabric. The same criterion was used to select work for this portfolio.

The next twenty-one pages feature work by architecture students from Judson University, Notre Dame, University of Miami, University of Arkansas, UNITEC Institute of Technology in New Zealand, the ICA&CA, Yale University, and the University of Bologna. Despite the differences in curriculum and school philosophies, every single example of work presented shows evidence of precedent research. Because of this approach, the unifying theme throughout the following · section is the desire to design enduring buildings. And as these buildings are products of a more urbanistic approach the outcome transcends labels of traditional or classical. Further, the range of schools represented here, including those not known for classical pedagogy, suggests an encouraging trend. — EC

The Institute of Classical Architecture & Classical America

CONTINUING EDUCATION: *"Invention and the Orders," Stephen Chrisman, instructor, fall, 2004.*

This course builds upon the canon of the Tuscan, Doric, Ionic, and Corinthian Orders to explore the treatment, use and application of the orders. The study of the orders does not end with the fundamentals but should be expanded dramatically to contribute to the wealth of the living language of classicism. Students studied the application of the orders including precedent, superposition, use of pilasters and piers, paired columns, entablature variation, use of ornament, and tectonics or fixture structure. The course also examines invention within the classical framework through the study of work by architects including Borromini, Bramante, Michelangelo, Hawksmoor, Latrobe, Lutyens, and modern examples.

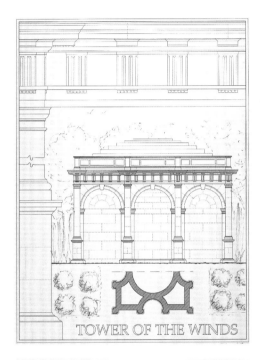

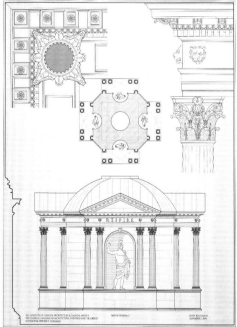

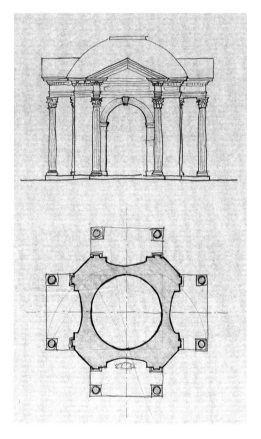

Top Left: Elisa Cuaron, Tower of the Winds; *Pencil on velum.*

Above: Scott Reed Dakin, Tower of the Winds; *Sketch on trace.*

Left: Scott Reed Dakin, Tower of the Winds Esquisse.

Opposite: Brian Connolly, Mutulary Doric Order; *Computer drawing.*

PROGRAM FOR THE AMERICAN
INSTITUTE OF BUILDING DESIGN
(AIBD): *"New Residence for Savannah,
Georgia,"* August, 2004.

The AIBD is a 50-year-old national organization for those who design residences but are
not licensed architects. Most members have
little or no architectural training yet they
are responsible for most of the residential
design in this county. In 2002, Christine
G. H. Franck, Board Director, and ICA&CA
Fellows Steve Bass and Gary Brewer met with
AIBD directors to create an educational
program that would improve the design quality of the AIBD members. Since the first
seven-week program in 2002, the program
has expanded and is one of the most effective
ICA&CA educational initiatives. The student
work that follows is from the AIBD
Southeast program in 2004.

Top: R. Clanton, Front Elevation; *Computer drawing.*

Bottom: R. Clanton, Entryway and Stair; *Computer drawing.*

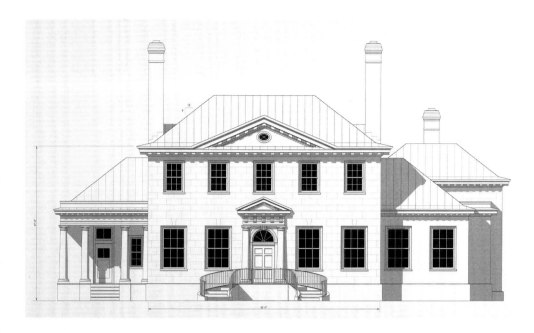

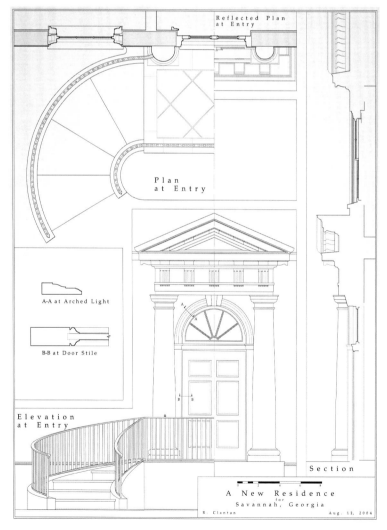

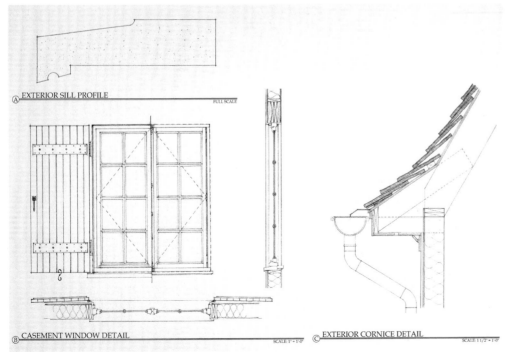

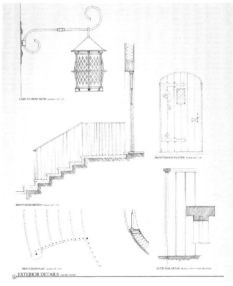

Top: S. L. Alden, Side Elevation; *Computer drawing.*

Above: S. L. Alden, Exterior Details; *Computer drawing.*

Left: S. L. Alden, Window Elevation; *Computer drawing.*

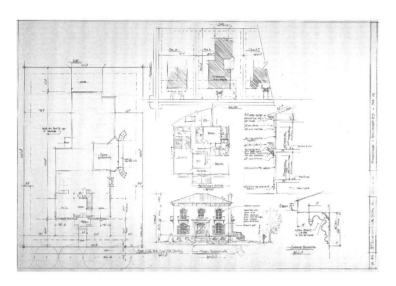

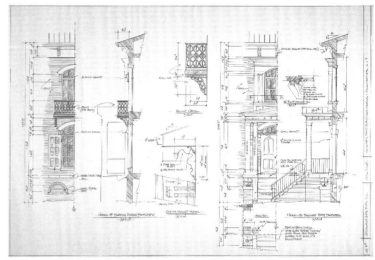

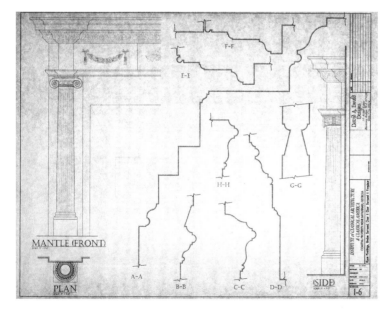

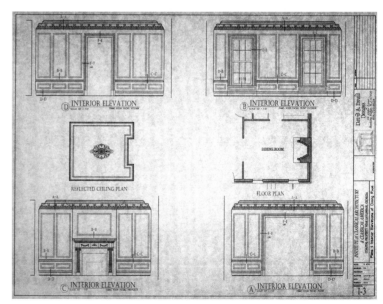

Top Left: Chris Eller, Esquisse.

Top Right: Chris Eller, Front Elevation Details; *Computer drawing.*

Bottom Left: David Ewald, Interior Details; *Computer drawing.*

Bottom Right: David Ewald, Interior Elevation for Dining Room; *Computer drawing.*

Judson University

ADVANCED DESIGN STUDIO: *"Library and Oratory; Piazza della Rotunda, Rome,"* *Christopher Miller, instructor, 2003.*

THE INSTRUCTOR'S STATEMENT:
Judson University's liberal arts character and the rich student interest in ethical service shape Judson's architecture program. The curriculum works to integrate the diverse approaches of its faculty including a value in the history of architecture in contemporary practice, and the importance of cultivating the tradition of urban environments. At present, opportunities for students to explore classical architecture and traditional urbanism are found in summer European study, in a civic architecture studio, in watercolor instruction, in a substantial history and theory curriculum at the undergraduate and graduate levels, and in independent and thesis projects.

This semester-long studio assignment required students to design a building that would assume the footprint of an existing palazzo facing the Pantheon. The architecture was expected to represent the multiple purposes of the building, including an oratory and a small library. At the same time, the building was expected to maintain the background character of the existing buildings that frame the piazza.

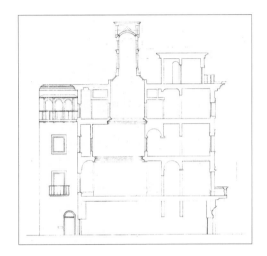

Top Left: Rozanne Stewart, Section looking south; *Graphite on vellum.*

Top Right: Rozanne Stewart, View looking west; *Graphite on vellum.*

Bottom: Rozanne Stewart, West Elevation; *Graphite and color pencil on vellum.*

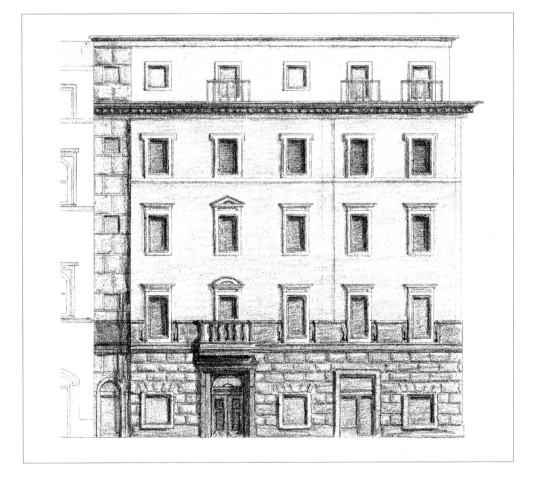

M. Arch Sixth Year Studio:
*"Doric Order and Corinthian
Order Studies in Watercolor,"
Craig Farnsworth, instructor, 2004.*

The Instructor's Statement:
From roughly the mid-1700s to the 1920s, architectural rendering was synonymous with controlled, precise watercolors that were created with considerable skill and artistic value. The result was a number of conventions and graphic standards that communicated architectural ambitions and intentions in an age before digital simulation and photography. But as architectural preferences shifted from Beaux-Arts-flavored classicism to Bauhaus modernism, the preferences for graphic portrayal of designs shifted as well. Watercolor in graded washes gave way to ink line drawings that emphasized masses and volumes rather than detail and ornament. The merits of various architectural styles aside, this change gradually led to a decline in the use of watercolor as a rendering medium. Later, the advent of colored pencils and permanent markers gave architects a quicker and more forgivable method of adding color to drawings. However, the unique, luminous qualities of watercolor were never adequately approximated by these other techniques.

In the 1980s, several architects and illustrators "rediscovered" the unique qualities of watercolor rendering and reintroduced those techniques to their work. In the process, they updated the old methods with new advances in paints and papers. Today, watercolor continues to enjoy a renaissance and has returned to prominence as a valued rendering medium within the architectural community.

Each student was to render two of the traditional Greek or Roman orders. A title and graphic scale were to be integral to the rendering. The shades and shadows had to be cast from the traditional 45 degree orientation. Each was drawn to scale on a separate 10" x 14" sheet of block paper.

CORINTHIAN ORDER
PORTICO OF THE PANTHEON

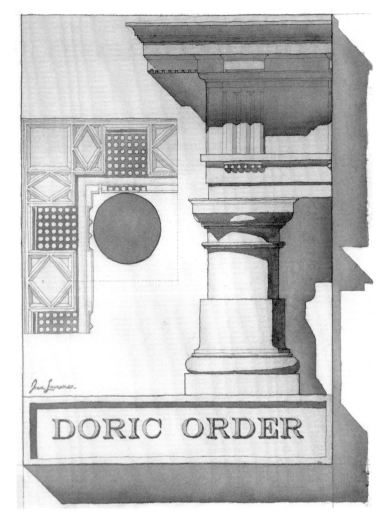

DORIC ORDER

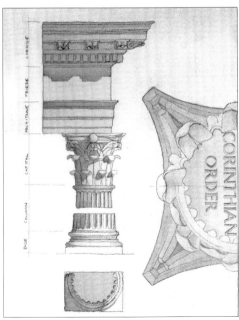

Opposite: Grant A. Saller, Ionic Order study; *Graphite and watercolor on paper.*

Top Left: Jim Fikkert, Corinthian Order study; *Graphite and watercolor on paper.*

Top Right: Jim Fikkert, Doric Order study; *Graphite and watercolor on paper.*

Bottom Left: Jesse Michael Lawrence, Corinthian Order study; *Graphite and watercolor on paper.*

Bottom Right: Jesse Michael Lawrence, Doric Order study; *Graphite and watercolor on paper.*

Unitec Institute of Technology

THIRD YEAR STUDIO: *"Project for the Completion of the Building of New Zealand Parliament in Wellington, New Zealand,"* Branko Mitrovic, instructor, fall, 1998.

The building of the New Zealand Parliament in Wellington was originally designed as a fine example of Edwardian Baroque but it was never completed according to the original plans. In the 1970s a modernist wing was added to the old building. For this project, students were invited to suggest a way to complete the old building and in particular to design a new dome for the original structure.

THIRD YEAR STUDIO: *"Gallery in Devonport, New Zealand,"* Branko Mitrovic, instructor, fall, 1999.

Davenport is one of the oldest parts of Auckland. The project was a design proposal for a gallery in this part of the city. Particular attention was paid to the composition of internal spaces and planning of internal volumetrics.

Top: Mark Boyack, Parliament Elevation; *Watercolor on watercolor paper.*

Bottom: Damon Brider, Davenport Gallery, Analytique; *Watercolor on watercolor paper.*

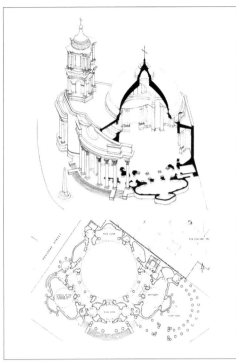

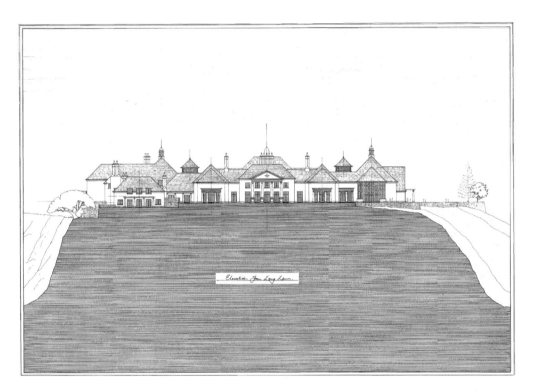

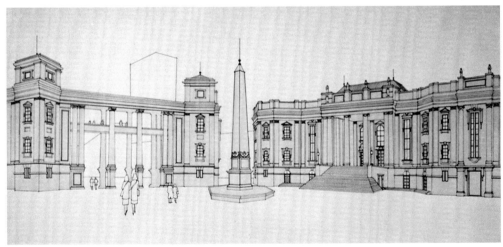

Top: Chad Hempelman, Elevation, Residence for the Governor General; *Ink on mylar.*

Top Right: Damon Brider, Axonometric and Plan, Cathedral for Auckland; *Ink on mylar.*

Bottom: Aleksander Achansky, Perspective View of Aotea Square; *Watercolor on watercolor paper.*

FOURTH YEAR STUDIO: *"Project for Aotea Square,"* Branko Mitrovic, instructor, fall, 2002.

Aotea Square is the main square center in Auckland, New Zealand. The extensive modernist intervention in the 1970s has caused it to be little used by the general public. The project was intended to critically reevaluate modernist urban planning and propose ways to revitalize this part of Auckland city.

FOURTH YEAR STUDIO: *"Residence for the Governor General, Auckland, New Zealand,"* Branko Mitrovic, instructor, fall, 2003.

The Governor General of New Zealand normally resides in Wellington; this was a project for a residence in Auckland. This project was awarded the school's prize for best student work in 2003.

FIFTH YEAR THESIS: *"Cathedral for Auckland, New Zealand,"* Branko Mitrovic, instructor, fall, 2002.

University of Arkansas

Fifth Year Design Studio:
*"A Baroque Theater," Greg Herman,
instructor, fall, 2000.*

The Student's Statement:
The project involved the design of a new theater to house a proposed Baroque Opera on the grounds of the University of Arkansas. Sarah Caldwell, founder of the Opera Company of Boston, and member of the University of Arkansas faculty, was the force behind the project, and commissioned specialists in Baroque theater to design the stage mechanisms, the proscenium, and the theater house. The remainder of the design was left to the student.

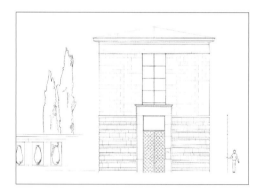

Right: Todd Furgason, Elevation Detail; *Pencil and colored pencils on vellum.*

Above: Todd Furgason, Front Elevation; *Pencil on vellum.*

University of Bologna

FIRST YEAR STUDIO: *"The Classical Orders, Geometry and Wash,"* Giuseppe Amoruso, instructor, fall, 2002.

Teaching the technical aspects of architectural drawing with the appropriate tools helps students understand the spatial implications of architectural design. Furthermore, the exploration of representational methods and the practice of graphic techniques provide students with the skills to communicate the visual and aesthetic aspects of architecture. Freehand drawing and graphic analytical skills are reached through field drawing exercises recorded in a sketchbook; rendering techniques are taught in the classroom following traditional methods.

A dedicated study is related to the representation of classical orders in the form of watercolor plates, whereby students begin to understand the relevance of geometric forms within complex architectural shapes. Each student prepares a hand-drafted sheet of an order of their preference. Once the pencil drawing has been mastered, each student continues the exercise by adding shade and shadow to a final watercolor rendering.

The requirements are the following:
1. Board size, 50 x 70 cm
2. Technique: china ink and watercolor rendering based on black-and-white schemes in Johann Matthaus Von Mauch, Peirre Joseph Normand, and Donald M. Rattner's *Parallel of the Classical Orders of Architecture* (New York: Acanthus Press, 1998).

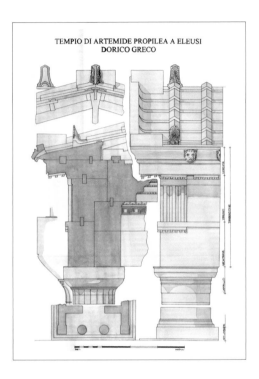

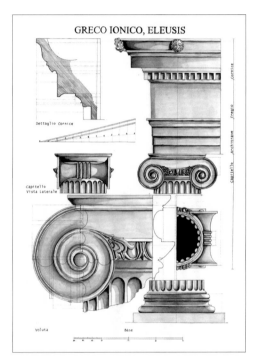

Top Left: Cynthia Mura, Analytique; *Watercolor rendering.*

Top Right: Daniela Poggiali, Analytique; *Watercolor rendering.*

Bottom: Elisa Bandini, Analytique; *Watercolor rendering.*

University of Miami

GRADUATE THESIS: *"The Amsterdam House,"* 2003–2004 *by Justin Ford*

ABSTRACT

New York is, perhaps, the greatest city in the world. It has a diversity of people, cultures, professions, architecture, street patterns, and communities. The focus of this project is on Lower Manhattan, which is the oldest section of the city and the locus of a number of varied neighborhoods. Most of these work very well, because they have a good mix of residential, commercial, retail, public, and park areas, all of which contribute to the making of a successful community. The Financial District, however, is one region of Lower Manhattan that lacks the most important components of a vital neighborhood: housing and public spaces. Understandably, the Financial District is home to many office buildings. But as a result, the area completely shuts down after the work day, becoming still and lifeless by seven o'clock at night. On weekends, the district attracts only tourists, who venture south to view such landmarks at Trinity Church, One Wall Street, the New York Stock Exchange, Federal Hall, the Bankers' Trust Building, and 40 Wall Street. This project proposes to restore 24-hour life to the area by adding a mixed-use skyscraper with residential units and public spaces, as well as an observatory. Together, these elements would create a more accessible and useable neighborhood that ultimately would also better connect to the surrounding areas of Bowling Green and Battery Park City.

SKYLINE ELEVATION LOOKING SOUTH *(above)*
This plate is a purely compositional one in which the New Amsterdam House appears with its taller neighbors. The drawing is at a scale of one inch equals twenty feet and starts at a height of about 525 feet. The six buildings (from left to right) include the Cities Services Building (810 feet), Twenty Exchange Place (684 feet), the New Amsterdam House (1,000 feet), the Bank of Manhattan (927 feet), One Wall Street (654 feet) and the Woolworth Building (793 feet).

OBLIQUE ELEVATION AND VIEWS *(opposite left)*
This plate focuses on a specific aspect of the project, which in this case is the top. The drawing in the middle of the composition is an oblique elevation portraying the building from its corner and is at a scale of three thirty-seconds of an inch equals one foot. The brick materiality of the project can be seen as can some other details such as windows, spandrels, parapets and railings. The transplanted New Amsterdam house type, with its stepped parapet and gabled roof, is also apparent and sits against a New York sky. The insets of the drawing also focus on the top, but do so from the truer vantage point of the ground. The view in the left inset portrays the New Amsterdam house with its surroundings. It is on axis with the corner from a spot on William Street south of Beaver Street. The inset on the right represents a view of the project taken from the intersection of William and Beaver streets looking straight up. The drawings show how the New Amsterdam house is visible from the ground.

NEW AMSTERDAM HOUSE
NEW YORK CITY

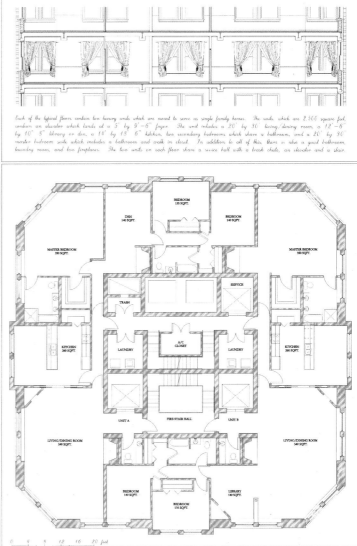

NEW AMSTERDAM HOUSE
NEW YORK CITY

RESIDENTIAL PLAN AND SECTION *(top right)*
This plate focuses on the typical floorplans of the tower portion of the building, which are located between the twenty-sixth and fifty-sixth floors. Is shows part of the project in a more detailed manner and is at a scale of one inch equals four feet. The floor plan depicts that there are two units on a floor, each of which is about two-thousand-five-hundred square feet. Every one of the units consist of an elevator which lands at an entry foyer, a spacious living/dining room, a large eat-in kitchen, a library or den, a master bed-room suite, two secondary bedrooms, as well as two-and-one-half bathrooms. The major-ity of the rooms have one or two windows. Other features include two fireplaces per unit as well as a private laundry room. In addition to all of this, each floor has a shared service hall which includes an elevator, staircase, and trash chute. The section of the plate portrays one wall of a unit. The drawing depicts the project's ten-foot high ceilings and six-foot six-inch tall windows. In addition to these finishing elements, the section begins to describe the materials, partition walls and structure which make up the building. The spaces depicted (from left to right) include the master bedroom suite, the master bath-room (with window), kitchen, and lastly the dining/living room.

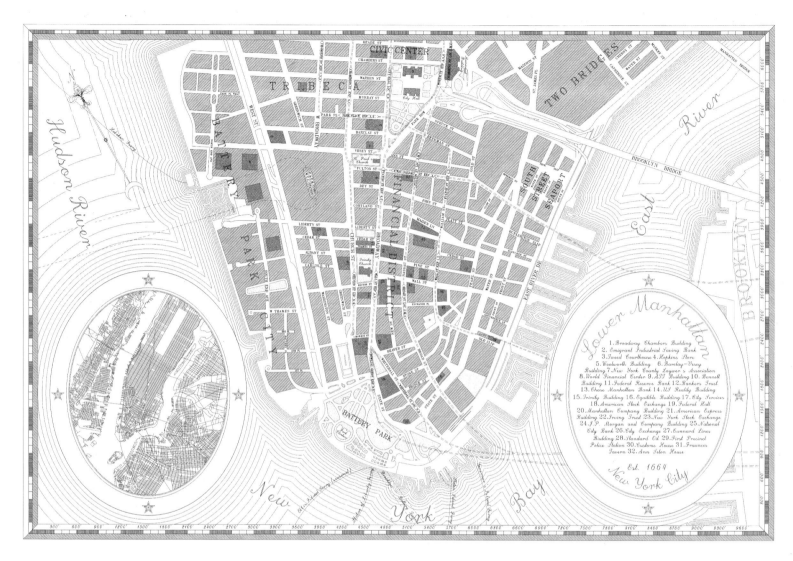

MAP OF DOWNTOWN MANAHATTAN *(above)*
This plate focuses on downtown Manhattan at a scale of one inch equals two-hundred-fifty feet. It depicts how Lower Manhattan is part of an island surrounded by three bodies of water. It also shows that the street layout is a medieval one which is quite random. In addition, the map labels the distinct districts of Lower Manhattan as well as land and water transportation lines. Lastly, the map labels the street and public spaces and designates interesting and historically important buildings and sites. The inset on the right side of the plate is a legend for these buildings, while the inset on the left depicts the full island of Manhattan with its street grid, putting it into its greater context of New York and New Jersey.

GRADUATE ROME STUDIES *(opposite top)*: *"Piranesi Studio," Teofilo Victoria, instructor, 2002.*

THE TEAM'S STATEMENT:
The Basilica di Massenzio was constructed between 308 and 312 A.D. under Massenzio, Emperor of Rome. Continuing the great Republican tradition of adding civic structures to the Forum Romano, the basilica was a gift on several levels: it housed a new market and judgment hall and provided the Forum Romano with its largest enclosed volume.

The building received inspiration from two uniquely Roman vernacular forms: the traditional basilica and the monumental frigidariums of the Imperial Roman thermal bathing halls. Accordingly, a new basilica type

was created. Whereas traditional basilica types featured a nave surrounded by two colonnaded aisles, the plan of Basilica Massenzio's central hall, like the baths, was surrounded by large rooms. Like the Imperial baths, the new basilica type featured innovative curvilinear volumetric forms. In a departure from the traditional basilica's flat or gabled ceilings, Basilica Massenzio's central nave ceiling flowed with monumental cross-vaulting. Apses were also overhead, but perhaps most striking, the side rooms were engulfed by gigantic soaring coffered barrel vaults. Despite their impressive stature, these majestic barrel-vaulted rooms, like their frigidarium predecessors, were not aligned with one another and were considered mere extensions of the central hall.

The Basilica di Massenzio was constructed between 308 and 312 A.D. under Massenzio, Emperor of Rome. Continuing the great Republican tradition of adding civic structures to the Forum Romano, the basilica was a gift on several levels it housed a new market and judgment hall and provided the Forum Romano with its largest enclosed volume (265'X 83'X 115' in the central hall). The building received inspiration from two unusually...

Jose Venegas and Graham Ivory, "La Basilica di Massenzio." The drawing presented is an oblique documentation plate, on which both team members worked for an entire semester; *Ink on mylar.*

View of the Marine Garden during the Conservation Assessment with Villa Vizcaya in the background. *Photo used by permission of Rocco Ceo.*

VIZCAYA DOCUMENTATION AND CONSERVATION ASSESSMENT (*bottom and next page*): *The Getty Foundation Architectural Conservation Grant, summer, 2003*

Project Manager: Professor Rocco Ceo
Student Team: Marcus Chaidez, Peter Nedev, Alice Oliveira, Veruzca Vasconez

This project is a documentation and conservation assessment of the Vizcaya Villa and Gardens for the Getty Foundation and Vizcaya Trust. During the summer of 2003 Rocco Ceo lead one of three project teams to document and assess the gardens of Vizcaya with particular emphasis on the Marine and Fountain Gardens. The work was conducted over nine weeks and included review of Vizcaya's archives, field drawing and photography, and the coordination and production of finished drawings. The final aspect of the project will be a report to the Getty Foundation and the Vizcaya Trust.

The garden team working with Professor Ceo consisted of four architectural interns from the University of Miami School of Architecture who worked full-time to assist in producing the 120 field drawings and nine final 30" x 60" sheets. (Three of the finished drawings are shown on the next page.) This work documents the landscape, locating plants in order to identify historic plant material, invasive and naturalized native plants, and the history of plantation on the site. This documentation formed the foundation for the materials assessment team from University of Pennsylvania.

The University of Pennsylvania team, headed by Frank Matero, was able to develop sophisticated mapping of stone and metal surface conditions and landscape material to understand what currently impacts the historic fabric, and for current and future monitoring of the site. This combined work formed the basis for an additional grant application for funds to implement conservation and restoration of the garden. The final report was due in January of 2004. It is hoped that the research will contribute to an additional collaborative effort, in the form of a book, about the construction of Vizcaya.

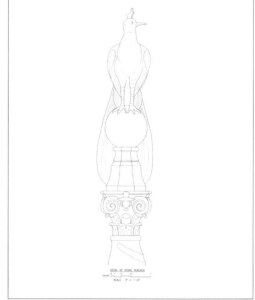

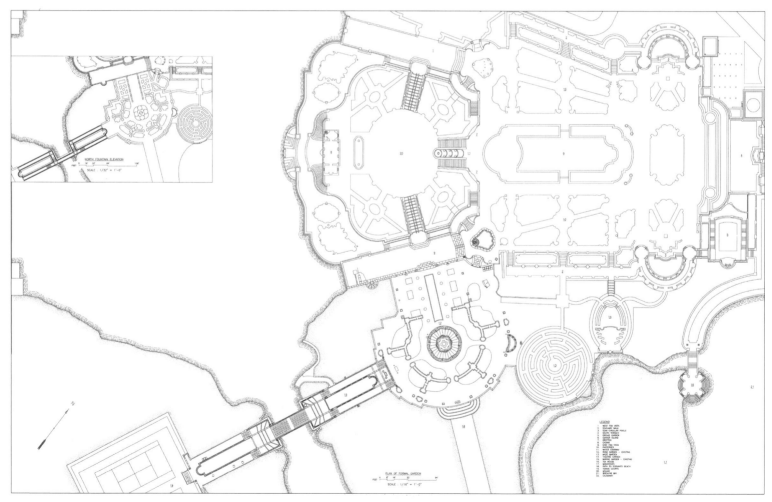

Three of the nine finished drawings for the Vizcaya Documentation and Conservation Assessment, summer, 2003.

University of Notre Dame

FOURTH YEAR STUDIO: *"Downtown South Bend," Norman Crowe, instructor, 2004.*

THE TEAM'S STATEMENT:
The Northeast Neighborhood Commons project was initiated by the University architects to develop a South Bend neighborhood just south of the University of Notre Dame Campus. The design strategy aims to better connect the campus and the community within a safe and walkable neighborhood. This was achieved by treating the greenbelt between campus and the neighborhood as an entrance rather than a barrier. Streets and roads were laid out to support residential and commercial investment. The avenue that delineates the campus from the neighborhood incorporates a boulevard and on-street parking during non-peak hours.

The proposal also provides the community with a mix of building types and uses to augment rather than detract from the neighborhood. The assortment of building types sustains and enhances the diversity of people and businesses that shape the neighborhood. Commercial and residential uses interact in public spaces provided by the streets, Eddy Square, and the park.

Above: Emily Burnett and Joseph Nickol, Site Plan and Street Elevation; *Watercolor rendering.*

Next Page Top: Emily Burnett and Joseph Nickol, Evening Perspective View of Eddy Square; *Photoshop rendering.*

Next Page Bottom: Emily Burnett and Joseph Nickol, Perspective View of Eddy Square; *Watercolor rendering.*

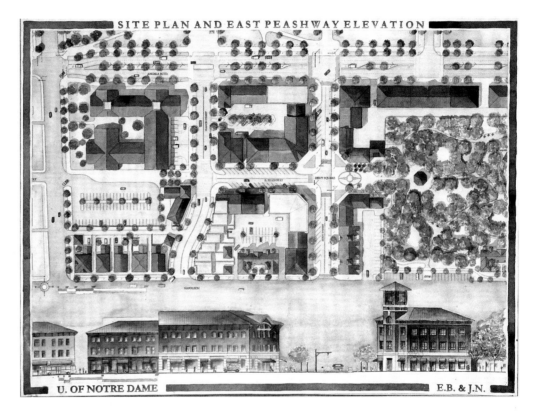

SITE PLAN AND EAST PEASHWAY ELEVATION

U. OF NOTRE DAME   E.B. & J.N.

THESIS PROJECT: *"Revitalization of Hospital Site in Ferrara, Italy,"* Michael Lykoudis, instructor, spring 2004.

THE STUDENT'S STATEMENT:

The site, which is currently occupied by a hospital, will probably be abandoned in a few years because of plans for relocation of the hospital. To that end, this project is a vision for an urban plan and architectural design as a substitution to the existing hospital.

Existing uses around the site were emphasized and integrated in the project: the south side keeps basic hospital functions while residences were added on the west side, and the university campus was expanded towards the north. This historical nucleus of the old hospital was then connected to its surrounding buildings through a main piazza, in front of which stands the focus of the second part of the thesis: a conference and exposition center.

The proposed conference and exposition center thus becomes a connection between the academic world, the historical hospital, and the citizens.

Its design was inspired by Ferrara's most typical features: materials like brick and white stone and architectural spaces like courtyards and arcades, aiming to create continuity and dialogue with the city and its traditions.

Top: Silvia Neri, Front Elevation; *Watercolor rendering.*

Bottom: Silvia Neri, Site Plan and Aerial Perspective; *Watercolor rendering.*

Next Page: Silvia Neri, First Floor Plan; *AutoCAD drawing.*

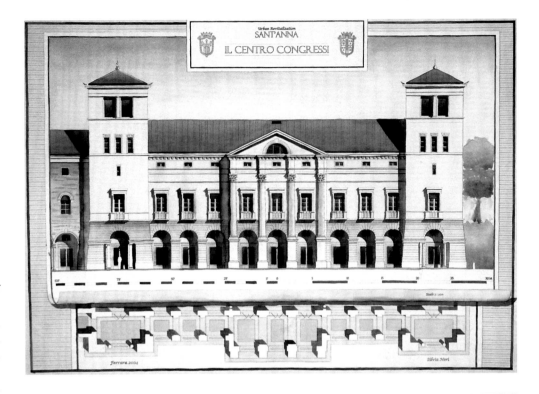

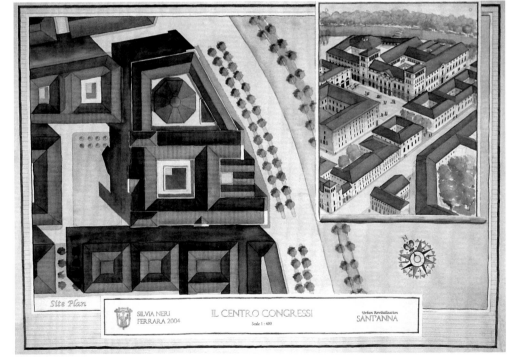

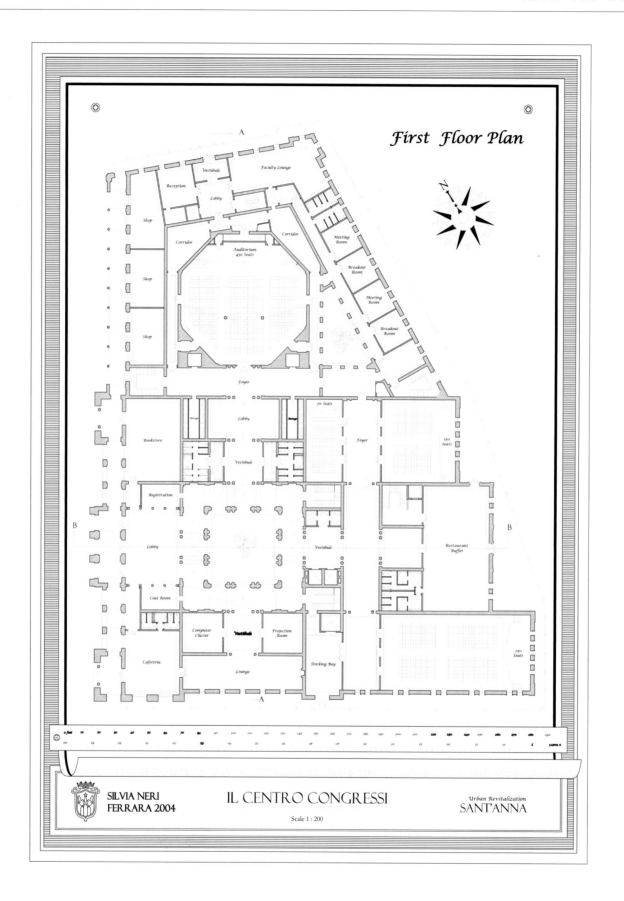

First Floor Plan

SILVIA NERI
FERRARA 2004

IL CENTRO CONGRESSI

Urban Revitalization
SANT'ANNA

Scale 1 : 200

THESIS PROJECT: *"Governor's Residence in Musick Point, New Zealand,"* Michael Lykoudis, instructor, 2004

THE STUDENT'S STATEMENT:

This project is a hypothetical; a possible proposal for a new Governor's residence in Auckland, New Zealand. A Golf Course currently exists on the site; a peninsula called Musick Point, which juts out into the Manukau Harbor.

The topography of the site provided a wide variety of challenges that drove much of the early planning stages. This included a much wider context of study with the planning of gardens, parks, and the arrangement of two important buildings—the Governor's Palace and the Governor's Villa—which enclose a large open court bracing a cliff along one side of the peninsula. The Governor's Palace was to serve as the primary public building containing the State Ballroom, State Dining Room, and accommodation for guests and offices. The Governor's Villa contains the more private living spaces for the Governor General and family.

A number of precedents were used as the basis for this project, but the most prevalent was the idea of the Roman villa. In particular, the concept of Pliny's Laurentine Villa of which we have only written descriptions. Study of Pliny's description and the typical planning of a Roman villa revealed a sequence of internal spaces that contained degrees of privacy created through the use of courtyards and hierarchy of space. Along this same line was the relationship of the villa to landscape, or how interior spaces related to exterior spaces with varying degrees of openness and enclosure.

The Governor's Villa is designed around a large open courtyard that is directly on axis with all major entrance spaces from the north and west. From the major internal courtyard there is a procession of openness as one moves east towards the cliff edge into a colonnaded court with a pool terminated by a large half-circular exedra. The façade was influenced by Greek and Renaissance styles; symmetry and asymmetry also played an important role. The three towers set up a tripartite rhythm linking the main building to

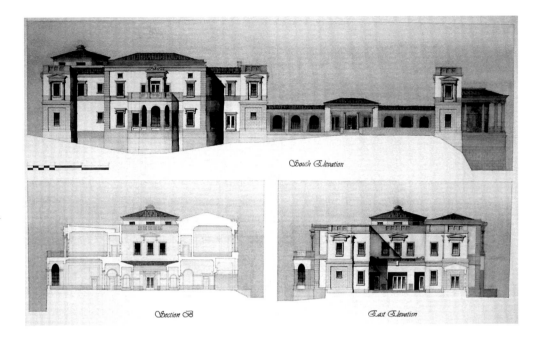

South Elevation

Section B

East Elevation

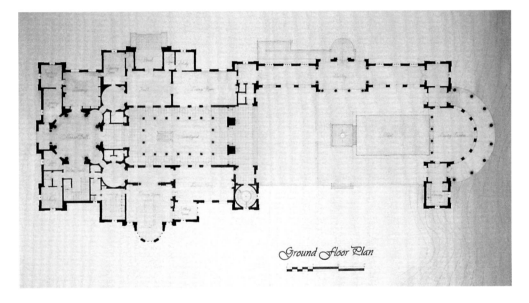

Ground Floor Plan

the outdoor living area and exedra. While there is an asymmetrical relationship of the main building to the outdoor area, these towers tie it all together and maintain the massing of the primary form.

The section "B" was taken through the main internal courtyard; it is a typical renaissance space enclosed by a single-story colonnade. From the east it is closed off by a single-height screen wall (can be seen on the east elevation) with doors that may be opened for direct continuity out into the private enclosed yard and exedra.

Top: Damon Brider, Governor's Villa: Elevations; *Watercolor rendering.*

Bottom: Damon Brider, Governor's Villa: Plan; *Watercolor rendering.*

Yale University

ADVANCED DESIGN STUDIO:
*"Redevelopment of Harleston Village,
Charleston, South Carolina," Andrés Duany
and Léon Krier, instructors, spring 2001.*

THE STUDENT'S STATEMENT:
This semester-long project was from the first
Transect design studio. The project began
with Transect-based field analysis of ten
American cities with quality urbanism, including Charleston, Savannah, New Orleans, and
San Francisco. Each student selected one of
the cities visited, and focused on an area of
the urban fabric which had been modernized
(corrupted; made anti-urban). The brief had
three parts: first, study the components of
quality urbanism, like streets, block sizes, and
frontage conditions; second, create a master
plan for the site; and third, develop the
master plan architecturally. Relating to the
Transect and an open concern for America's
prolific annual residential production, the
key building blocks consisted of student-
designed dwelling units for Urban Centre
(T3), General Urban (T4), and Suburban
zones." (*For more on the Transect please see D.V.
Marcantonio's article on pages 18–23.*)

The selected site was the Village of
Harleston, in Charleston, South Carolina.
Two items of special interest came from a
study of Charleston: the architecture of
Robert Mills and the side-yard house, an
intriguing model for a "flexible house." The
side-yard house is compelling because it
allows for a porch, parking, and a yard—a
total package which facilitates a particularly
American form of urbanism.

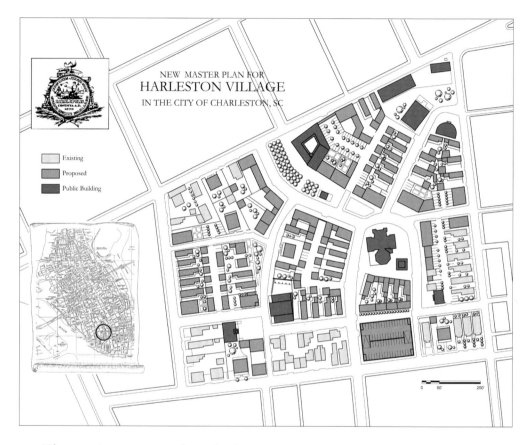

The project proposed replacing
Harleston's Robert Mills Manor housing
estate with a group of small urban blocks that
are similar to the neighboring blocks. The
blocks are developed with a syncopated
rhythm, mixing the three different Transect
zone units throughout the site, rather than in
segregated zones. A selection of appropriate
public buildings, closely following recognizable building types, are strategically located to
provide local facilities as well as neighborhood
landmarks. Also, in keeping with recent efforts,
the project proposed that the former City Jail
be reused as a School of Building Arts.

Above: Chris Pizzi, Masterplan; *CAD drawing.*

T4 GENERAL URBAN

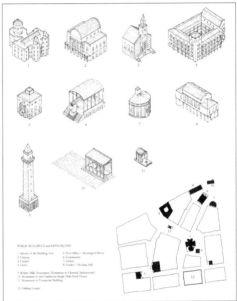

THE CHARLESTON SINGLE HOUSE
THE ORIENTED URBANISM OF THE "SIDE YARD" HOUSE TYPE

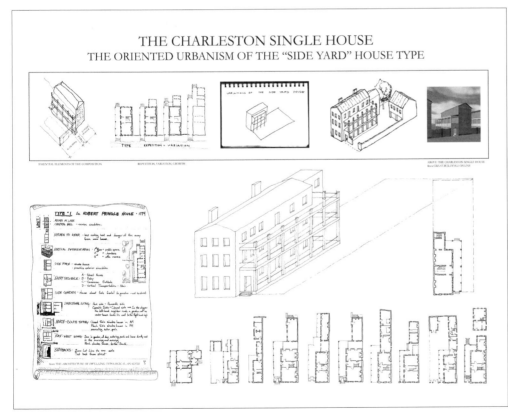

Top Left: Chris Pizzi, Study of the Side-yard House Type; *Hand sketches in ink.*

Top Right: Chris Pizzi, Public Buildings and Monuments; *Hand sketches in ink.*

Bottom: Chris Pizzi, T4 Zone: General Urban; *Hand sketches in ink.*

Competitions

Competitions

This issue of *The Classicist* continues the tradition of being one of the rare forums for presenting classically-designed competition entries. These projects, though unbuilt, can serve as useful precedents for how certain problems might be solved. They can also be inspirational, from a presentational point of view, as considered compositions, drawings, and renderings. The persuasiveness of a beautiful drawing cannot be underestimated.

If there is an overarching theme to this collection of proposals, it is design in the public realm. The size of these designs ranges from street furniture to houses, to monuments, to civic buildings with a strong urban component, to entire city quarters. The one entry for a new country house serves as an example of a rural counterpart to the traditional city.

These solutions demonstrate the versatility of the classical approach to problems of various sizes, making use of one of the qualities of traditional design most loved by its practitioners and laymen alike—the use of human scale. It is perhaps this aspect of traditional design, as well as the shared palette of moldings and details, that helps relate the street lamp to the building, the building to the

street, the street to the square, the square to the city. In this way, the traditional city becomes a harmonious whole made up of disparate parts.

This being the first issue of *The Classicist* published since September 11, 2001, we have included three entries for memorials to the victims of the attacks. They raise interesting questions with respect to character and how tragedy should be memorialized. One entry is based on the triumphal arch motif, one is an open, classical pavilion, and one is based on Sir Edwin Lutyens' cenotaph in London. This exemplifies the variety that almost always results, despite similar briefs.

Several entries also express an interest in a more sustainable, "green" approach to design. This is not to be seen as the use of a fashionable buzzword, but rather something that many traditionalists have long suspected: traditional design's use of locally available and natural materials, as well as local and regional typologies that have evolved over time to adapt to the local environment, results in naturally "green" buildings, thus making a compelling argument in favor of traditionalism. This is an element of civic responsibility or stewardship being increasingly required of design in the public realm. — CL

World Trade Center Memorial Design Competition

New York, New York; September 2002

Tiffany L. Burke

THE LOWER MANHATTAN DEVELOPMENT COMPETITION of New York sponsored this competition to design a memorial for the World Trade Center site. In this scheme the first object as you approach the site is a large obelisk, which marks the entry to the Memorial Site and it is the first in a timeline of monuments. This monument recognizes the victims of the February 26, 1993 terrorist bombing.

Visitors walk past the obelisk and down the escalator bank, and are on axis with the Memorial. It is a square temple with four Corinthian columns on each side, which represent rebirth and rejuvenation. Set within the capitals are eagles, which represent democracy. The use of four elements is representative of the four groups of people affected by this tragedy: the firemen, the police officers, the rescue officials, and civilians. At the top of the structure are four figures which represent the four virtues that must be observed in times of tragedy and conflict: Peace, Temperance, Justice, and Wisdom. In the middle of the temple there is a globe, for this was a global tragedy. And on top of the globe is a sculpture of Liberty holding the American flag and a dove of peace.

To the left of the Memorial is the footprint of the South Tower surrounded by tall, polished granite slabs. The granite slabs to the north and south have the names of all the victims carved into them. The east slab is the Liebskind waterfall, which pours into a pool below. The center is a green space with small trees and benches surrounding it. The green space represents a place of remembrance, but also of healing and hope for the future.

At the center of the north slab of the South Tower footprint is a small, private gate. This is the entrance to the area for the families and loved ones of the victims. Entering this space, one is surrounded by lush gardens and large canopied trees, which give a sense of enclosure and privacy. A picturesque path leads to a tholos. The exterior is surrounded by benches, and within the temple are the unidentified remains from the World Trade Center site.

The North Tower footprint is also surrounded by polished granite slabs. This footprint has a single large opening, a metaphor for how vulnerable to the attacks we were. Liebskind's Cultural Building is overhead, creating a large shadow. "A Shadow Over American History" is the theme for this footprint. Engraved on the granite walls is a timeline of the events leading up to September 11. The North Tower footprint is a place of reflection, and in the center are two adjacent reflecting pools

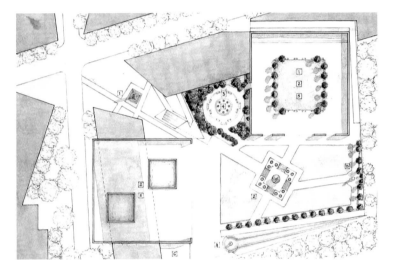

placed in a representation of the placement of the two towers.

Upon exiting the North Tower footprint, visitors see a round pool with a constant stream of water flowing into it. In the center of this pool is a monument to the firefighters. Engraved on two arched walls to the left and right are the names of all the fallen heroes. A statue in the middle depicts a firefighter, poised in uniform.

Opposite: Tiffany L. Burke, Detail of the Corinthian capitals in the World Trade Center Memorial; *Watercolor on board.*

Top: Tiffany L. Burke, World Trade Center Memorial Elevation Detail; *Watercolor on board.*

Middle: Tiffany L. Burke, Site Plan; *Watercolor on board.*

Bottom: Tiffany L. Burke, Site Section; *Watercolor on board.*

International Ideas Competition for the Hellenikon Metropolitan Park and Urban Development

Athens, Greece; March 2004

IN EARLY 2004 THE HELLENIC MINISTRY of the Environment, Planning and Public Works launched an international ideas competition for the design and urban development of the Hellenikon Park. The transfer of Athens airport from Hellenikon to the Mesogeia plain, in 2001, made available a large piece of prime land close to Athens, ten kilometers from the Acropolis and very close to the Saronic Coast. The planning and management of this extensive area, nearly 530 hectares, is a unique opportunity for Athens to reclaim a green area badly needed to improve the quality of the city's environment, and to project new strategies for urban development.

PROJECT CREDITS
Name of Team: Notre Dame Urban Design Team
Team Leader: Richard Economakis
Design Team: Richard Economakis, Sandra Vitzthum, Michael Lykoudis, David Mayernik, Roberto Soundy, John Griffin, Mwangi Gathinji, Wendan Tang
Consultants: Douglas Hunt, Holladay Properties, South Bend, Indiana

The proposed new Hellenikon neighborhood development seeks at once to convey architectural richness and a sensitization to the particular yet timeless qualities of Athenian vernacular and neo-classical architectural morphologies. Although projecting a high degree of urban and architectural specificity, this proposal is intended to convey general strategy and broad conceptual ideas for the organization of the site and program. The elevations of the new neighborhood reflect not particulars but the intended character of a new town. This urban village would materialize as lots are sold and developed by numerous clients, and as architects—operating creatively and in accordance with an established architectural code—guarantee the quality and consistency necessary for the creation of a memorable sense of place.

The masterplan envisions the new quarter at the northeastern side of the site. By concentrating the urban component here, the greatest possible area is made available for the metropolitan park, which is now conceived as incorporating the existing golf course and Agios Kosmas athletic complex. The entire site of the old airport is thus divided into a new neighborhood, which includes a cultural and academic district (including the former East Air Terminal and FIR buildings), a health and athletic district, and the park, which comprises a number of distinct areas.

The new urban quarter is designed to incorporate a principal north-south commercial spine, and a secondary east-west commercial street. The urban blocks include service alleys and parking structures, which keep vehicles away from street curbs, and allow arcades along the commercial spines.

The planning strategy that has been applied to the project is based on new urbanist principles and is comparable to numerous new traditional developments, which have demonstrated clear social and economic benefits. Pedestrian-friendly development encourages the growth of tightly-knit communities, a sense of place and belonging, and by extension, greater real estate value. Traditional patterns of settlement are also environmentally beneficial, as they do not generate sprawl across the countryside, and do not expect the citizen to be as reliant on the automobile for everyday needs. With regard to construction, the use of locally available, natural materials is both beneficial to the local economy and environmentally friendly. Furthermore, traditional construction techniques and materials are known to last longer, and permit a high degree of adaptive re-use.

ELEVATION OF PRINCIPAL COMMERCIAL STREET

ΠΡΟΤΑΣΗ ΑΝΑΠΤΥΞΗΣ ΠΑΛΑΙΟΥ ΑΕΡΟΔΡΟΜΙΟΥ ΕΛΛΗΝΙΚΟΥ
A PROPOSAL FOR THE HELLENIKON SITE, ATHENS
ΜΑΡΤΙΟΣ · 2004 · MARCH

AERIAL VIEW OF NEW NEIGHBORHOOD DEVELOPMENT

Top: Notre Dame Urban Design Team, Elevation of Principal Commercial Street; *Ink and color pencil on watercolor paper.*

Right: Notre Dame Urban Design Team, Aerial View of the New Neighborhood Development; *Ink and color pencil on watercolor paper.*

Above: Notre Dame Urban Design Team, Plan of the New Neighborhood Development at the Northeastern Corner of the Old Airport Site; *Ink and color pencil on watercolor paper.*

Opposite Top: Notre Dame Urban Design Team, View of Main Square; *Ink and color pencil on watercolor paper.*

Opposite Bottom: Notre Dame Urban Design Team, View of Central Intersection; *Ink and color pencil on watercolor paper.*

Ruth Wittenberg Memorial Competition

New York, New York; 1997
Fairfax & Sammons, PC

THE RUTH WITTENBERG Memorial Competition was sponsored by the Greenwich Village Society of Historical Preservation to honor a leading pioneer of that movement.

This design reflected the convergence of the history of the Village with the physical context. The triangle is the site left over at the Christopher Street, Greenwich Avenue, and Sixth Avenue intersection. In the eighteenth century, Greenwich Avenue was originally a country lane known as "Monument Lane" as it leads to the Monument for General Wolfe, who died in the battle of Quebec during the French and Indian War (the Seven Year War).

The Monument, long missing, was in the form of an obelisk and sat near 14th Street at the opposite end of the avenue from the site.

This proposal creates a latter-day companion to the long lost obelisk in the form of a three-sided pyramid or tetrahedron, which reinforces the triangular site and recalls the original purpose of this diagonal avenue.

The materials to be used would follow the traditional fabric of the village bluestone and cobblestone pavement, brick and brownstone for the walls and a slate cap. This palette also reflects Calvert Vaux's adjacent Jefferson Market Courthouse. The design incorporated a time capsule behind the Greek revival stone tabernacle and inscription.

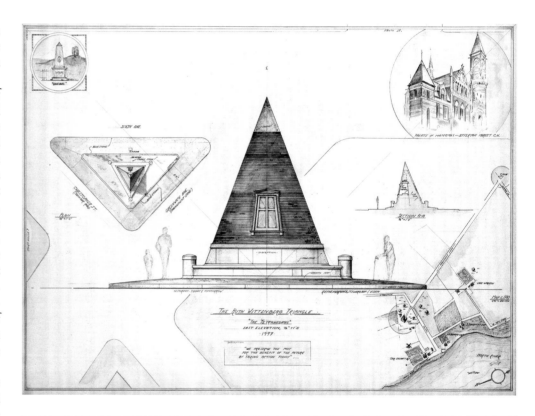

Above: Fairfax & Sammons Architects, PC, Competition Board; *Watercolor.*

New York City Streetlight Competition

New York, New York; 2004
Fairfax & Sammons, PC

THE NEW YORK CITY Streetlight Competition was sponsored by the City of New York to design a new street lighting system standard for the city. The goal was to seek out and identify new ideas for public street lighting and to obtain the flexibility to apply an integrated streetlight design on a block-by-block, street-by-street, or district-to-district basis within the city's five boroughs. The design competition process was used as a tool to improve and enhance the New York City streetscape.

The cast iron streetlights of the nineteenth century, such as the Bishop's Crook, have long been a favorite with the public and have become an icon of a more genteel New York City. Cast iron, being a very robust material, gives a sense of permanence and quality that speaks to the tradition of New York street furniture (i.e., fire plugs, call boxes, park benches, and other streetlights). Fairfax & Sammons broadens the choice within the range of traditional streetlights by providing a design in keeping with the nineteenth century character, but with more graceful proportion and simplicity of detail. The removal of the detail more suited to carving than casting should translate into some economy over the ornate Victorian designs and free it from that association. A sequence of crisp, well-defined moldings is the only ornament. In an ever-changing city it is important to maintain consistent patterns to give the streetscapes coherence.

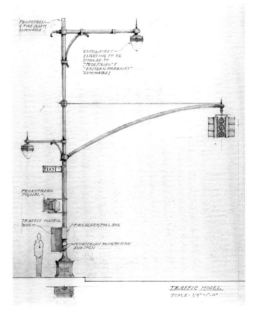

Top Left: Fairfax & Sammons Architects, PC. Proposed Streetlight with Surrounding Buildings; *Watercolor.*

Top Middle: Fairfax & Sammons architects, PC. Detail of Streetlight; *Watercolor.*

Top Right: Fairfax & Sammons Architects, PC. Park or Pedestrian Streetlight; *Watercolor.*

Left: Fairfax & Sammons Architects, PC. Typical Streetlight; *Watercolor.*

Above: Fairfax & Sammons Architects, PC. Traffic Model Streetlight; *Watercolor.*

Pentagon Memorial Design Competition

Arlington, Virginia; September 2002

Dino Marcantonio and Paloma Pajares

THE U.S. ARMY CORPS OF ENGINEERS sponsored this competition to design a memorial for the victims of the September 11, 2001, attack on the Pentagon. The site chosen for the memorial is a two-acre plot of land adjacent to the crash site itself, with the Pentagon building to the east and Washington Boulevard to the west.

The design is a cenotaph, a sepulcher set on a high pedestal, modeled after Sir Edwin Lutyens' Cenotaph at Whitehall, in London. It stands high enough so as to be visible from the interstate over the Pentagon's rooftops, thereby establishing itself firmly in the family of monuments that characterize Washington. The cenotaph is monumentally scaled and ornate to separate itself from ordinary construction, but calibrated to defer to the more important monuments of the Mall.

For visitors to the site, the cenotaph is found within an enclosure demarcated by a stone bench and iron gate. It stands at the end of the entrance axis, at the head of a reflecting pool flanked by Japanese cherry trees. Three steps, with lions standing perpetually on guard to either side, lead to the raised platform of the cenotaph. Its stepped pedestal is relatively austere, decorated only with the names of the dead, while the marble sepulcher above is decorated with anthemia and palmettes in its plinth, garlands in the center register, and acroteria and eagles at the top. The site of the plane crash is visible looking west from the enclosure and to the east a dense stand of trees veils the outside world.

Below: Dino Marcantonio, Paloma Pajares. Perspective view of the scheme looking toward the crash site at the Pentagon building; *Digital image.*

Opposite: Dino Marcantonio, Paloma Pajares. Analytique plate submitted for the competition; *Digital image.*

MEMORIAL
TO THE DEAD AT THE PENTAGON
IX·XI
MMI

THIS MEMORIAL IS COMPRISED OF A CENOTAPH SET
WITHIN AN ENCLOSURE. IT STANDS HIGH ENOUGH
TO BE VISIBLE FROM A DISTANCE, APPEARING ABOVE
THE ROOF LINE OF THE PENTAGON. THE
REFLECTING POOL IS FLANKED BY CHERRY TREES,
AND THE GATE HAS A BENCH AT ITS BASE. IN THE
CENOTAPH PEDESTAL ARE INSCRIBED THE NAMES
OF THE DEAD.

September 11, 2001 Memorial Design Competition

New Jersey; June 2004
Tomas Ramirez

THE STATE OF NEW JERSEY sponsored this competition to design a memorial "to reflect the legacies of those whose lives were lost, that their unfulfilled dreams and hopes may result in a better future for society" (Family & Survivor Advisory Committee).

The site chosen for the Memorial is a 1.6 acre area located in Liberty State Park, along the Hudson River, right across the historic Central Railroad Terminal of New Jersey (CRRNJ).

The project for the proposed memorial is composed of three parts: the Entry Court, the Place for Reflection, and the Gardens. The Entry Court is characterized by a commemorative elliptical arch that represents the monumental gateway to the park. Two obelisks recalling the Twin Towers of the World Trade Center rise on the attic pedestal over the arch. The elliptical shape of the stone arch recalls the one made of steel in the adjacent CRRNJ Terminal. The rusticated pylons, the continuous entablature and the attic pedestal echo the language of the nearby Ellis Island buildings, but use materials that match the color of the Terminal.

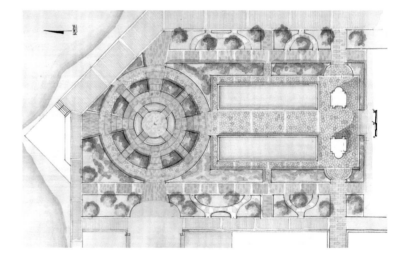

The Place for Reflection is a square that contains twin reflecting pools surrounded by granite stone coping. Inscribed along the edges are the names of the 691 New Jersey victims. The pools reflecting the two obelisks are meant to symbolize the Hudson River reflecting the World Trade Center towers.

The design of the Gardens is based on alternating concentric rings of landscaping, red brick herring bone patterns, and white granite grid patterns.

Top: Tomas Ramirez, Imaginary view of the monument in front of Manhattan skyline.

Middle: Tomas Ramirez, Site plan showing from right to left the sequence of Entry Court with its monumental.arch; the Place of Reflection with the two pools; and the Gardens; *Watercolor rendering.*

Bottom: Tomas Ramirez, Side and front elevations of the monumental elliptical arch; *Watercolor rendering.*

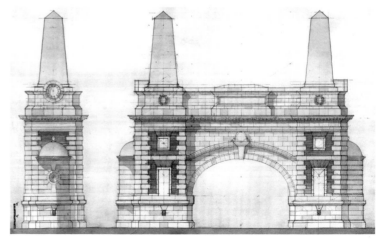

Competition to Contribute to the Tradition of the English Country House

Glouchestershire Valley, England; November 2001
Michael Rouchell

THE ENGLISH COUNTRY HOUSE COMPETITION was sponsored by the Royal Institute of British Architects (RIBA), and its purpose was to select an architect for the Cardale Family home. The site is located near Ozelworth, Gloucestershire, England.

The design program called for a large family home that would also be used for entertaining and accommodating guests. The various rooms had site orientation requirements and adjacency requirements that strongly influenced the layout of the plan.

The design intent was to adhere to the program requirements to the greatest extent possible while creating a design that continues the classical tradition. The house is "L" shaped, wrapping around an enclosed basement pool, but is intended to present a symmetrical elevation on the approach sides of the house. The simplified classicism of John Nash was an influence in the design. The axial arrangement and the building's relationship to its garden recall the work of the Edwardian architect Edwin Lutyens.

The north façade of the main house has a tripartite composition with a central engaged tetrastyle temple front of Tuscan Doric columns. The east façade has a similar tripartite composition with the conservatory in the form of an engaged octagonal tempietto with paired Doric columns. Below the conservatory is an octagonal wine cellar.

The formal entrance hall, which was requested in the program, is a grand two-story space with a large stair that lies beneath a south-facing arched window. To the west is the drawing room; a corner display on the opposite wall of the fireplace maintains the room's symmetry. The drawing room opens out to the formal garden on the west side with additional windows on the north side.

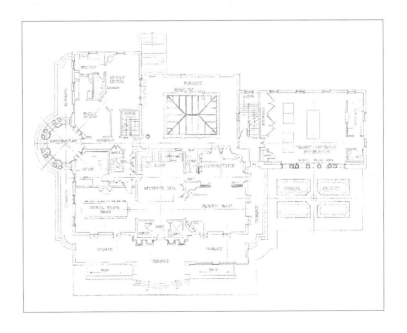

Top: Michael Rouchell, North Elevation; *Pencil on vellum.* The north façade has a tripartite composition with a central engaged tetrastyle temple front of Tuscan Doric columns.

Middle: Michael Rouchell, East Elevation; *Pencil on vellum.* The main element of the east façade is the conservatory that forms an engaged octagonal tempietto with paired Doric columns. Below the conservatory is an octagonal wine cellar.

Bottom: Michael Rouchell, First Floor Plan; *Pencil on vellum.*

International Design Competition for a General Urban Layout Plan for the Bertalia-Lazaretto Area

Bologna, Italy; October 2000

John Simpson & Partners Ltd.

THE FINANZIARIA BOLOGNA METROPOLITANA S.P.A., a company that has members like the Bologna Municipality and the University of Bologna, was the sponsor of this competition. The remit of the competition was twofold: first, to design a general urban layout for a vast area on the north-west outskirts of Bologna, which is only partly urbanized; and second, to design, on the same site, the University of Bologna's Faculty of Engineering's department and services.

The area to be planned has a land surface area of about 730,000 square meters and an available surface area potentially suitable for building of about 210,000 square meters. The designated uses of the area, besides that of the University, comprise residential use, offices, commercial facilities, and green areas.

John Simpson & Partners' overall design creates a new urban quarter that is still recognizable as part of Bologna, but also has a specific identity of its own and an authentic urban character. The masterplan creates a traditional mixed-use neighborhood, with the University buildings integrated into the block structure together with residential, commercial, and public uses.

The form and character of Bologna was taken as a model to inform the urban design with basic street, block, and building types; the typical arcades of Bologna continue into the new quarter to ensure a genuine extension of the urban grain of the existing city, and to free the citizen from the necessity of the car.

The center of this university quarter is marked with the tower of the main library. A 5,000-seat auditorium is proposed to take advantage of the location of the site between the airport and the city center. Together with the range of meeting rooms available to the faculty it would help create a first-class venue for conferences in Bologna.

Special attention is given to the landscape in order to pick up views of a local landmark, the San Luca church and its dome on a nearby hill.

Due to its position, the new quarter would become the major approach into Bologna from the airport and it would inevitably be the visitor's first experience of the city. The view from across the country park and lake of the University library tower and auditorium rotunda with San Luca and the mountains as a backdrop, would become an image with which the quarter is identified.

Top: Simpson & Partners, Aerial view; *Watercolor rendering.*

Bottom Left: Simpson & Partners, Perspective view of the main piazza; *Watercolor rendering.*

Bottom Right: Simpson & Partners, Urban plan of the core of the intervention; *Digital image.*

The New Urban House: Proposal for the Community of New Amherst in Cobourg, Ontario

Ontario, Canada; October 1998
De la Guardia Victoria Architects; Trelles Architects

THIS COMPETITION WAS SPONSORED by Max Le Marchamp and by the architecture and town planning firm of Andrés Duany and Elizabeth Plater-Zyberk, which also designed the Community of New Amherst based on the leading-edge urban design principles known as "New Urbanism."

New Amherst is a community planned for 271 acres of land located on the west side of the Town of Cobourg, Ontario, which will include 1,600 to 2,000 homes, as well as commercial, institutional, and recreational components. Cobourg is located on the north shore of Lake Ontario, sixty miles east of the downtown center of the City of Toronto. New Amherst is designed to create an architecturally exquisite, high-quality pedestrian environment that complements the existing character and architectural charm of the old town. Human scale and a mix of residential, business, and civic uses, in carefully focused neighborhoods woven together by generous parks, bike paths, and a finely graded network of streets, are the characteristics that will define this community. The competition called for designs of townhouses, as well as midsize and large house types.

This project by De La Victoria and Trelles Architects was the winner of the competition. The submission consisted of two designs for each of the three house types: townhouse, medium size detached (cottage), and large size detached (house).

According to the competition requirements all units have full basements and all designs include outbuildings. Construction documents for selected proposals had to conform to the 1997 Ontario Building Code.

DESIGN TEAM
Jorge Trelles, Luis Trelles, Teofilo Victoria

PROGRAM

TOWNHOUSE
Lot size: 24' x 98' min
Finished Floor Area: 1150–2000 sq. ft.
Construction cost ceiling—main building: $120,000
Construction cost ceiling—outbuilding: $30,000

MEDIUM SIZE DETACHED/COTTAGE
Lot size: 36' or 40' x 98' min
Finished Floor Area: 1250–2400 sq. ft.
Construction cost ceiling—main building: $156,000
Construction cost ceiling—outbuilding: $30,000

LARGE SIZE DETACHED/COTTAGE
Lot size: 40' to 48' x 98' min
Finished Floor Area: 2400–3600 sq. ft.
Construction cost ceiling—main building: $234,000
Construction cost ceiling—outbuilding: $40,000

Next Page: New Amherst Townhouse and Shop-front. Drawn by Jeremy Lake, Matthew Lister, Rafael Fornes, Nicolai Nedev, Edgar Sarli, Mu'ayad Abbas, Elizabeth Cardona, Arnaldo Sanchez, Ricardo Lopez, Erin Pryor, Emily Baker, Mimi Le Fevre, Jorge Trelles, Luis Trelles, Teofilo Victoria; *India Ink on Mylar, 24" x 36".*

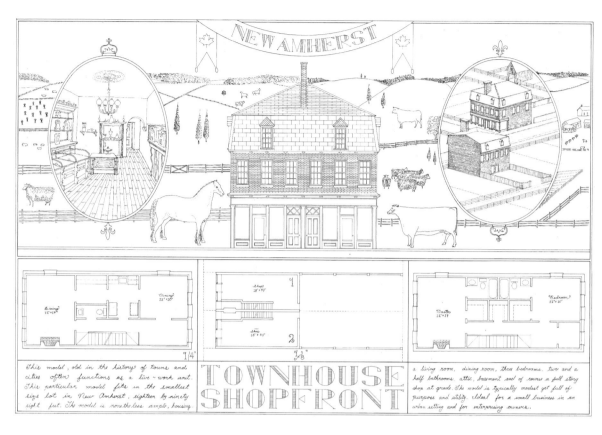

This model, old in the history of towns and cities often functions as a live-work unit. This particular model fits in the smallest size lot in New Amherst, eighteen by ninety eight feet. The model is nonetheless ample, housing

TOWNHOUSE SHOPFRONT

a living room, dining room, three bedrooms, two and a half bathrooms, attic, basement and of course a full story shop at grade. The model is typically modest yet full of purpose and utility. Ideal for a small business in an urban setting and for enterprising owners.

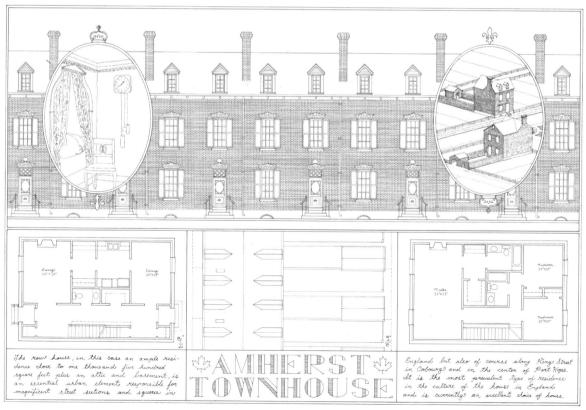

The row house, in this case an ample residence close to one thousand and five hundred square feet plus an attic and basement, is an essential urban element responsible for magnificent street sections and squares in

AMHERST TOWNHOUSE

England but also of course along King Street in Cobourg and in the center of Port Hope. It is the most prevalent type of residence in the culture of the house in England and is currently an excellent choice of house.

The New Williamsburg Town Plan Design Competition and the New Williamsburg Courthouse Building Design Competition

Williamsburg, Virginia; 1996
De la Guardia Victoria Architects; Trelles Architects

THE PEACEABLE KINGDOM

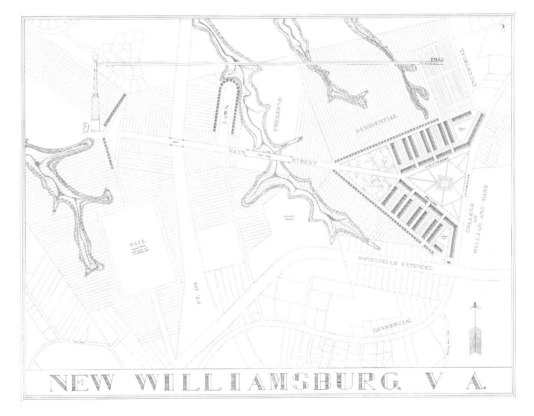

NEW WILLIAMSBURG, V. A.

Two COMPETITIONS WERE CONDUCTED simultaneously. The town plan competition asked participants to prepare a new town to be built adjacent to the College of William and Mary that would include a new courthouse for the region. The building design competition presented the program for the courthouse.

DESIGN TEAM:
Jorge Trelles, Luis Trelles, Teofilo Victoria, Mu'ayad Abbas, Adib Cure, Cari Penabad, Vincent Yueh, John Seaman, Bill Cate, Eric Osth

Above: The Peaceable Kingdom. Skyscraper, Row Houses, and Georgian Houses make up the town center of New Williamsburg; *India Ink on Mylar, 30" x 42".*

Right: New Williamsburg, Virginia. One-mile-long Main Street extends from the town center site, where the new courthouse is sited, to the inn; *India Ink on Mylar, 30" x 42".*

The West Palm Beach Library Competition
West Palm Beach, Florida; spring 2001

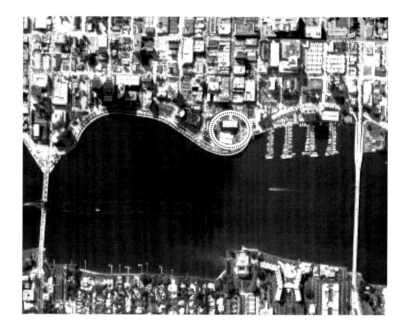

IN 2001, THE CITY OF WEST PALM BEACH in Florida invited four architectural teams to compete for a new public library design in downtown West Palm Beach. The four invited architects were Merrill-Pastor (now Merrill, Pastor & Colgan), Michael Graves & Associates, Rodriquez Quiroga with Léon Krier, and Porphyrios Associates. The competition site is located on a triangular piece of land presently housing the existing outdated library and open green space, at the boundary between the downtown district and the waterfront park area. The extensive brief requested a large flexible library with various community facilities.

A masterplan for West Palm Beach, the largest municipality in Palm Beach County, was completed in 1994 by Andrés Duany and Elizabeth Plater-Zyberk, two leaders of the New Urbanism movement. Consistent with a 1923 plan for West Palm Beach by a previous planner, John Nolen, they emphasized the importance of planning a city around its squares, parks, and civic buildings within properly focal settings. Duany and Plater-Zyberk found the Library site and the adjacent Flagler Park to be the most important civic site in West Palm Beach, given the significance of Clematis Street, historically the main street of the city, as an axis terminating there.

Clematis Street, leading to the site from the west, is now a small scale street of restaurants among larger blocks of five- to nine-story buildings towards the water. A triangular fountain at the west end of the site, just a few years old, has quickly become a gathering point for the community. The eastern part of the site has been the main staging area of a yearly music festival called SunFest that attracts tens of thousands of people, and for shows such as the Antique and Jewelry Show and the Boat Show.

The criteria for the project included several urban considerations. The city wanted to connect Clematis Street and the existing Centennial Fountain plaza with the waterfront, while simultaneously commissioning a workable library facility three times the size of the existing library. They wanted to continue to accommodate the annual music festival and to maintain the fountain. And they wanted to create a civic symbol for their city. The library program called for a café and community outreach spaces for after-hour meetings, research, and exhibits. Consequently, there was a good programmatic opportunity to engage the activity of the fountain plaza. The design committee minimized the need for surface parking, as so many existing parking structures were within a few blocks of the site.

Above: The West Palm Beach Library Competition. Aerial of the vicinity of the site, a prominence facing the home of Henry Flager across Lake Worth in Palm Beach.

The West Palm Beach Library Competition
Michael Graves & Associates in Association with PGAL

MICHAEL GRAVES & ASSOCIATES (MGA) proposed a bold design "to capture hearts and minds worldwide" and many elements of their entry were highly praised even though it placed fourth in the design competition. The scheme responded to its greater surroundings; the building's amenities as proposed by MGA included public steps and a plaza at the edge of the Intercoastal Waterway with views across to Palm Beach. The design allowed for an amphitheater at the end of Clematis Street with the required area parking underneath. The center of the Library was given a transparently glazed character that would allow views through the building to the water from upper Clematis Street.

The building proposed by MGA contains five levels: a level of parking below grade with 65 parking spaces; the First Level with the Main lobby, circulation desk, community spaces (café, auditorium, galleries, art studios, library store and bookstore); the Mezzanine, which contains staff offices, workrooms, boardroom, genealogy collection and seniors' area; the Second Level, which contains the Children's Library and Multimedia Area; and the Third level, which contains the Adult Library.

The building is crowned by pergolas topped with hardwood trellis, providing shade at the third floor terraces. Precast panels at the ground level create a base for the building in a rusticated running bond pattern. Cast stone is used on the upper stories. The open framed tower is sheathed in painted metal panels finished in a custom color.

The MGA design would have accommodated the special local annual event called SunFest, with the library as a backdrop for the stage facilitated by the presence of electrical service. The entire library was seen as a beacon—literally, with its open framed central tower—for its business community and the Clematis Street area, stimulating business activity by drawing people to Clematis Street for all kinds of indoor and outdoor events.

Above: Michael Graves & Associates, Aerial View from West; *Computer Rendering.*

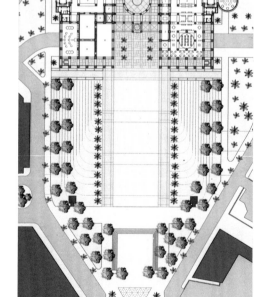

Top Left: Michael Graves & Associates, South Elevation; *Computer rendering.*

Top Right: Michael Graves & Associates, Perspective of Internal Rotunda; *Computer rendering.*

Bottom Left: Michael Graves & Associates, Section; *Computer rendering.*

Bottom Right: Michael Graves & Associates, First Level Plan; *Computer rendering.*

The West Palm Beach Library Competition
Merrill, Pastor & Colgan in Association with Gensler

THE INCLINATION OF THIS TEAM was to organize several buildings around a new courtyard, and to create a new terrace on the east (river) side, both spaces located on an extension of the Clematis Street axis. By this means, they proposed to draw people from the crowded street and fountain plaza, through a series of intimately scaled but varied spaces, to the seriously underused river esplanade. The two larger buildings were connected on the second level. The outreach meeting spaces and the café were placed in a freestanding building. The plaza level café sits on both the fountain plaza and the new library courtyard.

The buildings are composed and sited to serve the creation of the new spaces. They are a picturesque group of structures meant to be attractive from all sides and intended to make pedestrian movement through the site fun and stimulating. The courtyard and the river terraces extend the axis of the existing street, teasing crowds by degree from the popular fountain plaza to the waterfront, and thereby fulfilling the project's primary urban responsibility.

The design derives from specific regional traditions, building practices, climate and culture, without aspiring toward parochialism. The project would be among larger and bulkier commercial buildings at the waterfront. The basic composition of the pieces, the monumental language of the buttressed walls of the buildings, the typology of the constituent elements, and the iconography were all developed to convey the highest public aspiration for an important civic building on a prominent site.

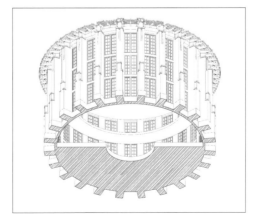

Top: Business Library from the Upper East River; *Ink and color pencil.*

Bottom: Worm's-eye View of Business Library; *Ink and color pencil.* The business library, with its own entrance, operates somewhat independently of the other buildings, but its rotunda also provides passage to the other buildings. There are two levels of enclosed rooms around a high central space. The floor of the central space is at the second level, but an opening in the floor allows views of the entire height of the space from the ground level. Recessed porches at the center of the three sides further help to light the ground floor. The eaves and the piers serve to shade the glass of the central space from all angles.

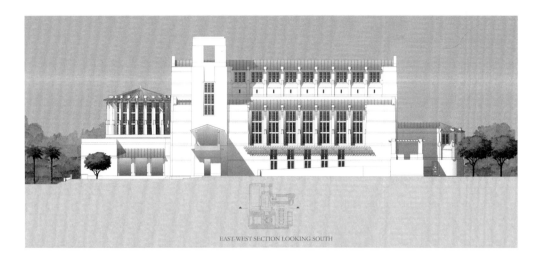

EAST-WEST SECTION LOOKING SOUTH

WEST ELEVATION

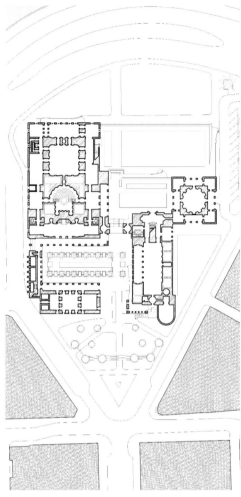

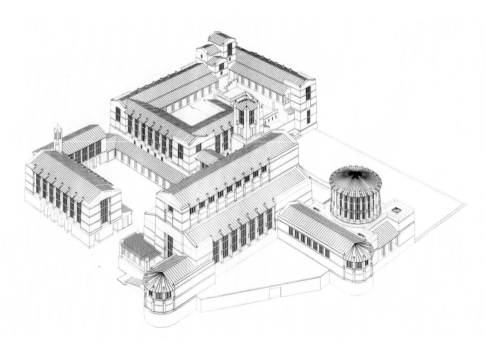

Top Left: East-West Section looking South; *Computer rendering.*

Above: Site plan of Library and Surrounding Blocks; *Ink and color pencil.* Clematis Street approaches the immediate site from west (*bottom*). The fountain plaza at the west end of the site was to be kept, and Clematis was to be reconnected with the waterfront of the Lake Worth at the top of the drawing. The three principal pieces of the library form a new courtyard and waterfront terraces at the east side of the site.

Middle: West Elevation; *Computer rendering.*
Bottom: Axonometric of the Entire Library from the Southwest; *Computer rendering.*

Images courtesy of Merrill, Pastor & Colgan.

The West Palm Beach Library Competition
Porphyrios Associates

Above: Porphyrios Associates, Aerial Perspective; *Watercolor.*

THIS WINNING SUBMISSION explored designs for both the urban and civic realm as well as a public library that provides for traditional reading rooms, flexible interactive technology, and community spaces.

The library is located at the western end of the site, enclosing and configuring the existing Centennial Square into the "Piazza Clematis," giving it a civic presence and signature. In this way, it holds the streets to the north and south, enhancing the character of this unique triangular site.

The design features a number of building volumes of different scales and character broadly divided into two main parts centered on an open entrance court. In this way, it also extends the visual axis of Clematis Street, affording access to the Lake Worth waterfront. This progression of spaces seeks to imbue the new development with a flowing continuity between internal and external spaces, and interlaces the new library with its landscape, enhancing the sense of place in the park and extending toward the waterfront, creating a naturally linear promenade. The library, and in a more literal sense, its tower, also act as a beacon from both the waterfront and downtown.

To the north, the main library establishes large legible areas of open-access book and multimedia areas on two main levels, providing for a multi-sensory interactive library environment. There is also a large, more formal reading room; reference and study areas of various sizes and character, which provide for quiet reading and contemplation; a children's story room; and shaded outdoor reading areas overlooking the eastern outdoor amphitheatre towards the inland waterway.

To the south is the main community foyer with a café, large gallery for visiting exhibitions, a number of meeting rooms, a two-hundred seat auditorium, and computer workshops, providing unique educational facilities as well as spaces for social gathering.

The library design encourages green methods of energy conservation, which make the building pleasant and user-friendly, and minimize energy demands.

Porphyrios & Associates' unique design will become both an integral part of the urban fabric and a signature for the City of West Palm Beach.

TEAM:
Design Architects: Porphyrios Associates
Executive Architects: Spillis Candela & Partners Inc.
Landscape Architects: Sanchez & Maddux

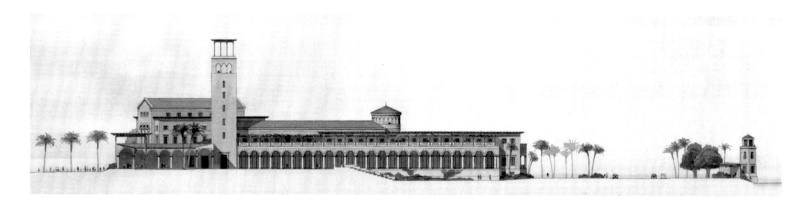

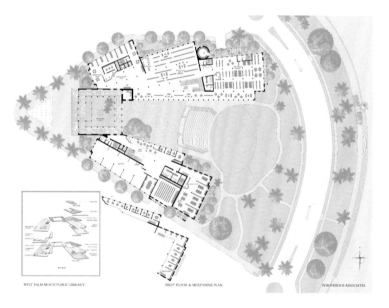

Top: Porphyrios Associates, West-East Section; *Watercolor.*

Middle Left: Porphyrios Associates, First Floor Plan; *Watercolor.*

Middle Right: Porphyrios Associates, East Perspective; *Watercolor.*

Bottom: Porphyrios Associates, West Perspective; *Watercolor.*

The West Palm Beach Library Competition
Rodriguez and Quiroga Architects, Chartered,
with Léon Krier and Rafael Portuondo

RODRIGUEZ AND QUIROGA Architects, Chartered, is located in Coral Gables, Florida. The firm was established in 1983 and is known for its aesthetic standards with innovative and practical responses to programmatic and economic requirements for urban planning, architecture, and interior design. Rodriguez Quiroga, along with Rafael Portuondo of Portuondo Perroti Architects, also of Coral Gables, collaborated with Léon Krier, the well-known architect, urban planner and educator, on a proposal for the West Palm Beach Library Competition.

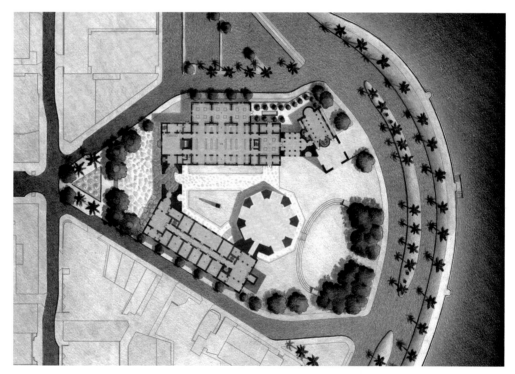

Clockwise from Top: Southeast Perspective;
Site Plan; Perspective from Underneath the Arcade;
East Elevation; Front Perspective.

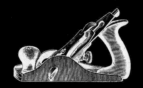

Good Practice

The Shared Language of Architecture:
Architectural Woodwork and Millwork

By Peter Talty

Perhaps it is a well-worn concept to consider the language of architecture as a distinct enterprise comprised of its own vocabulary and grammar. However, a great merit of classical architecture is the extent to which this vocabulary is communicable to many, across generations grounded in reality, and transcendent in meaning and purpose. This article will look at the work of four different architects and how they express this shared vocabulary in architectural millwork drawings. The four come from as many different countries—France, Scotland, England, and America— and they are all well-versed in the essentials of the classical idiom. While each country may have different systems for the development of architectural millwork, it is remarkable the degree to which each architect conveys architectural information in a compatible and transferable language.

Architectural millwork is broadly defined as the development of paneling, casework, trim, base, and cornices to create a fully-detailed room or setting. The control and understanding of this process requires the highest level of sensitivity, knowledge, and experience in design as well as in the fabrication process and installation. To achieve exemplary results requires a firm commitment in detailing, an understanding of documentation, and coordination of all parts and trades.

The correct composition and assembly of these parts is best achieved by establishing a hierarchy of elements. These elements are presented in plan, section, and elevation, and are most effective on drawings that register these three conditions simultaneously. Architectural millwork at its highest level demands detailing which describes the junctures of wall, opening, floor and ceiling.

The synthesis of all of these disparate parts within a coherent millwork "package" must be grounded by an overall aesthetic sensibility and a clear intent. This intent must be maintained throughout the development of the drawings, beginning with concept sketches and moving through preliminary architectural drawings, detail drawings coordinated with hardware or mechanical equipment, shop drawing review, fabrication, installation, and shop, or on-site finishing. It is the

distillation of all of these elements, understood in minute detail, which eventually serves to reinforce the overall composition that establishes the groundwork for beauty.

We begin here by considering the work of the French architect Laurent Bourgois, who is based in Paris. His sketch [FIGURE 1] of a library for a Parisian flat captures the intended elements and character of the room and evokes a furnished setting. Even in this early "atmospheric" study he suggests the tectonic logic that will govern the millwork: he sets up the elementary division of base; the wall and entablature are established; the architrave dividing upper and lower setting of the bookshelves echoes the opposing door architrave; and all this reinforces an implied order superimposed upon the wall surface.

The elevation sketch of the bookcase wall [FIGURE 2] delineates these architectural elements of base cabinets (dado), column (stiles), and entablature (cornice). Accommodation of furnishings is suggested, and some consideration in plan detail is shown referencing the columnar element. Compositionally, Bourgois has established the proportions of the wall unit, balancing both casework and opening accordingly. The base cabinet establishes a datum, and reads as a solid element reinforced by the cabinet doors. The narrow band of pilasters adjusts the scale of the room for a domestic feel, and the suggestion of the cornice completes the arrangement and solidifies the composition.

The transition from the sketch elevation into an architectural detailed drawing [FIGURE 3] may have an antiseptic feel. But in reality the drawing is part of a rational process initiated with the sketch and developed into an architectural drawing, which will ultimately lead to a detail drawing, fabrication, and installation. Greater specificity as to elements is achieved in this drawing, e.g., planted or flattened relief on the pilasters, delineation of grills on cabinet doors, and voids in the skirting board to accommodate air movement across the heating elements housed behind them.

We could continue with Bourgois's development of detailed drawings, but the commonality of purpose behind the example set by all of these architects allows us to travel, as the Bourbons of old might have, to the shores of Edinburgh and the practice of Simpson & Brown

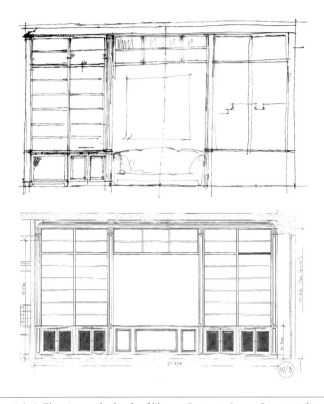

Figure 1: Sketch perspective of library in Parisian flat. *Drawing courtesy of Laurent Bourgois Architect.*

Figure 2 (top): Elevation study sketch of library. *Courtesy of Laurent Bourgois Architect.*

Figure 3 (bottom): Detailed architectural drawing. *Courtesy of Laurent Bourgois Architect.*

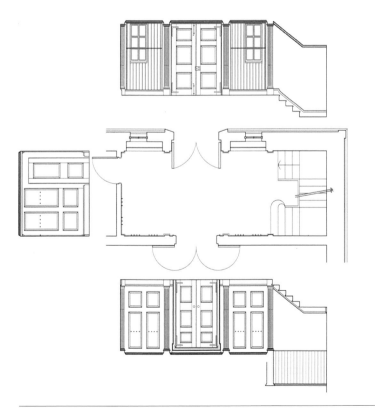

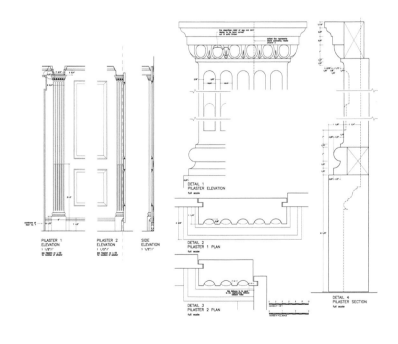

Figure 4: Layout drawing. *Courtesy of Simpson & Brown Architects.*

Figure 5: Lobby pilaster details. *Courtesy of Simpson & Brown Architects.*

Architects. The example of their work that we will consider here is a chapel they designed and built an ocean away, in Canada!

The Location drawing [FIGURE 4] elevates the four walls around the floor plan—at 1/2"–1'-0" scale. (American readers will appreciate the irony of a European architect drawing in feet and inches.) This Layout drawing (as the Scots call it)—literally "L" drawings—around the floorplan can seem confusing, but by grounding the proposed elevation in its respective locations, clarity of intent is reinforced, and more so in the subsequent drawings. The Assembly—or "A" drawing—Lobby Pilaster [FIGURE 5] provides details in plan, section and elevation for the principal order, in this case Roman Doric. As the drawings transition to show more developed detail, instruction for the fabricator takes precedence. Specific dimensioning is established as well as identification of areas of equality, which allows the installer some flexibility in assembly. Indeed, only the most inexperienced detailer does not allow for such variance and flexibility.

Ian Parlin, the project architect from Simpson & Brown's office, achieves an economy of drawings by focusing attention on the surface details, and is not distracted to consider how pieces are to be assembled, nor how the elements are to be secured to the sub-wall surface. There is an active debate among practitioners about the level of assemblage detail that an architect should provide. I am not certain a single correct answer exists. It is, however, prudent to acknowledge that the architect should at least understand how the final product is achieved; and it is the domain of the fabricator to provide the means to the desired end. The failure on either side is the degree to which the architect tells the fabricator how to do his work, or the fabricator limits what can be achieved simply because he has never done it that way before. There is no clear solution to these two positions. Rather, respect and confidence in each professional realm should rule.

Parlin profiles and locates the architectural elements as his chief concern. He provides dimensioning of the critical elements, thus allowing the fabricator the flexibility of resolving site constraints within the body of the pilaster. The relationship in plane between the pilaster and panel is noted in both vertical and plan section, and then the specifics of the raised panel are provided on a subsequent drawing [FIGURE 6] at 3"–1'-0" and full scale. Again, Parlin delineates the critical dimensioning of the elements, allowing "float" to exist within the body of the panel. Please note that he establishes the relationship of the wall plane, i.e., paneling and door opening, by referencing back from the crown to the door architrave and frieze. This point will be amplified in the next example.

We travel south to London, to consider the work of the architectural firm Julian Bicknell & Associates. In detailing architectural millwork, one of the more challenging aspects is resolving the relationship of wall to opening. In the previous example, the relationship between wall and opening is established in two dimensions by linking

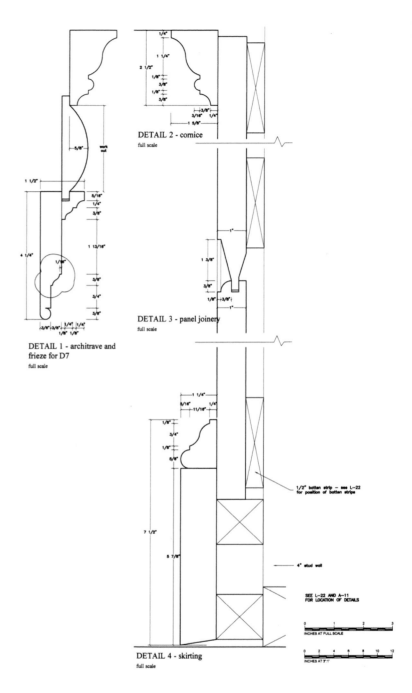

Figure 6 (above): Panel detail. *Courtesy of Simpson & Brown Architects.*

Figure 7 (opposite): Great Room window features. *Courtesy of Julian Bicknell & Associates.*

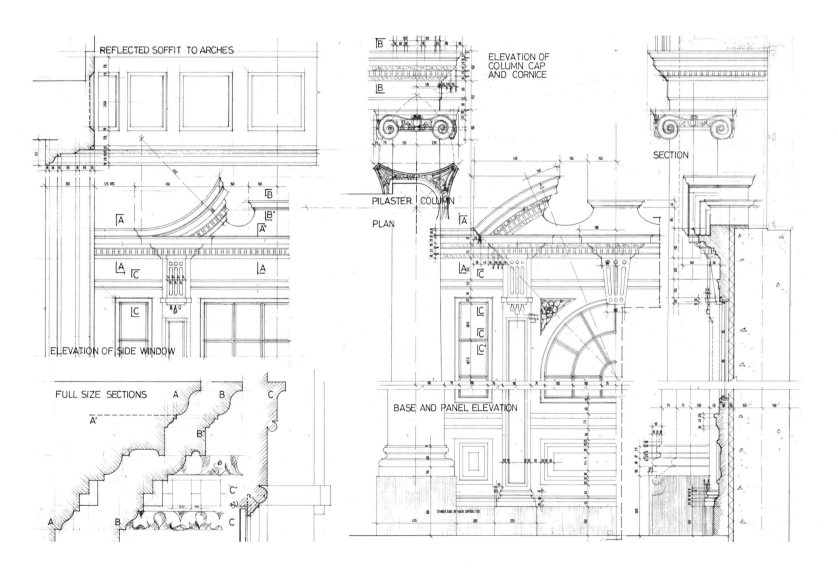

REFLECTED SOFFIT TO ARCHES

ELEVATION OF SIDE WINDOW

FULL SIZE SECTIONS

PILASTER COLUMN

PLAN

ELEVATION OF COLUMN CAP AND CORNICE

SECTION

BASE AND PANEL ELEVATION

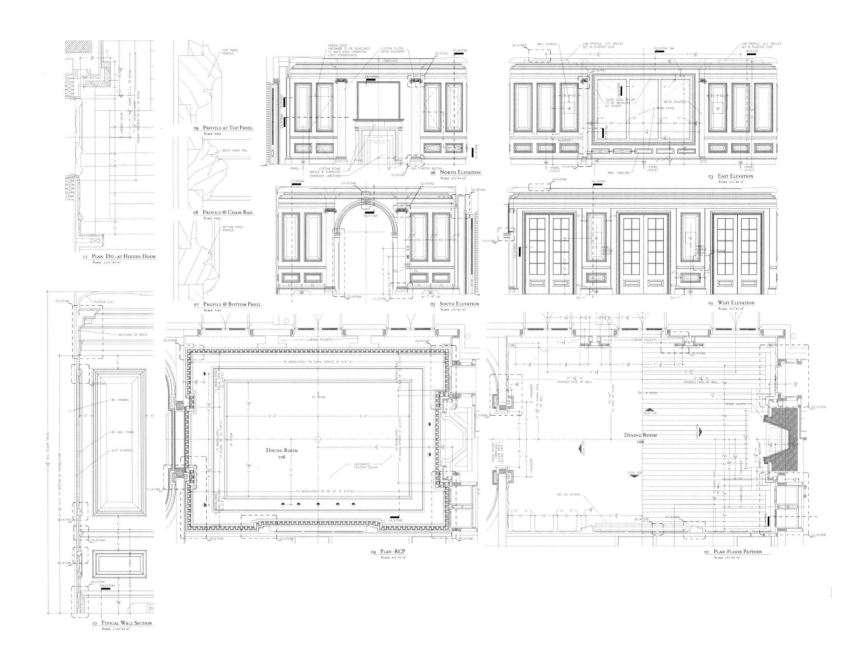

wall paneling with door architrave. Bicknell's office takes a more robust approach in their attempt to clarify that relationship: for them, the juncture between wall and opening is where a fundamental architectural condition is pronounced. The challenge is how best to resolve the architrave—the element which distinguishes an opening—from the wall surface, which is the basis for the architrave's structural integrity.

In "The Great Room: Window Features" [FIGURE 7], Bicknell provides an elevation and vertical section to help clarify the architrave condition. Compositionally, he distinguishes between an upper Ionic order as the principal columnar element in contrast to the minor order detailed at the window opening. The entablature is delineated at full scale in the lower left-hand corner and base and plinth detailed on the opposing right-hand side. The inner pilaster at the window frame captures dado and fielded elements of the lunette and casement sash. In hindsight, and if possible, a plan section would have secured and clarified the relationship in plane between these different surfaces. As in the previous example, the principal elements are dimensioned clearly, and float is provided in the lengths of the column and pilaster.

Now we cross the ocean westward to the Houston, Texas-based architectural firm of Curtis & Windham and their drawings for a dining room in a Houston home. Their example provides a good opportunity to coalesce many of the above points. The drawing depicts the millwork package for a well-appointed dining room [FIGURE 8]. The plan, with accompanying elevation drawings, provides immediate reference to the subject. The plan shows the flooring layout as well as reflected ceiling information. The principal vertical section detail secures dimensioning, and helps to confirm the overall relationship between base, wall, and cornice. The Ionic order, effectively deployed at both chimneybreast and at the opposite wall entrance, clarifies the transition between wall surface and opening. Curtain pocket details at the exterior French doors are only understood by comparing plan and elevation: here, a detailed plan section might have been helpful. Specifics relative to location of electrical outlets, sconces, and HVAC skirting vents are delineated in elevation and noted as to their relationship to base moldings; panels or in reflected ceiling; and cornice.

The sequence of presentation by the four architects could have easily been reversed. All began their work with a concept sketch, which developed into more detailed drawings, which then culminated in specific drawings prepared for fabrication. To maintain the character and intent of premium architectural millwork from concept sketch through installation is a serious task. At this high level, there is very little margin for error. Coherence of approach, understanding of materials, comprehension of detail, and the ability to visualize the final results is required throughout. ◄

Peter J. Talty, Director of Properties for Belvedere Property Management LLC, has been a Fellow and instructor of the ICA&CA since its inception and has also been a contributor to The Classicist. *Mr. Talty received a BA in American History from the University of North Carolina, a Master's in Liberal Education from St. Johns College, and a Master of Architecture from the University of Virginia. For the past ten years he has managed a domestic and international property portfolio for an individual client.*

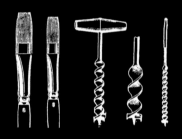

The Allied Arts

Classicism within the Realism of Claudio Bravo

By John Woodrow Kelley

Claudio Bravo, more than any other living representational painter, exemplifies the classical tradition of extracting seemingly ideal beauty from a close observation of the real world. He is quoted as saying, "I've followed classicism all my life, I consider myself to be a classical artist." In marked contrast to the strict objectivity of the contemporary realist school, Bravo's humanistic sensibility imbues his figures with a belief in the nobility of the human individual. While at first glance his paintings might seem to adhere to the realist coda, one is immediately aware of a concurrent paradoxical beauty born of this humanistic approach. Although this paradoxical, even surrealist, contrast gives his work a very contemporary tension, it also allies it with that of some of the great humanist realist painters of the past, such as Caravaggio and Velasquez.

The surrealist element in Bravo's painting is especially evident in his still life work, where objects are arranged in such highly significant ways that one is immediately intrigued with the hidden spiritual meanings implied. Order is contrasted with disorder; elements from nature are placed with the man-made; ancient artifacts are coupled with modern ones; there is always a suggestion of meaning beyond the beautifully-rendered surfaces. Many of Bravo's still life arrangements become anthropomorphic in their suggestion of the human form, furthering the evidence of a humanistic sensibility at work. Quite often an object from the Greco-Roman ancient world, such as a bust, torso, or marble urn, is included as a reminder of the classical origins of Bravo's approach to painting.

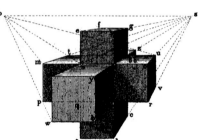

The most compellingly classical still life element in all of his paintings, however, is his extraordinary drapery. The symbolist juxtaposition of drapery with the human form is a tradition that goes back to the wall paintings of ancient Rome. This appreciation of symbolist potential in the careful rendering of drapery was revived in the Italian Renaissance and in the Baroque, and introduced to the mainstream of modernism by such artists as Salvador Dali and René Magritte.

To look at Bravo's drapery is to feel an excitement about the suggested meaning, which always furthers the impact of the larger narrative of the painting. The subjects of many of Bravo's major paintings, scenes from Greek mythology or the Judeo-Christian tradition, act as perfect vehicles for the sensational combination of drapery with figures. At first viewing one might imagine that these are paintings from the past; but then one notices contemporary elements and begins to sense the extremely contemporary aura born of the tension between realism and classicism. In this way Bravo weds his very un-modernist love of beauty with his profound understanding of the ambiguity of the modern world.

Claudio Bravo was born in Valparaiso, Chile, in 1936. One of seven siblings, he was the eldest son of a successful businessman and landowner. His father was unhappy about his son's interest in art and obliged Claudio to work on the family farms throughout much of his youth. His mother had been a painter before marriage and was more sensitive to advancing the cultural education of her children; she took them to museums from an early age. Although his mother died at the age of 49, she lived to see Bravo's early success as an artist. Bravo's real training began when he attended a Jesuit boarding school in Santiago, where his drawing ability attracted the attention of Father Dusuel, the school's prefect. Dusuel took Bravo to Santiago's only art teacher, Miguel Venegos Cienfuentes, and financially supported his student's lessons and art supplies. Venegos gave Bravo a sound academic training, beginning with drawing from plaster casts of ancient Greco-Roman statues and copying old master paintings. This early training was augmented by his independent study of the Italian Renaissance, the most fundamental influence in his career. In his early twenties Bravo manifested the definition of the Renaissance man, painting portraits, writing poetry, working in the theatre, and even dancing with the Compania de Ballet de Chile. In this period Bravo developed his interest in the work of Salvador Dali, which would inform the rest of his career. During his first years out of college,

Bravo lived in the coastal town of Concepcia, where the poet and philosopher Luis Oyarzun deeply influenced his intellectual and spiritual development.

In 1961 Bravo left Chile for a ten-year residency in Madrid, where his success as a portrait painter not only provided financial security but also served as an introduction to Madrid's highest social, political, and intellectual circles. Bravo's residency in Madrid allowed him to thoroughly absorb the influence of paintings by Velasquez, Zurberan, and Titian, which are monumentally represented in the collection of the Prado Museum. During this period he also developed an interest in still life painting, with the series of paintings of packages wrapped in paper and string that eventually brought him international fame. The first show of these innovative paintings was at the Galleria Fortuny in Madrid in 1963, followed by additional Madrid shows throughout that decade. His package paintings debuted in New York at the Staemplfi Gallery in 1970, which proved to be a popular and critical success, and led to periods of New York residency. The growing interest in Bravo's new expression of the figurative tradition during the seventies brought additional shows at Staemplfi Gallery, as well as participation in prestigious group shows such as "Documenta 5," in Kassel, Germany.

In 1972, from a desire for a quieter, more contemplative life, and in flight from his portrait painting career, Bravo moved to Tangier, the port city of Morocco. The peaceful isolation and extraordinarily beautiful light of this new location enabled Bravo to expand his deepening interest in creating his highly symbolist still life and figure paintings. The 1980s began with the first of many shows he was to have at Marlborough Gallery in New York. The astoundingly prolific outpouring of paintings and drawings from the next two decades includes still lifes, figure paintings of friends and household staff, Judeo-Christian subjects, and Greek mythology and allegory, all of which exhibit his uniquely humanist quality.

His work may be found in the permanent collections of the Museum of Modern Art and The Metropolitan Museum of Art in New York City; The Philadelphia Museum of Art; The Art Museum, Princeton, New Jersey; The Peter Ludwig Museum, Cologne, Germany; and many other public and private collections. In addition to other recent prestigious exhibitions, the Institut du Monde Arabe has mounted a show of Bravo's work that demonstrates his sympathetic understanding and observation of the Muslim world in which he lives. This show represents an effort to create a culture bridge between the Muslim world and the west; the reconciliation between these two cultures implicit in Bravo's mature work grows in importance in the face of today's international crisis.

Blue Package of 1968 [FIGURE 1] is characteristic of the wrapped package paintings that first brought Bravo international acclaim in the 1960s. The phenomenal attention to carefully rendered detail displayed in these paintings certainly continues the still life tradition of the Spanish baroque artists Bravo had studied, such as Velasquez and Zurberan. A closer analysis, however, reveals Bravo's interest in the color field abstract work of some of his contemporaries, such as Rothko, whom he is known to have admired in New York. The ordi-

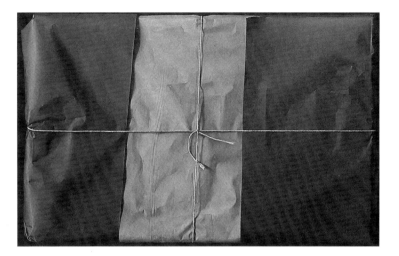

nary, everyday aspect of the subject matter also relates to the Pop Art movement, in which Bravo was immersed during his New York years. The viewer is immediately aware of Bravo's assimilation of the prevailing contemporary art movements, making his interpretation of the figurative tradition uniquely of his time. Ultimately, however, it is the provocative contrast between the modernist objectivity of the presentation and the classical love of carefully rendered detail which creates the beauty of these packages.

The Bacchanal of 1980 [FIGURE 2] is a pivotal painting in Bravo's career and displays his fully developed interest in the human figure, born of his interest in the classical figurative tradition of the Renaissance and Baroque. Bravo has said that this work was painted to prove that it is possible to create classical paintings that are unique to the twentieth century. Bravo further cites the bacchanal painting of Bellini, now in the National Gallery of Art in Washington, D.C., as the prototype for this work. As with all of Bravo's work, one immediately feels the love of the classical tradition infused with a keen observation of the contemporary world. To quote Bravo, "It's an homage to life in all its plentitude. In my *Bacchanal*, the people are modern. They've, perhaps, just left a discothèque, and are continuing their homage to Bacchus in a field." Many standard bacchanalian characters dating back to the ancient world are present, starting on the left of the composition with a goat-legged satyr pouring wine for a rather youthful, drunken Silenus. Flanking the composition on the far right, the old comedy of an amorous satyr admiring a sleeping nymph takes place. In the center an embracing couple represents the triumph of love. A couple in the background, seemingly engaged in philosophical discussion, are cast in shadow, suggesting that this is more a time for honoring the irrational side of human nature, the basis for the ancient Bacchic religious rites. The composition continues with revelers inviting one another to join the dance, culminating in a glass wine vessel triumphantly held high. Looking at the painting, one may at first view the occasional article of contemporary clothing as a nod to modern

Figure 1: Blue Package, 1968, oil on canvas, 33 ¾" x 57 ¾"

iconoclasm, until one remembers that many great painters from the past, such as Veronese and Titian, frequently clothed their classical figures in the clothing of their own time. The strongly humanist manner in which the contemporary elements are painted allies this Bacchanal with those from the past.

Minerva y Arachne of 1981 [FIGURE 3] also displays Bravo's specific desire to reinterpret Greek mythology with contemporary imagery. Arachne, a mortal girl with a tremendous gift for the art of weaving, has challenged the divine master weaver, the goddess Minerva, to a competition. The story, most movingly told in Ovid's *Metamorphoses*,

concludes with the defeat and death of the foolish mortal. Minerva, however, shows mercy and turns Arachne into nature's eternal weaver, the spider. Bravo's interpretation, once again, transforms contemporary models through his classical sensibility. The classical feeling is furthered by the frieze-like, planar quality of the composition, reminiscent of ancient Greek sculptural frieze work or vase painting. In addition, the drapery is monumental in its richly rendered vertical folds, morphing into classical columns before our eyes. This analogy between the human figure and the classical column is the very definition of humanistic classical architecture.

At the height of ancient Greek culture, athletic events were a part of religious festivals, most famously at Olympia, but also at the Pan Athenaiac festival in Athens and the Pythian games at Delphi. In *Antes del Fuego* of 1983 [FIGURE 4] Bravo reminds the viewer of the divine heritage of sporting events evident in contemporary soccer players. Again, the composition refers to the planar quality of ancient art. Furthering the classical allusion, the central figure has assumed the *contra posto* pose of the canon *The Doryphoros* by the fifth-century sculptor Polykleitos, the quintessential classical statue from the golden age of ancient Greece. He is flanked by figures assuming the more naturalistic poses of recognizable Hellenistic statues. The figure to the right is sitting in the pose of *The Spinario* from the Capitoline Museum in Rome. Behind him a soccer player strikes the pose of *Cincinnatus* of the Louvre in Paris, a product of the fourth-century B.C. school of Lysippus. The highly animated figure on the left resembles *The Dancing Faun* of Pompeii. The rendering of the anatomy of the athletes displays the humanistic approach to realism that Bravo admires so much in the work of Velasquez, with direct references to *The Forge of Vulcan* in the Prado Museum. As in all of Bravo's work, the viewer experiences a shock of recognition by sensing the underlying classical beauty in this contemporary scene.

Bravo's most recent paintings concentrate more on the still life tradition, but often with anthropomorphic suggestions in the composition, and always with his meticulous rendering. All of Bravo's interests come together in *Roman Heads* of 2002 [FIGURE 5]. The Roman period of the ancient world saw the highest development of the portrait bust, with its emphasis on realism, as well as a "Greek Revival" movement imitating the ideals of fifth-century B.C. Greek art and architecture. In Bravo's painting, a collection of busts, representing the full range of Roman art, is set up in an arrangement suggesting a dialogue about the terrible fate of Roman civilization, and, by extension, concern for all mankind. They are all connected by a purple cloth, rendered in a characteristically symbolist manner, this time seeming to represent the river of time. The bust on the far right looks back at the others with an expression of horror, perhaps at their fate of being fragments of a dead society, represented by the fallen bust of a goddess at his side. In the center, an idealized bust of Apollo stares straight ahead, oblivious of his surroundings. To the left of Apollo a very battered Roman portrait bust of a general or senator looks back and seems to answer the first with a message of stoicism. The composition concludes on the far left with another portrait bust, one of great calm shining through the acute Roman realism. This bust leaves the viewer reassured of Bravo's faith in the beauty of mankind, and, in the midst of ruin, hope for the future.

Drapery, the ancient vehicle for many meanings in art, has increasingly become the subject of Bravo's paintings in recent years. Cloth, one

Figure 2 (opposite): Bacchanal, 1981, oil on canvas, 78 ¾" x 94 ½"

Figure 3 (top): Minerva y Arachne, 1981, oil on canvas, 64 x 51 ⁷⁄₁₆"

Figure 4 (bottom): Antes del Fuego, 1983, oil on canvas, 78 ½" x 94 ¼"

of the earliest products of civilization, is associated with every phase of human life. It embraces the newborn baby, it veils the bride in marriage, and it wraps the body in the burial ceremony. Bravo's manner of rendering drapery evokes the emotional nature of these associations. *Johanes* of 1998 [FIGURE 6] embodies all the serenity and mystery of his early package paintings, but in this more timeless material. In contrast to many of Bravo's drapery paintings, which employ the full range of colors, *Johanes* is white, redolent of classical allusions. Again, the composition is frieze-like, with the reference supported by the swag arrangement, a popular motif in classical art. The swag, or festoon, was a celebratory, jubilant symbol in the ancient world. The hidden message in this painting is optimism and joy, emphasized by the beautiful rendering of the drapery itself.

It is significant that Bravo's retreat from the complexities of urban life led him to the perimeter of the Arab world, with all its serious cultural and socio-economic conflicts. The images that he sends back remind us of our classical heritage, but also of the real world, imbued with a provocative, sometimes disturbing enigma. Bravo invites us to enjoy the beauty of the world, but he also challenges us to understand its many realities and to look always beneath the surface. ✦

John Woodrow Kelley, an architect turned painter, divides his time between his studios in New York City and Tennessee. He studied at Pratt Institute, The Art Student's League, and The New York Academy. He is a fellow of The Institute of Classical Architecture & Classical America and teaches drawing for the Institute's continuing education and summer programs. His Greek mythology paintings are on view in galleries in Chicago and Milan and were recently the subject of a retrospective show, "Greek Mythology Now," at the Parthenon Museum in Nashville, Tennessee.

All images reproduced courtesy of Marlborough Gallery, Inc., New York, New York.

Figure 5 (top): Roman Heads, 2002, oil on canvas, 29 ½" x 78 ¾"

Figure 6 (bottom): Johanes, 1998, pastel on paper, 43 ¼" x 29 ½"

Recent Work by Two Master Cabinetmakers

By Daron Builta

Since this journal's inception, it has highlighted the classical resurgence in the allied arts and a number of collaborations between artists, craftsmen, and architects. Fine cabinetry, a part of this resurgence, has survived to a greater extent than the fine arts as an unbroken tradition, despite the cultural trends of the past century. Many of the best traditional furniture makers today learned their skills in the repair and restoration of fine antique pieces. These skills have survived primarily due to twentieth-century taste for antiques, a reaction against modernist aesthetics and mass production.

The connection between furniture restoration and new commissions is illustrated by the work of Gary Armstrong and William Ralston. Both craftsmen were trained in established cabinet shops that restored as well as reproduced top-quality antiques. Gary Armstrong, who lives in Exeter, New Hampshire, is a recent immigrant from the United Kingdom. His training and focus are within the European tradition, specializing particularly in mid-eighteenth-century English design. William Ralston works out of Cooperstown, New York, and learned his craft from a German immigrant master craftsman in Georgia. He works primarily in the late-eighteenth-century American Federal style.

I. GARY ARMSTRONG: ORGAN CASE

In 2003, Gary Armstrong was asked to design and produce an organ case for a royal Middle Eastern client. Originally housed in an oak upright piano-style case, a modern, computerized organ was to be transferred to a new enclosure better suited to its surroundings. The organ was to be the focal point of an octagonal reception hall, and the challenge of the commission was to make a piece of furniture to complement a collection of European eighteenth-century antiques already in the room. The program also required that the organ be re-housed in a decorative church organ-style case.

The biggest hurdle was that of successfully transferring a piece of modern technology into a new, more aesthetically appropriate housing while still allowing it to perform its intended function. This came down to a series of problems that Armstrong had to resolve. First, the gilded organ pipes were to be the central showcase of the new design. Real

Above: This organ case by Gary Armstrong is made of mahogany and Amboyna Burr with boxwood, and ebony inlay. Armstrong's knowledge of mid-eighteenth-century English cabinetry work shows in the broken pediment with finial, the carved moldings, and the Ogee feet. Size: 192" tall, by 72" wide, by 42" deep. *Photograph by Gary Armstrong.*

organ pipes, however, would have been made in lead, which cannot be gilded. Extensive research led to an experienced engineer-fabricator who was prepared to make them in brass. Manufacturing the organ pipes was a four-step process. The pipes had to be milled to a fine, blemish-free finish and highly polished before being nickel plated and finally gilded in 24-karat gold leaf.

Next, the original organ music stops, made of a black resin composite and an integral part of the electronics, were to remain. In order to seamlessly incorporate the stops into the overall structure and design, these simple but nevertheless essential components had to go through a special vacuum gilding process, ensuring a flawless match to the gilded pipes.

Finally, the case was designed with the goal of concealing the high-wattage organ speakers behind a gilt lattice grille with pleated silk backing. However, the high-output acoustics resulted in the fabric vibrating against the grills. To overcome this problem, a rubber gasket was fitted between the grill and the fabric panel to absorb and prevent the vibration.

The design of the case shows the influence of William Vile, the English mid-eighteenth-century royal cabinetmaker. It is made of Amboyna Burr with inlays of ebony, boxwood, and mahogany. The cross-banding is of mahogany curls and the fluted mahogany columns have gilt bronze bases and capitals. The client desired that the case convey a sense of stature equal to his position; and the design, proportion, and material selections all reflect this concern, making it worthy of the royal coat of arms centered on the music lectern.

II. Gary Armstrong: André Charles Boulle 'Bureau Plat'

This *Bureau Plat* is a copy Gary Armstrong was commissioned to make after an original by André Charles Boulle that sold at Sotheby's New York, in 1999. Boulle was one of the first great French *ébénistes*; he was appointed *ebéniste et marqueteur du roi* under Louis XIV in 1672. Armstrong was fortunate to have access to the original desk during its restoration and was able to make detailed measurements and take digital photographs to aid his replication process.

Following the initial construction of the mahogany desk carcass, Armstrong worked alongside master gilders, carvers, and tanners to reproduce the table. All details were copied faithfully with the exception of the tortoiseshell inlay, which was substituted with black lacquer. The greenback and hawksbill turtles, the original source for the inlay, are now both protected species.

The technique used in fabricating arabesque Boulle marquetry has changed since the eighteenth century. Originally, the marquetry pattern would have first been laid out and engraved onto a brass sheet. The sheet would then have been glued to a sheet of ebony or tortoiseshell and the layers cut through, separated, and recombined to produce a "first-part" combination of brass on a dark ground, and a "counter-part" combination of a dark design on a brass ground. The effect of this process has been modernized to compensate for the scarcity of the original materials, but the concept remains the same. A common frustration in this process is getting the brass to stick to the black groundwork. An age-old remedy for this is to apply a freshly cut lemon

Above Left: This detail of the keyboard and gilded organ stops also shows a corner column with gilt bronze base and capital, carved moldings, and brass grill with silk panel that covers electronic speakers. Armstrong spent a great deal of time incorporating the functional requirements within the new design of the case. *Photograph by Gary Armstrong.*

Above Right: This detail of the music lectern shows an Amboyna Burr panel surrounded by boxwood and ebony shadow banding and cross-banded by crotch mahogany. Centered on the lectern is the royal coat of arms of Armstrong's client, which is engraved on a gilt bronze plaque and set within an oval of book-matched crotch mahogany. *Photograph by Gary Armstrong.*

Opposite Top: This *Bureau Plat*, made by Gary Armstrong after an André Charles Boulle original, is in mahogany with ebony and brass Boulle marquetry and ormolu mounts. Size: 31" high, 63" wide, and 38" deep. *Photograph by Gary Armstrong.*

Opposite Bottom: End view of the *Bureau Plat* shows the ormolu mounts: a female mask with feathered headdress centered between the legs and bearded male masks at the corners. The marquetry designs and the headdress of the female mask show the design influence of Jean Berain who was *architecte dessinateur de la Chambre et du Cabinet du Roi* and provided designs for Boulle in his cabinetry work. *Photograph by Gary Armstrong.*

Above: This Hall Chair was designed by A.J. Davis for Lyndhurst in 1841 and reproduced by William Ralston in 2001. Ralston used computer-aided technology to lay out and cut the rose window design on the chair back. The holes in the seat rails are to receive caning. Wood: white oak; size: 36" high, 18 ½" wide, 17" deep. *Photograph by Richard Walker.*

Opposite: This Bench is from a pair interpreted by William Ralston after an original A.J. Davis designed for Lyndhurst in 1865. The National Trust found an 1880s photo of one original bench that showed that the design closely matched the dining chairs made for George Merritt, the second owner of Lyndhurst. Wood: white oak; Size: 18" high, 40" wide, 20" deep. *Photograph by Richard Walker.*

Opposite Top: In 2001 William Ralston was commissioned to reproduce this sofa by The National Trust. An existing sofa by A.J. Davis was the model and now the pair of sofas furnish the restored drawing room at Lyndhurst. Davis's design shows a rococo revival influence in the use of curves on the back and the arms. Wood: white oak; Size: 41 ¼" high, 79 ½" wide, 28" deep. *Photograph provided by Lyndhurst, a National Trust Historic Site.*

across the surface, allowing the juice to evaporate, which eliminates oils that can prevent the glue from sticking.

One particularly challenging aspect of the project was the accurate replication of the detailed mounts, which were large bearded male masks at each corner and two female masks with feathered headdresses at each end. These masks are emblematic of Boulle's work, and replicating exact copies using only photographs required the carver to have a keen sense of proportion. The mounts involved three different disciplines. First, they were carved in wood, then casts were made in bronze, and finally the castings were gilded.

The resulting piece of furniture is remarkably true to the original, and the many disciplines and precious materials involved in its making insure that it will remain a valued object well into the future.

III. WILLIAM RALSTON: LYNDHURST WORK

In 2001, William Ralston was commissioned to reproduce three missing pieces for Lyndhurst, a property of the National Trust. One of America's finest Gothic revival mansions, Lyndhurst was completed in 1842 by A.J. Davis for William Paulding Jr., a former Mayor of New York. The National Trust was restoring the drawing room to be re-opened to the public and needed to replace missing original furnishings. The original plans for this room by Alexander Davis called for a pair of sofas. It was not specified which sofas were actually used, but a single sofa by Davis existed within the house and the National Trust chose to reproduce it, creating a pair for the room. In order to create the impression of an original pair, replicating the sofa required exact attention to every detail of the form and finish.

Ralston also reproduced a pair of window seats for the same drawing room. The original furnishing plan called for these window seats as well, but the exact model was not known. In 1865, Alexander Davis remodeled and expanded Lyndhurst for the second owner, George Merritt, who bought the estate from William Paulding's son Phillip. Davis added the five-story tower and dining room wing, and converted the old library into a picture gallery. An 1870s photograph showed a pair of window seats in the gallery which the National Trust chose to reproduce for the drawing room. At first, their design was unclear, but later a better photograph was found showing that the design of the benches closely matched Davis's dining chairs of the same date, and Ralston was able to use them as the model for the bench's details.

Although these two pieces were recreated using traditional joinery, a private commission done during the same time period gave Ralston the chance to incorporate modern technology into his construction methods. One of Davis's most notable furniture designs for Lyndhurst is the set of hall chairs done in 1841 for Paulding. These incorporate a Gothic rose window design in their backs. Ralston was asked to make a pair of these. He decided that this was an ideal pattern to fabricate using a computer-generated layout of the twelve-segment back; he would then cut it using a computer-controlled router. By changing the blade on the router he was also able to cut the molding profiles. This enabled him to get uniform segments and even moldings. The rest of the considerable carved details were then completed by hand. In this instance, modern technology proved to suit the design most appropriately, and Ralston was able to incorporate this technology without compromising the quality of the outcome or the aesthetics of traditional joinery.

Whether a piece is an exact reproduction or a new interpretation within the classical or traditional idiom, once a design is settled upon it is ultimately the quality of the workmanship that gives it lasting value. Fine craftsmanship has an ability to speak to the human spirit. Armstrong's and Ralston's work are testimony to the strength and flexibility of the cabinetmaker's tradition, a method of working that can deal with new problems and technologies while maintaining the high quality standards of the past. ❧

Daron Builta graduated from Pratt Institute in 1988 and is currently a furniture and interior designer in New York City. He studied the history of European decorative arts at Sotheby's Institute in London, and classical architecture at the ICA&CA. Daron is also currently a Fellow of the ICA&CA.

Administration,
Sponsors & Membership

ADMINISTRATION

BOARD OF DIRECTORS
Anne Fairfax, *Chairman*
Richard Wilson Cameron,
    Vice-Chairman
Henry Hope Reed, *Scholar in Residence*
Margaret Halsey Gardiner, *Secretary*
Christopher H. Browne, *Treasurer*
Gregory Shue, *Fellows President*
Marshall G. Allan
Marc Appleton
Adele Chatfield-Taylor
Jacob Collins
Jeffrey L. Davis
Richard Driehaus
Christine G. H. Franck
Ray Gindroz, FAIA
William H. Harrison
Kathryn Herman
John Massengale
Peter Pennoyer
Elizabeth Plater-Zyberk, FAIA
Barbara Sallick
Suzanne R. Santry
Gilbert P. Schafer III
David M. Schwarz
Roy S. Zeluck

DIRECTORS EMERITI
Rodney Mims Cook, Jr.
David J. Cohen
Philip K. Howard
Clem Labine
Robert Pirie
Thomas J. Salvatore
Bunny Williams

FELLOWS
Gregory Shue, *Fellows President*
Steve Bass
William H. Bates III
Lisa Boudiette
Martin Brandwein, AIA
William Brockschmidt
Aimee Buccellato
Daron Builta
Stephen T. Chrisman
Courtney Coleman
Brian Connolly
Melissa Del Vecchio
Phillip James Dodd
Erik Evens
Petra Garza
Jeffrey P. Hall
Edward J. Halligan
Kristen Johnson
John Woodrow Kelley
Tom McManus
Francis Morrone
Leonard Porter
Steven W. Semes
Sean Tobin
Heather R. von Mering
Anne Walker
Seth Joseph Weine

FELLOWS EMERITI
Gary Brewer
Vicky J. Cameron
Victor Deupi
Lawrence Dumoff
Grace Hinton
Thomas Kaufman
Nora Martin
Manuel Mergal
David Netto
Damian Samora
Gilbert P. Schafer III, AIA
Peter J. Talty
Henrika Taylor

COUNCIL OF ADVISORS
Robert Adam
Boris Baranovich
Michael Bierut
John Blatteau
Louis Bofferding
Gary Brewer
Alexander Creswell
Stefania de Kennessey
Elizabeth Dowling
Richard H. Driehaus
Andrés Duany
David Anthony Easton
Nancy N. Green
Allan Greenberg
Mac Griswold
Inge Heckel
Eve M. Kahn
George M. Kelly, Sc.
Léon Krier
Michael Lykoudis
Myron Magnet
Arthur May
Sarah Medford
Hugh Petter
Carlos A. Picón
Demetri Porphyrios
Dick Reid
Jaquelin Robertson
Foster Reeve
Witold Rybczynski
Richard Franklin Sammons
Edward Schmidt
Thomas Gordon Smith
Robert A.M. Stern
Peter Trippi
Simon Verity
A. Russell Versaci
Darren Walker
Eric Watson
Carroll William Westfall
Jean Wiart

CHAPTER PRESIDENTS
Brent Baldwin, *Tennessee*
Chris Barrett, *Southern California*
Nir Buras, *Mid-Atlantic*
Eric Daum, *New England*
David Grace, *Southeast*
Alvin Holm, *Philadelphia*
Michael G. Imber, *Texas*
Charles Furman McLarty, *Charlotte*
Geoffrey Mouen, *Florida*
Ralph Muldrow, *Charleston*
Suzanne Tucker, *Northern California*

STAFF

OPERATIONS
Paul Gunther, *President*
Henrika Taylor, *Managing
    Director/Editor*
Randy Acosta, *Finance and
    Communications Manager*

EVENTS AND MEMBERSHIP
Joanna Berritt, *Special Events Manager*
Brendan Connelly, *Membership and
    Special Events Assistant*

EDUCATION
Victor Deupi, *Arthur Ross
    Director of Education*
Michael Gormley, *Associate Director
    of Education*
Leah Aron, *Education Programs
    Coordinator*
Justine Kalb, *Coordinator, Grand
    Central Academy of Art*

OFFICE AND
CLASSROOM SPONSORS
Arthur Ross Foundation
Balmer Architectural Mouldings
Bauerschmidt & Sons
Benjamin Moore & Co.
Gary Brewer
Christopher H. Browne
Brockschmidt & Coleman
Budd Woodwork
E.R. Butler & Co.
David Cohen and the I-Grace
    Company
Decora Electric Co., Inc.
DFB Sales
LaPolla, Inc.
Lutron Electronics
Amanda Haynes-Dale
Morris and Alma Schapiro Fund
Scalamandre
Robert A.M. Stern Architects
Stephanie Tegnazian
Simon Verity
Amy Weinstein
Roy and Kevin Zeluck,
    Zeluck Windows & Doors

THE CLASSICIST NO. 7

*The publication of The Classicist No. 7
has been made possible thanks to the generous
contributors of the following sponsors:*

BENEFACTORS
Agrell Architectural Carving, Ltd.
Andrew Skurman, Architect
Ariel, The Art of Building
Balmer Architectural Mouldings
Brockschmidt & Coleman
Bunny Williams Incorporated
Carnegie Hill Books
Chadsworth's 1.800.Columns
The Classic Group, Inc.
Curtis & Windham Architects
Decora Electric Co., Inc.
Dyad Communications, Inc.
E. R. Butler & Co.
Eric J. Smith Architects, PC
Fairfax & Sammons Architects PC
Fenestra America
Ferguson & Shamamian Architects, LLP
Franck & Lohsen Architects
G. P. Schafer Architect, PLLC
Grand Central Academy of Art
FJ Hakimian
David D. Harlan
Historic Doors
The I-Grace Company
Ike Kligerman Barkely Architects, PC
Jacob Froehlich
James Bleecker Photography
John Blatteau Associates
John B. Murray Architect, LLC
LaPolla, Inc.
Leonard Porter Studio
Les Metalliers Champenois
Mark P. Finlay Architects, AIA
Peter Pennoyer Architects
Restore Media, LLC
Robert A. M. Stern Architects
Robert Orr & Associates, LLC
Robin Bell Design, Inc.
Robinson Iron
Rodney M. Cook Interests
Syon Studio
Thoughtforms Corporation
Traditional Cut Stone Ltd.
Urban Archaeology
Wadia Associates
Zeluck Incorporated

PATRONS
Appleton & Associates, Inc.
Ken Tate Architect
Lantern Masters, Inc.
White River Hardwoods, Inc.

DONORS
A.J. Rogac Ltd.
AJ.T Architect PC
DMS Studios Ltd.
Eric Watson Architect PA
Alvin Holm, AIA
James F. Carter, Inc.
Michael G. Imber, Architects
Michael Simon Interiors
    Incorporated
Merrill and Pastor Architects
Moor & Associates, Architects PA
Peter Cosola Incorporated
Steven W. Semes, Architect
Timothy Bryant Architect

INDIVIDUAL MEMBERS

LATROBE SOCIETY

Marshall G. Allan
Norman Askins
Mark Appleton & Joanna Kearns
David G. Baird, Jr.
F. Ronald Balmer
Jon Berndsen
Christopher H. Browne
E.R. Butler
Gibert and Ildiko Butler
Richard Cameron
Dick Clegg
David Cohen
Jacob Collins
Jeffrey L. Davis
Richard H. Driehaus
Anne Fairfax and
    Richard Sammons
Mark Ferguson
Elizabeth and Patrick Gerschel
Mr. & Mrs. George J. Gillespie III
Ray Gindroz
William T. Golden
David Grace
William M. Hablinski
Jim Hanley
William H. Harrison
Amanda Haynes-Dale
Kathryn Herman
Charles Heydt
Michael Imber
Mr. and Mrs. Charles Johnson
Clem Labine
Tom Maciag
Steven J. Maun
Mr. and Mrs. William J.
    Michaelcheck
Aidan Mortimer
John B. Murray
Joe Nye
Yong Pak
Greg Palmer
Peter Pennoyer
Elizabeth Plater-Zyberk
Leonard Porter and Qian Yi
Foster Reeve
Suzanne Rheinstein
R. Douglass Rice
Jaquelin Robertson
William Rondina
Mr. and Mrs. Alfred Ross
Arthur Ross
David M. Schwarz
Barbara Sallick
Suzanne and David Santry
Gilbert P. Schafer III
Oscar Shamamian
Andrew Skurman
Eric Smith
Nick Stern
Robert A.M. Stern
Todd Strickland
James W. Sykes, Jr.
Aso Tavitian

Helen Tucker
Suzanne Tucker
D. Clay Ulmer
The Hon. & Mrs.William J.
    vanden Heuvel
Dinyar Wadia
Jean Wiart
Bunny Williams
Kevin Zeluck
Roy Zeluck

BENEFACTORS

Joan Johnson, White River
    Hardwoods Inc.
Richard Krysiak, Tradewood
    Windows and Doors, Inc.
Ric and Suzanne Kayne
Dell Mitchell Architects, Inc.
Frederic Rheinstein

PATRONS

Diane Beattie
Kevin P.A. Broderick
Edward Lee Cave
Mr. and Mrs. Christopher Davis
Robert Halper
Elizabeth Lenahan
Michael Lykoudis
G. Michael Merritt
Nancy Brown Negley
Gregory L. Palmer
Katharine J. Rayner
Mr. and Mrs. William P. Rayner
Paige Rense
Allison Roeder
Gilbert P. Schafer, Jr.
Sandra Seligman
Eric J. Smith
Scott Snyder
Wesley R. Vawter III
Daniela Holt Voith

SPONSORS

Betsy A. Allen
Michael Allen
Tim Barber
Constance Goodyear Baron
Karen Becker
Paul Beirne
Maria V. Bielins
Russell Bloodworth
Maureen Bluedorn
Lisa Singleton Boudiette
Thomas Anthony Buckley
Janna Bullock
Vincent J. Buonanno
James F. Cooper
Richard Crum
Jean de Merry
Dean Dordevic
Eleanor Edelman
Seth Faler
Christopher Forbes
Becky Gee
Mary Campbell Gallagher J.D., Ph.D.
Patricia Glazer

Christabel Gough
William Guthy & Victoria Jackson
Damon Hein
Frederick H. Herpel
Richard Kossmann
Mr. and Mrs. Richard Kramer
Jill Lloyd
Thor Magnus
Christian Maroselli
Mr. and Mrs. Peter May
Jim McDonough
Mr. and Mrs. W. R. McNabb
George P. Mills
Mr. and Mrs. Tom Mitchell
Paula Nataf
Nancy Newcomb
Eric Rustan Osth
Ben Page, Jr.
Valerie Paley
S. Edward Parker
Todd Alexander Romano
Stephen Salny
Thomas J. Salvatore
Frances M. Schultz
Gregory Shue
Michael Simon
Michael S. Smith
Lynn Tamarkin Syms
Peter J. Talty
Helen S. Tucker
Riccardo S. Vicenzino
Russell Windham

FRIENDS

Emerson Adams
Jon Adir
Frederick L. Ames
Hugh Anderson
O. Kelley Anderson
Robert Anthony
Edgar O. Appleby
Collette Arredondo
Andrew B. Ballard
Barbara Barry
T. Pamela Bathgate
Kay Bearman
Patricia Benner
Osvaldo Bertolini
J. Goodwin Bland
Abbey Blum
Michael C. Booth
Emily R. Bourgeois
John Bralower
Robin Browne
Sondra Browning-Ott
Catherine Cahill & William L.
    Bernhard
Dr. and Mrs. John Cameron
Vincent Cappello
Chris Carson
Susan Cowen Coleman
Mary Kay Crain
Andrew Cullinan
Scott Reed Dakin
Timothy Deal
Laura DePree

David Dowler
Richard Dragisic
Gavin Duke ASLA
Thomas Edelman
Russell Ervin
David Esterly
Neil Flax
Richard Ford
Ned Forrest
Emily Frick
Todd Furgason
Heather Hoyt Georges
John Gicking
David H. Gleason
Debra Godsoe
Marvin Goodman
William Green
Peter Louis Guidetti
Albert Hadley
Jeffrey Hall
Stephen Harby
Thomas S. Hayes
Suzanne L. Haynes
Julie Higgins
Roger H. Howard
Mr. & Mrs. Thomas J. Hubbard
Gordon Hyatt
William B. Irvine III
Ann Johnson
William F. Johnson
Howell Jones
Meg and Lawrence Kasdan
Frances Kent
Scott R. Layne
Mr. & Mrs. Alan P. Levenstein
Jenny Levion
David Lewandowski
Calder Loth
Sandra Mabritto
Robert MacLeod
Robert C. Magrish
James C. Marlas
Helen Marx
John D. Mashek, Jr.
Vicki McCluggage
Mark W. McClure AIA
Donald B. McDonald
Susan McFadden
Susan C. Meals
Albert S. Messina
Brenda H. Mickel
Chas A. Miller III
Richard D. Miller
Tim Miller
William L. Mincey, Jr., AIA
Philip Morris
Grace Mynatt
Margaret and Thomas Noble
Thomas V. Noble
William D. B. Olafsen
Robert Orr
Kristen and Sanford Panitch
Noble Gregory Pettit
Paul R. Provost
Willem Racke
George A. Radwan

William Dean Randle
Lawrence H. Randolph
Jacqueline Ressa
Rosalie W. Reynolds
Richardson Robertson III
Alan Rogers
Marc Rosenberg
Robert Rosenberg
Siamak Samii
John Robert Savage
Sophia Duckworth Schachter
Mr. and Mrs. Stanley DeForest
    Scott
Steven W. Semes
Paul Francis Shurtleff
Catherine Sidon
Harold R. Simmons
Sandy Sorlien
Mr. and Mrs. L. Caesar Stair III
Keary Sullivan
Jack Taylor
William Barry Thomson
Noreen Tomassi
Richard John Torres
Susan and Coleman Townsend
Nancy R. Turner
Nancy and Jim Utaski
John Varriano
Lavelle Walker
Luanne Wells
Carroll William Westfall
Paul Whalen
George Bell Whitney
John H. Whitworth, Jr.
Dr. and Mrs. Robert D. Wickham
William Ridley Wills III
Erich Winkler & Nancy Allerston
Cecilia Winston
Richard Wissmach
Nalla Wollen
David Michael Wood
John Yunis
Fred S. Zrinscak, Jr.
Amy Zwicker

SUPPORTING/ DUAL MEMBERS

Dr. and Mrs. Malouf Abraham
Tamara Acosta
Carl Adams
Kim Alexandriuk
William Allison
Jhennifer Amundson
June Anderson
Marvin Anderson
David Anderson
Martha Angus
Charlotte P. Armstrong
Mary Ascheim
Frederick W. Atherton Assoc. AIA
Robert J.S. Attiyeh
Charles Bagby
Mr. and Mrs. Thomas G. Bagg
Brent Baldwin
Elliot Banfield
Anthony Baratta

Betsy Barbanell
Chris Barrett C.I.D.
James Barry III
D. Troy Beasley
Lynne Beavers
Chris Becker
Mr. and Mrs. Thomas Beeby
Myron Beldock
Patsy Ann Bell
Mr. and Mrs. Jordan Bender
Claudia Benvenuto
Raffi R. Berberian
Susan K. Berland
Roy Bernat
Amy Bernstein
Seth P. Bernstein
Gregory Bettenhausen
Marguerite Bierman
Jonathan Bliss
Louis H. Blumengarten
Larry E. Boerder
Tom Boland
Brandt A. Bolding
Charles P. Bolton
John Bossard
Suzanne L. Botts
Denis J. Boylan
Holland Brady, Jr.
Sandra Breakstone
Patricia Breen
Mr. and Mrs. Craig Brewerton
William Brockschmidt
Mr. and Mrs. Alexander Brodsky
Harry P. Broom, Jr.
Connie and Morrison Brown
Franklin Browne
David Brussat
Mark Buchanan
Peter Budnik
Nir Buras
John Burgee
Andrew Burke
Mr. and Mrs. James Burke
Laini Byfield
Tim Call
Thomas Callaway
Christian B. Calleri
Mr. and Mrs. Thomas A. Cassilly
Jane Causey
Arthur Chabon
Ellen M. Cheever
Mr. and Mrs. Joel Chen
Monica Cheslak
Mr. and Mrs. Gaetano Cichy
Blanche Cirker
Daniel Clancy
John Clark
Kenneth Clark
Michael Clifford
Dr. and Mrs. Steven R. Cohen
Steven Cohen
Gary L. Cole AIA, Esq.
Anne Moore Colgin
Josyane Colwell
Robert Condon
Patricia Conlin

Brian Connolly
Morgan Conolly
Helen Adams Cook
Robert Couturier
John Craig
Tony Crane
Gregory Cranford
H. Beck Crothers II
Daniel Clayton Cuevas
John Dale
William Daniels
Howard Davis
Tina Davis
Leslie Davol
Adrine Davtyan
Mike Day
Marina Forstmann Day &
    Paul Livadary
Megan M. De Roulet
Robert M. Del Gatto
Antoinette Denisof
Joseph Dennan
Stewart Desmond
William Diamond
Curt DiCamillo
Elizabeth Dinkel
Kathryn Dinkel
Gregory Dixon
Joseph Dixon III
Alden Lowell Doud
Robert Douglass
Mr. and Mrs. Michael Doumani
Elizabeth M. Dowling AIA
William Drakely
Fred Drohsler
Peter Dunham
Mary Laurence Dunne
Chantal Dussouchaud
Peggy Earle
Leslie Edelman
Don Edson
Laura Egelhoff
Whitney Rietz Eller
Audun Engh
Justin Falango
Richard N. Faust
Matthew Fitzgerald
David Flaharty
Laura W. Fleder
Ronald Lee Fleming
Patrick Flood
Mr. and Mrs. Paul G. Flynn
Patrick Folan & Bill Biondolino
Ruth Frangopoulos
Violanda Franzese
Charles J. Frederick, Jr.
Elizabeth Boggs Freund
Tres Fromme
Oliver M. Furth
Hamid Gabbay
Yassi Gabbay
Robin Garrett
Stephanie Gash
Theresa Ghevondian
Callum Gibb
Linda Gillies

Cynthia Goldsmith
Kay Golitz
Toni K. Goodale
Steven Goodwin AIA
Alexander Gorlin
Betsy Gotbaum
Kristine Gould
Eric Greenberg
Nancy Greenberg
Dr. and Mrs. Vartan Gregorian
A. Michael Griffith
Michael Grimes
Jeff Groff
Jane M. Gullong
Mr. and Mrs. Kenneth Gunther
Theodore Gutmann
G. William Haas
John M. Haas
Mr. and Mrs. Robert Hack
The Hon. and Mrs. Craig Haffner
Philip M. Hahn
Erik Haig
Joseph K. Hall
Edward J. Halligan, Jr.
Paul and Audrey Hanneman
Pam Hargett
Mr. and Mrs. Kirk Henckels
Emilie Henry
Evelyn Henry
Ronald G. Herczeg
William Heyer
Mr. and Mrs. Richard D. Higbie
Albert P. Hildebrandt
May Brawley Hill
Jeffrey Hitchcock
Lorin Hodges
Christopher Holbrook
Richard Holt
Stephen R. Holt
William Hopkins
Chery Sumner Horacek
Kazuko Hoshino
Don Hudson
Cheryl Hurley
Timothy Husband
Barry Hutner
Mildred Q. Iacovetti
Carol Innes
Mark Irizarry
Mr. & Mrs. Keith Irvine
Roger P. Jackson AIA
Laurence Janson
Thomas Jayne
Michael Jefcoat
William Rush Jenkins
Richard H. Jenrette
Britton Jewett
Richard John
Mr. and Mrs. David Johnson
George Johnston
Michael Juckiewicz
David Karabell
Raymond Kaskey
Michael Kathrens
Jeff Keenan
Gary R. Keim

Michael Keir
Rose and Nora Kenny
Margaret Derwent Ketcham
Mark L. Khidekel
Michelle Kinasiewicz
Theodora Kinder
Bruce C. King
Lauren S. King
Laura King
Stephen Kirschenbaum
D. Dean Kiser
Suzanne Klein
Dimitrios Klitsas
Tasos Kokoris
Kathi Koll
Barbara Kraebel
Karen Kreitsek
Kirk E. Kreuzwieser
Anthony Kronman
Thomas Kruempelstaedter
Kenneth S. Kuchin
Annette Kuyan
Peter A. LaCava
D. E. Lafave
Robert J. Lancelotta, Jr.
Richard Landry
Thomas Landry
George Lanier
Fred Laser
Nora Lavori
Clay Lawrence
Veronica and Walter Leipert
John Leonards
Alan LeQuire
J. Scott Leurquin
Jennifer Levin
John Liang
Mr. and Mrs. Robert Lindgren
Wayne A. Linker
Charles Lockwood
William Long
Joaquin Lorda
Nancy Lovas
Thomas Lucas
Susan Lustik
Donald MacDonald
Arlette Magee
William Malmstedt
Thomas Fleming Marble
Hannah Marks
Andrew Martin
Jenna Martin
Richard D. Martin
Van Jones Martin
James Marzo
Haskell R. Matheny
Patricia J. Matson
David McAlpin
Scot McBroom
Deedie McCarthy
Mary Ryan McCarthy
Gordon McClure
Holly McCord
Thomas A. McCrary
Patrick S. McDonough
Dennis C. McGlade

Elizabeth McMillian
Denis McNamara
Lisa McTernan
Martin Meek
Michael J. Mekeel
Callie Melton
Alan Metz
Thomas Michie
Paul Milana
Christopher Miller
Orloff and Elisabeth Miller
Susan Miniman
Naomi Mirsky
Edgar K. Mitchell
William R. Mitchell, Jr.
Dina Morgan
Edward B. Morgan
Susan C. Morse
Mr. and Mrs. Robert Mueller
Sara Muller-Chernoff
Mr. and Mrs. Richard Mulligan
Trish Munro
Ward Murphy
Andrew Muscato
Lyn R. Muse
David L. Nagrodsky
Donald J. Neely
Mr. and Mrs. Garrett Nelson
Christine Ness
Louis Newman
George Nichols
John Nieman
Sean Patrick Nohelty AIA
Greg Nott
Dottie O'Carroll
Bob Ray Offenhauser AIA
Winfield Ogden
Kevin K. Ohlinger
Mr. & Mrs. Dennis O'Kain
Sean O'Kane
Mark Olives
Peter O'Malley
Paul Onstad
Joseph I. Onstott
Susan Orlando
Mr. and Mrs. Alex B. Pagel
Daniel Parolek AIA, CNU
Gordon Pashgian
Patricia S. Patterson
Richard Paulson, Jr.
David Pearson
Russell P. Pennoyer
Linda Peters
Ahna and Geoffrey Petersen
Jim Pfaffman & Katherine Pearson
Patrick Pigott
Steve Poe
Susan Poland
Edward and Marianne Pollak
Patricia Pope
Marc Porter
Annabelle F. Prager
Thomas Proctor
Vito C. Quatela
Chip Rae
John W. Rae, Jr.

Seema Reznick
Barry Rice
Donna Rich
Robert W. Rich
Ron Richardson
David Rimmler
Samuel Rindge
Richard E. Roberts
Francine Rodriguez
Colleen M. Rogers
Eavon Rolich
Danielle Rollins
Alison and Larry Rosenthal
John Rosselli
Phillip H. Rubin
Robert C. Russek
Margaret Russell
Marie Salerno
Edward Savard
Mr. and Mrs. Henry Schacht
Kibby Schaefer
Molly Schaefer
Eleanor Schapa
Arthur Schlesinger, Jr.
Darrell Schmitt
Les Sechler
George Seddon
Ann G. Seidler
Adele Seltzer
Eric Shaikewitz
Jasminka Shaikewitz
Elliot Shalom
Lesley-Anne and Eytan Shapiro
Bailey Sharp
Gail Shaw
George Shelden
Bruce and Lauren Sherman
Elizabeth D. Shevlin
Audrey Shinn
Brian Shore
Barbara J. Siemon
L.M. Silkworth AIA
Robert A. Silver MD
Teresa Silverman
Daniel Sinclair
John Sinopoli
HoweK. Sipes III
Philip L. Sleep
Jeanne Sloane
James Smiros
Laura Smiros
Scott Smissen
Ian H. Smith
P. Allen Smith
David R. Snider
Laura and George C. Snyder
Salli Snyder
Maria R. Sola
Pat & Walter South
F. T. Spain
Joseph Peter Spang
Barrie Curtis Spies
Cheryl Ann Spigno
Tjasa Sprague
D. Scott Springer
John Steigerwald

Marcia D. Stemwedel
Mia Taradash
Dr. and Mrs. Jay Tartell
Michelle Tate
Dr. and Mrs. Richard Tavernetti
Crawford Logan Taylor III
Jonathan Matthew Taylor
John Tee
Collin Tinsley
Sean J. Tobin
Karen Topjian
Paul D. Trautman
William Trautman
Paul R. Tritch
Mark Umbach
Mr. and Mrs. James Upham
Donna Vaccarino, AIA
Mike Vegher
Ruard Veltman
Linda Vinson
Gerald T. Vitagliano
Joe Wagner
Arthur Wallander
J. Randal Wallar
William Robert Ward
Daniel Ward
Patricia G. Warner
Charles Warren
Mr. & Mrs. William B. Warren
Michael Watkins
Kirk Watson
Wendy Watson
Sam Watters
Scott Weaver
Lamar T. Webb
Sydney Weinberg
Frank Wen & Diana Mulder
Tony Weremeichik
Carol and Bill Wermuth
Steadman H. Westergaard
Timothy Whealon
Bruce W. Whipple
Brooks S. White
Henry M. White
Mac White
Jana Whitley
Roby and Robert Whitlock
Gretchen Willison
Marguerite Anne Wilson
Mr. and Mrs. Rod Wilson
Valerie S. Wilson
Barbara J. Wiseley
B. Stephen Wiseman
Christopher Wiss
Nancy L. Wolf
Christine Wolfe-Nichols
Robert L. Woodbury
Douglas C. Wright III
Robert R. Wright
Mei Wu
Karen S. Yannett
Mr. and Mrs. John Young
Michael J. Young

MEMBERS

Gerald Abbott
Alisha Acevedo
Duval B. Acker ASID
Beth Adams
Guy Aiman
Jacob Albert
Donald Albrecht
Drury B. Alexander
Mr. and Mrs. James M. Alexander
Mr. and Mrs. Michael J. Algieri
Suzanna Allen
Mark Amey
John H. Anderson
Robert Anderson
Edward D. Andrews
Debra Antolino
Michele Arboit
Mike E. Arzouman
Ann Ascher
Nick Atkinson
Patsy Ault
Helene Aumont
Laurence J. Aurbach, Jr.
Paul V. Averbach
Anne Aziz
Cory Babb
Larry Babbio
Laurie Bachman
Terry Bailey
Marc C. Bailly
Denise E. Baime
Candice R. Bales
Leonora M. Ballinger
Ramiro A. Baptista
Anthony Baragona
Gena Bardwell
Penelope Bareau
Ann Stewart Barker
Angela Barretto
Vicky Barshay
William Barth
Britton Bartlett
Ann Barton
Yvonne Bartos
Thomas Paul Bates
Nancy F. Battaglia
Bulent Baydar
Kristin Bayruns
Maria Becerra
David A. Beckwith
Deborah Belcher
Christina Belmonte
Ronald Bentley
John Bergan
Cassandra Berger
John L. Beringer
Inez Bershad
James T. Best
Jenny Bevan
John Bews
Sander Bijker
Philippe Bilger
Michelle Bird
Nora M. Black
Roderick H. Blackburn

Richard Blumenberg
Paul Bockenhauer
R. Louis Bofferding
Glen B. Boggs II
Mr. and Mrs. Alexander L. Bolen
Deborah Bonelli
Jeb Bonner
Samuel Bonnet
Valerie J. Boom
Daniel Borden
Steven P. Borelli
Richard A. Bories
Sarah Bouchier
Daniel J. Bowen
Darren A. Bowie
Linda Boyce
Benjamin Bradley
Caroline Bradshaw
Diane Brandt
Ms. Christine Brennan
Victor Brighton
Yuliya and Andrey Brizhan
Mr. and Mrs. Alexander Brodsky
Nathaniel Brooks
Jan Hall Brown
Lisa Brown
Vance Browning
William Bruning
Robert Bryant
Christopher Budinger
Barbara Buff
Mary A. Burke
William Burke
Jean Burn
Jonathan P. Butler
Mirelys Calise
Frances Campbell
Mitchell Campbell
Sharon Campbell
Thomas Rex Campbell
Ana L. Canton
Mitchell Cantor
Kristine Carber
Scott Carde
Valerie Carney
Susan Carr
Gloria Carrera
Christopher M. Carrigan
William L. Cary
John Casarino
Lisa R. Cassidy
Catherine Casteel
Fernando Castro
Patricia J. Ceglia
Rocco Ceo
Roger Cerasoli
Robert L. Chapman III
Skye Patricia L. Chapman
Winston B. Chappell
Nicolas Charbonneau
Benjamin W. Cheney
Katherine Chez
Jason Childers
William H. Childs, Jr.
Lucylee Chiles
Josh Chuzi

Carol Clark
Kevin P. Clark
Timothy F. Clark
Edward Clarke
John H. Cluver
Andrew B. Cogar
J. N. Colburn
Mary Cole
Courtney Coleman
Diane Collins
Leah Collums
Elizabeth Condrick
Dana & Clayton Conger
Daniel W. Cook
Michael Cook
Michael G. Copeland
Kristin Costa
Patrick Cox
Robert Craig Cox
Mark Crawford
Anthony Crisafi
Elizabeth Curry
Annise B. Curtis
Amy V. Dachs
Donald Dale
Jeffery F.C. Dalzell
Lindsay Daniel
Nicholas Daveline
Jack Davis
Katherine Davis
Sheryl Davis
Randall Dawkins
John E. Day
Helen E. Dayton
A. Francyne de Buck
Ronald de Salvo
Angelina Deaconeasa
Michael Defty
Orestes del Castillo
George Delanuez
Marjorie Deninger
Jean Bernard Denis
Molly K. Denver
Samuel J. DeSanto
Perry Des Jardins
Peter F. Dessauer
Robert J. Deveau
Lori DeWaal
Lucio Di Leo
Clarisa Diaz
Stephen Dietz
Mason H. Disosway
Nada Djordjevic
John M. Dodd
Todd Dolan
Gerald E. Dolezar
Del Donati
Paul Donnellan
Murray Bartlett Douglas
Abigail Dowd
Stuart A. Drake
Robert W. Drucker
John Drum
Andrew Dulcie
Timothy Dunleavy
Kelly Dunn

Mr. and Mrs. Robert Dyck
Gary I. Dycus
Christie Dyer
Mr. and Mrs. Ben F. Easterlin IV
George H. Eatman
April Eberhardt
James Eckel
Joshua J. Eckert
Roy Eddleman
Ralph E. Eissmann
Patty Elias
Elton Elperin
Annalee Emanuel
Kenmore H. Emerson
Mary Jane Emmet
Norma Englert
Nord Eriksson
Tania Espinoza
Mary Anne Eves
Mark Dillen Failor
Sara C. Fair
William Fair
David Falk
Jacques Farasat
Marlene Farrell
Daniel Feinstein
Haley B. Felchlin
Ilene Feldhammer
Laurie Gunther Fellows
Happy Fernandez
Louis N. Ferrero
Jack Fetterman
April Fey
David Finlay
Pilar Fitzgerald
Richard Fitzgerald
Bill Fleck
James Joseph Fleming
Russell Flinchum
Cynthia Flood
Heather Flood
Robert Flood
Maureen Wilson Footer
Tracy Forsythe
Carolyn Foti
Jane Frankel
Philip Franz
Devanee Frazier
Robert Fry
Thomas P. Fuchs
Rick Fujita
Wilson Fuqua
J. Francois Gabriel
Patrick Gaffney
Jim Galloway
Susan Galvani
Sherri Garber
Brooke Gardner
Susan Garino
Jay-Michael Garrell
Kitt Garrett
M. Lee Garrison
Rachel Gasta
Patrick Gaughan

Celeste P. Gebhardt
Joanna Giannopoulos
Nicholas L. Gianopulos
Dennis Gibbens
Grant Gibson
Kurt Gibson
Richard Giesbret
Lynn Gilbert
Joe Gillach
George Gillespie
Gregory Gilmartin
Tracy Gilmore
Edward Giordano
Raymond Givargis AIA
Jan Gleysteen
Ronald Gold
Jason Gonzalez
Carol Goodman
Jessica Goodyear
Jeff C. Goolsby
Kevin C. Gore
Marc Gorman
Michele Grace
Bonnie Grant
Kellie Gravel
Leonard Greco
Bryan Green
Nancy Green
Sonya Green
Susan Green
Maria Greenawalt
Beverly Greenwald
Lucia Griffith
Sally Grossman
Suzy Grote
Max M. Guenther
Catherine Gulevich
Dale R. Halaja
Edward Hall
Buzz Halliday
Jeffrey P. Hamilton
Burks Hamner
Robert G. Hancock
Vanessa Hanson
Taylor Harbison
Cynthia Hardwick
Edwin Hardy
John Harra
Kevin L. Harris
Laura E. Harris
Peter Harrison
Teresa M. Hartford
Julian Hartzog
David Hathcock
Diana Hawes
Adriana Hayward
William Hayward
Huyler C. Held
Aaron Helfand
Steven Heller
Mary Helpern
Chad Hempleman & Glenda
   McKenzie
Robert W. Herald

Richard Hershner
Deborah Hershowitz
Frank F. Herz
Mark Higbie
A. Tobias Hildebrand
Katherine Hillock
Damian Hils
Kathryn Hobart
Shane Hobgood
Gayle Holmes
H. Randolph Holmes
Alana Homesley
E. Randolph Hooks
Carter Hord
Diana Houlihan
Barbara Howard
Natalie Howard
Clinton Howell
Richard H. Howland
Gregory D. Huber
Meisha Hunter
Ernest Watson Hutton, Jr.
Ivonne Ibarra
Ames Ingham
Alfred Izzo
Prudence Jackson
Robert Jaeger
Betsy Jaques
John M. Jascob
Deborah Jensen
Laura Jereski
Daniel R. Johnson
Elizabeth Glasgow Johnston
Andrew Berrien Jones
Brian Kent Jones
Carey Jones
Corinne Jones
Grace Jones
Kellie Jones
Marianne Jones
Susan Jones
Predrag Patrick Jovanov
Sidney Joyner
Eve Kahn
Susan Kahn
Majda Kallab
Jay Kallos
Dorothy Kamenshine
Anahid Kapoian
Renee Kaufman
Gersil N. Kay
Thomas Keeling AIA
Christian K. Keesee
Arthur Keller
John Woodrow Kelley
James Kelly
Patrick Kelly
W. David Kelly
Margaret Kendrick
Margaret Ketcham
Christina Khadivar
Marina Khoury
Suzanne Kinser
Roy Kirby

William Kirwan
Stephen Klimczuk
Corinna Knight
Paul Knight
Mr. and Mrs. Kevin Knight
Mary Knowles
Greg Koester
Dojie Kohn
Kevin Kolanowski
Debra Kossar
Maria Kostoulas
Trian Koutoufaris
Joseph Kowalski
Brian Kramer
Brian N. LaBau
Salvatore LaFerlita
Salem Richard LaHood
Mitch LaPlante
Roberto Lara
Jean Larette
Patrick Larkin
Marilyn R. Lasecki
Keith Lashley
Andrew Laux
Anne O. Lawrence
Shelly Lawrence
Priscilla Lee
Clifford L Lefebvre
John C. Lei
Rocco Leonardis
Erik Lerner
Andreas Letkovsky
Joy Lewis
Julie Liepold
Kent Lineberger
Frances Litvack
Carrie Livingston
Jeff Livingston
John Lloyd
Wendy Lloyd
Lee Loomis
Ricardo Lopez
Thomas E. Low AIA
David Garrard Lowe
Paul M Lucier
Kelly R. Luke
James Lumsden
Valera W. Lyles
Catherine Lynn
George Lynne
Warren Mack
Joyce Macrae
Henry Jonas Magaziner FAIA
John A. Magee
Christine Mainwaring-Samwell
John Thomas Maisano
Robert Maisano
Vaishali Makim
Bhoke Manga
Heather Mangrum
Rosario Mannino
Elizabeth Mantikas
Tom Marano
Tripp March

Susan B. Marcus
Jeffrey Alan Marks
Harold Marsh III
Diego Uribe Martinez
Toni Martucci
Elizabeth Mathes
Nancy Matthews
Jeffrey R. Matz
John Mayfield
Stacey McArdle
William McBain
Daniel McCarthy
Chris McCoy
Molly M. McDonald
Justin McEntee
Dennis McEvoy
Clancy McGilligan
John P. McGrath
Mary McGrath
Beverly McGuire Schnur
James R. McKeown
Charles Furman McLarty
Elizabeth A. McNicholas
Christie McRae
Bill McWhorter
Robert Meiklejohn
Carlos Mejia
Ronald Melichar
Walter Melvin
Marcelo C. Mendez
Tino Mendrzyk
Jean Mercier
Manuel Mergal
Louise Merola
J. Rodney Merrick AIA
Richard Messmann
James Meyers
Lisa Marie Milat
Dr. and Mrs. James Milgram
DeAnne Millais
John F. Millar
Adam Miller
Briana Miller
Brian B. Miller
Greg Miller
Jeffrey L. Miller
Marian Miller
Patricia Miller
Walter Miller
Bruce B. Mills
Justin F. Minieri AIA
Victor Misarti
Pauline M. Mohr
Maureen Monck
Andrew Moneyheffer
Michael S. Montgomery
Bo Moon
Stephen M. Moore
Josephine Morales
Angel Moreno AIA
Stephen H. Morley
Barbara H. Morrison
Richard Morrison
David Morton

Maria E. Mosca
Matthew J. Mosca
Beverly B. Mosch
Elias Moser
Paula Moss
James E Mulford
James Mundy, Jr.
Richard Munsey
Kenneth R. Nadler
Nancy Nahon
Michelle Nassopoulos
Josh Nathan
Susan Nathan
Gracia Navarro-Figueroa
Andrew G. Nehlig
Marena Nellos
J. Mark Nelson
Merise Nelson
Rick O. Nelson
Sonja Nelson
MarkW. Nester
Alan Neumann
John Neumann
Dana Newman
Daniel Nicolle
Carl Nittinger
Michael Nolen
Nathan Norris
Lincoln Norton
Oroma Nwanodi
Christine O'Brien
John O'Brien
Kazumasa Oda
John James Oddy
Bill Olafson
Daniel Osborne
Kate Ottavino
Joseph Owczarek
Laura Pacchini
Nelly Pajarola
Lisa Pak
Manuel Palos
Jennifer Paloski
Hema Pandya
Daniel Pardy
Jonathan Parisen
Bret Parsons
Tal Parsons
Daniel Partridge
Lenore Passavanti
Rajeev M.A. Patel
Rita Patel
Pradeep Pathak
Rose T. Patrick
Drex Patterson
Guy Pearlman
Thomas J. Pearsall
Jeanne Pearson
Michael Paul Pendergrass
Carol M. Penn
Betty Perlish
BJ Peterson FASID
Hugh D.M. Petter
Van Meter Pettit

Marc Phillips AIA
Patrick Pinnell
Cody Pless
Pearl Potter
Gwen Pottiker
Patti Poundstone
Jeffrey Povero
Dean L. Pratt
Robert E. Price
Lynn Pries
Lynette Proler
George Punnoose
Susan Emery Quinby
Suzanne Rabil
Jan S. Ramirez
Paul Andrija Ranogajec
Paulette Rapp
Patrick Rauber
Gale A. Rawson
John Reagan
Andrew B. Reed
Constance F. Reed
Stephen F. Reilly
Judith E. Reines
Richard Reinhart
Max Rendon
Robin Renfroe
Christine Retlev
Raymond Reynolds
Carol Reznikoff R.A.
Robert A. Rhodes
Mary Richardson Kennedy
Jennifer D Rimlinger
Dorrie Massaria Roberts
Sarah Robertson
Kathleen A. Robison
Rob Robinson AIA
Helen Rockwell
Frank Rogers
Lee Rogers
Joshua Roland
Jane Ellen Rosen
Kevin Rosser
Michael Rouchell
Patricia Rowland
Roslyn Rubin
Donald H. Ruggles
Lynn Russell
Suzanne Ryer
Lucrecia Sachs
William Sacrey
Lynda Safron
Victor H. Salas
Samantha Salden
Alan Salz
David Sammarco
Anne Samuel
Brian M. Scandariato
Anne Scardino
Marcia M. Schaeffer
Helen Schatiloff
Victoria Ann Schlegel
Gloria Schofner
Jack Schreiber

Jennifer K. Schreiber
Janet Schwartz
Joel A. Schwartz
Kelly Scibona
Peter Seidel
Tor Seidler
Annie Selke
John L. Sellers
Kenneth Robert Shane AIA
Steve Shard
Anne Shea
James Shearron
Mary A. Sheondin
Judy Sheridan
Gail Shields-Miller
Lisa Shire
Scott L. Shonk
Jeffrey Shopoff
Lara Shortall
Larry Sicular
Catherine Sidor
Sandra Silverman
Karen K. Simmons
Arlene Simon
Michael Simpson
Diane Sipos
Rita Sklar
Terri Slone
Anne Smith
Clinton Ross Smith
Demetra Canna Smith
Douglas A. Smith
Sarah Smith
Jeremy Sommer
German C. Sonntag
Jeffrey P. Soons
J. Leslee Sosa-Basualdo
Geoff Sosebee
Donna Southwick
Patricia Sovern
Steven Spandle
Brian Speas
Julie Sprague
Michele Sprietsma
Elsie St. Leger
Ann Stacy
Rob Stanford
Stephanie Stauffer
Carl Steele
Thomas Stegeman
Thomas Steiner
James Steinmeyer
Alan H. Stenzler
Martha Roby Stephens
Lani Sternerup
Suzanne Green Stevens
John Stewart
Edward Stick
David W. Stirling
Elise Stirzel
Stacy Stoffell
Nina Strachimirova
Mark C. Stromdahl
Holly Suich

Jerome J. Suich
Todd Sullivan
John Blaine Summitt AIA
Darren Sumner
Jerl Surratt
Phil Sutter
Richard Swann
Brian W. Sweny
Bart Swindall
Caroline Taggart
Galina Tahchieva
Tommy Talbot
Mark Taylor
Stephanie Tegnazian
Thomas Telesco
Victor Templeton
Brian Ten
E. Clothier Tepper
David Thiergartner
Janice E. Thill
Bruce Thomas
Hannah Thompson
Mark B. Thompson
Judy Frear Thorpe
Scott Tiffany
Margaret Anne Tockarshewsky
Thayer Tolles
Bill Toombs
Darius Toraby
A. Robert Torres
Michael Traines
Domenick Treschitta
Peter B. Trippi
Lucas J. Trunnell
Linda Tudisco
Andrew Tullis
Matthew Turner
Jennifer Turpin
John K. Turpin
Michael J. Tyrrell
Amie E. Uhrynowski
Marco A. Ungarelli
Cindy Urbanik
Adam Van Doren
Jannis Vann
David Vazquez
Yevgeniy Verbitskiy
Galo Verdesoto
Doreen Vermeersch
Raymond Vinciguerra
Mario Vitorino
Sandra Vitzthum
Adelene Vogel
Damian Wach
James Waite
Marshall Wakefield
Benjamin L. Walbert III, AIA
P. Jane Walmsley
Marigil M. Walsh
Paul Walter
Christopher V. Ward
Mr. and Mrs. Stanford
    Warshawsky
John Waters

Joan Watkins
Louise Weaver
David Webster
Mike Weich
Ruthzaly Weich
Amy A. Weinstein
Barbara Weinstein
Margot Wellington
Terry C. Wendell
Stacey Lee Weston
Johnsye White
Scott White
Terry Wildrick
Jann Williams
Robert Williams
Emily Williamson
Donald Windelspecht
Gail Caskey Winkler
Eric Witkowski
Kevin Wolfe
Peter H. Wollenberg
Kate Wood
Douglas W. Woods
John M. Woolsey
James Phillip Wright
Jonathan D. Wright
Howard Yaruss
Dean Yoder
Caroline Young
William Young
Shaun H. Yurcaba
Brandon Zabell
Gabriel Andres Zamora
Paula Zanes
Debra Zanoni
Jim Zanz
Nancy Zigelbaum
Nancy Zito
Charles Zivancev
Bob Zoni

PROFESSIONAL MEMBERS

CORPORATE SPONSORS

Balmer Architectural Mouldings, Inc.
The Burton Construction
  Corporation
Clark Construction Corp.
Oliver Cope Archiect
DSA Builders, Inc.
The D.H. Ellison Co.
Fairfax & Sammons Architects, PC
Ferguson & Shamamian Architects,
  LLC
Giannetti Architecture & Interiors,
  Inc.
The I. Grace Company
Victoria Hagan Interiors
Historical Concepts, Inc.
Alvin Holm Architects
K. Hovnanian Enterprises Inc.
Ike Kligerman Barkley Architects
Jenkens & Gilchrist LLP
Glenn Merlin Johnson
Kean Williams Giambertone, Ltd.
Kohler Company
Leyland Alliance LLC
London Boone, Inc./
  Mimi London, Inc.
Mayfair Construction Group LLC
Peter Pennoyer Architects, PC
Project Solutions, LLC
Foster Reeve & Associates
RD Rice Construction, Inc.
Ritner Architectural Group
Robinson Iron Corporation
SBD Kitchens, LLC
G.P. Schafer Architect, PLLC
David M. Schwarz Architectural
  Services, Inc.
Seaside Community Develpoment
  Corp.
Somerset Partners, LLC
Symm Group Limited
Ken Tate Architect, P.A.
Traditional Cut Stone, Ltd.
TVK & Associates dba Robinson
  Finishes
Unico, Inc.
University of Notre Dame School
  of Architecture
Urban Design Associates
Ellen Valentine
Voith & McTavish Architecture
Wadia Associates, Inc.
Waterworks
Zeluck, Inc.
Zepsa Architectural Woodwork
  and Stairs

CORPORATE FRIENDS

Alisberg Parker, LLC
Jane Antonacci & Associates
Appleton & Associates, Inc.
Ariel, The Art of Building
Armstrong World Industries, Inc.
Artistic Doors and Windows
Babey Moulton Jue & Booth
Biglin Architectural Group
BSF Properties
James F. Carter, Inc.
Cooper, Robertson & Partners
Cowtan and Tout
Cullman & Kravis, Inc.
Curtis and Windham
Drake Design Associates
Mark P. Finlay Architects, AIA
Fokine Construction Services
The Green-Wood Cemetery
The Grubb Company
Hablinski + Manion Architecture
  LLP
Harrison Design Associates
Hilton-VanderHorn Architects
Hobbs, Incorporated
Edmund D. Hollander Landscape
  Architect Design PC
Hottenroth & Joseph Architects
Laura Hunt Inc.
Interiors Unlimited
Jamb Limited
Jones Footer Margeotes & Partners
KAA Design Group, Inc.
Kais Custom Builders
L.M.C. Corp
Brian J. McCarthy, Inc.
Greg Mix Associates Architect, Inc.
Charlotte Moss Interior Design
Deborah Nevins & Associates
New York Builders Supply Corp.
New York School of Interior Design
Mark Ostensen
Katherine Pasternack
Restore Media, LLC
Danielle Roberts Interiors
Robert Sinclair
Richard Skinner & Associates, PL
Ryan Associates
Stancil Studios
Eric Stengel Architecture
John Stewart Designs, Inc.
Tendura
Thoughtforms Corporation
Eric Watson Architect, P.A.
Windsor Mill
The Wiseman Group
CVM Engineers

CORPORATE MEMBERS

Robert Bentley Adams AIA
ADL III Architecture PC
Aedicule Fine Framemaking
Agrell Architectural Carving, Ltd.
AJ.T Architect PC
Albert, Righter & Tittmann
  Architcects
Stephen Alesch
American Traditions by Tara, Inc.
Kristin Anderson
Richard Anderson
Anderson Architectural &
  Construction Management
Anthemion Construction Services,
  LLC
Aaron Anthony, Inc.
Architectural Detail Group Inc.
Architectural Details and Millwork,
  Inc.
Architectural Marketing &
  Management
Walter S. Arnold
Arttus Period Interiors
Eve Ashcraft Studio
Austin Patterson Disston Architects
Authentic Pine Floors
Authentic Provence Inc.
B&D Studio LLC
William T. Baker & Associates
Ball and Ball Hardware
Ballash Construction
Pamela Banker Associates, Inc.
Charlie Barnett Associates
Marco Battistotti Inc.
Mircea Bazac
Karen Beam
Robert Beard
Bob Becker Construction
  Management
The Beehive Foundation
Robin Bell Design Inc.
Benchmark Design International,
  Inc.
Robert Bennett Architect
B Five Studio LLP
Minor L. Bishop
Jill Biskin Fine Arts
FL Bissinger, Inc.
BKSK Architects LLP
Laura Blanco Interiors
Geoffrey Blatt
John Blatteau Associates
James Bleecker Photography
Peter Block & Associates
  Architects, Inc.
Bogden Design Studio
Joan Boone Architect Planner
Nancy Boszhardt Incorporated
Bourgeois Bohème
Mark Bradley Designs
Rebecca Bradley Interior Design
Dennis Brady
Brady Design Associates
Anne Brant Spaces
Breakwater Renovation & Design,
  LLC

Brett Design, Inc.
Ronald Bricke & Associates, Inc.
Jim Brown
Jonathan Browning Studios
Bryan & Contreras, LLC
Timothy Bryant Architect
Mario Buatta
Building Science Associates, Inc.
Daron Builta
Bump Construction
Michael Burch Architects
Brian P. Calandro Associates, LLC
Calhoun Properties
Calori Architects
Dean Camenares
Cameron Asociates
Campbell Design Associates Inc.
Campbell/Smith Architects
Cannon Design
Carolina Residential Design
Susanne Earls Carr, Inc.
Laura Casale Architect
Heather Cass
Catalano Architects
Charrette Design Group
Chesney's
Christie's Los Angeles
Churchill Brothers, LLC
Classical Home Design, Inc.
A Classical Studio for Residential
  Architecture
Clawson Architects
Catherine Clay
Dale Cohen Design Studio
Eric Cohler Design, Inc.
Cate Comerford AIA
Classic Garden Ornaments Ltd.
Philip Colleck, Ltd.
The Commonwealth Fund
Christopher Corcoran Incorporated
Core Home, LLC
Cornice & Rose Int., LLC
The Cotton District
Craft Architecture, PC
Creme Fresh, Inc.
Crisp Architects
Crone Associates Architecture, LLC
Cronk Duch Partners
Crowe Design & Associates, LLC
Marianne Cusato
Elizabeth Cutler Design
Mark Darley
Darnell & Company
DASA Plc.
Robert Dean Architects
Decorative Artworks
Allan Cooper Dell Interiors
Dennis D. Dell'Angelo
Denning Cabinetry
Derrick Designs
Athalie Derse
Design Concepts Plans, Inc.
Designer Doors, Inc.
Designer's 2
Designer Wall Finishes
David Desmond, Inc.

Donald H. Dewey
Peter DeWitt Architect PLLC
Di Biase Filkoff Architects
Dickson Development Corp.
The Studio of M.A. Dixon, FAIA
Stanly D. Dixon Architect
Kim Doggett
Dorosinski Campbell Design
  Associates, Inc.
James Doyle Design Associates LLC
Gillian Drummond Interior Design
DSI Entertainment Systems
Ralph Duesing, AIA
Don Duffy Architecture
Douglas Durkin Design, Inc.
Susan Durrett Garden Design
DVisionOne, Architects, LLC
Dwyer & Sae-Eng, Inc.
Eberlein Design Consultants
Lynette Edmonds
Edwards Architecture
Helene Eklen Interior Design
Elizabeth Elsey
Equinox Antiques & Fine Art
ERG Architect
William R. Eubanks Interior
  Design, Inc.
European Copper, LLC
Ervin, Lovett, & Miller, Inc.
Estudio J. Loyzaga
EverGreene Painting Studios, Inc.
Emmanuel Fillion
Fischer & Jirouch
Christopher Flacke
Flower Construction
Franck & Lohsen Architects, Inc.
Frazier Associates, Architects
  & Planners
Robert Frear Architects
Angela Free Interior Design
Jacob Froehlich Cabinetmakers, Inc.
M. Jane Gaillard Inc.
Kathleen Galvin
Kaja Gam Design
Larry W. Garnett & Associates, Inc.
Garrell Associates, Inc.
G. George & Co.
Thomas Gibb
John Gilmer Architects, Inc.
The Giust Gallery
Robert Glickman & Associates, Inc.
GMA Architects
Charles Paul Goebel Architect, Ltd.
Gold Coast Metal Works, Inc.
Michael Goldman Architect, PC
GOOD/Architecture
Dan K. Gordon Associates, Inc.
Gorton Associates, Inc.
Mitchell Gosar Fine Art
Thierry Goux
The Grand Prospect Hall
Grand River Builders, Inc.
R.S. Granoff Architects PC
Cindy Grant Architecture
Graphic Builders, Inc.
Grenfell Architecture PLLC

Griffin Interiors
Griffin Warehouse Associates
Group 3 Architecture-Interiors-
   Planning
GuildQuality Inc.
Gullans and Brooks Associates, Inc.
Jim Hackett
Shannon Hall Designs
Hallberg-Wiseley Designers
Hammond Beeby Rupert Ainge, Inc.
Alice Hancock
David D. Harlan, Architects
Chuck Harrison Residential Design
Hartman-Cox Architects
Hartmann-Sanders/Dixie Pacific
David Hatcher
Haven Properties
Keven Hawkins Inc.
Kitty Hawks Inc.
Constance T. Haydock
   Landscape Architect, PC
H.T. Hayslett & Co.
HB&G Building Products
HDB Architects Inc.
Hedrick Brothers Construction
George T. Heery, FAIA
Laura Heery, Architecture &
   Planning
William Hefner LLC
Heiler Fine Woodworking
Judith F. Hernstadt
Jack Herr Design Associates, Inc.
Hickox Williams Architects
Hiland Hall Turner Architects
Historic Doors
Historic Housefitters Co.
Kenneth Hitchens Architect
Richard Holz, Inc.
Howard Design Studio, LLC
Harry Gandy Howle Architect &
   Associates, PA
Jeffrey M. Housley
Hull Historical Restoration
Antonia Hutt & Associates, Inc.
Michael G. Imber, Architects
Interior Design Solutions
International Classical Architecture
International Fine Art
   Conservation Studios
I'On Group
Isabelle's Table
Molly Isaksen Interiors, Inc.
Jesenko Isanovic
Island Diversified, Inc.
Ivy Walk, Inc.
Clifton Jaeger LLC
Ashley Roi Jenkins Design
Ken Jennings Design, Ltd.
Kate Johns AIA
Ricky A. Johnson
Robert S. Johnson
Benjamin Jones & Associates
   Architecture and Planning
David Jones Architects
Scott Joyce Design, Inc.
Gary William Justiss, Architect

KAHA Architectural Elements
Robert Kaler Architect
KANON Roman Architecture
Barry Katz Homebuilding
KDA Development Corporation
Jack Kelly & Partners
Virginia W. Kelsey, AIA
P.S. Kennedy-Grant Architect
Kensington & Associates
David Kidd Studios
J.R. King III Custom Homes &
   Designs, Inc.
King Architectural Metals
Kiskaddon Architects, PLC
KMNelson Design
Mary V. Knackstedt
Knick Custom Home Design
Brent A. Kovalchik
Peter Kramer Architecture
The Lane Group, Inc.
Lantern Masters, Inc.
Joel Laseter Architect
Lawrance Architectural Presentations
Daniel Lee Architect
Jonathan Lee Architects
Legacy Design Group, Inc.
Leitenberger/Bronfman Architects
James Leslie Design Associates
Leverone Design
Jeffrey Levinson
Lichten Craig Architects LLP
William B. Litchfield Residential
   Designs, Inc.
Gregory Lombardi Design, Inc.
Maricris Longo
Looney Ricks Kiss Architects, Inc.
Loop Worx
Jonathan Love
The Lotus Collection
Low Tide Designs
Ludowici Roof Tile
Madison Cox Design Inc.
Madison Spencer Architects
David R. Mango Design Group, Inc.
Margolis Inc.
C. Mariani Antiques
G.D. Markey
Marlay Design Ltd.
Marquiss, Inc.
Mallory Marshall Interiors
Thomas P. Matthews, Architect LLC
M-Boss, Inc.
Virgil W. McDowell, Inc.
Kenneth McCook
R.J. McCormack Architect, Inc.
Leslie McCormick
McCoy Construction
McCrery Architects, LLC
McKinnon and Harris, Inc.
Duncan McRoberts Associates
MDL Lighting Design
Meleca Architecture
Merrill and Pastor Archictects
Merrimack Design Associates
Meyer & Meyer Architects
Meyer Architecture

Peter Mikulik
Eric Milby
Clinton Miller & Associates
Jonathan Miller Architects
Miller Architecture
Deborah Mills Woodcarving
John Milner Architects, Inc.
Mitchell Studio LLC
Richard Mock Designs
Moor & Associates, Architects, P.A.
Morales-Keesee Design Associates
The Morgan Company of
   Charleston, Inc.
Malcolm G. Morris
Shelley Morris Interior Design, Ltd.
Craig Morrison Architect
Moser Design Group
Barbara Moss Design
Geoffrey Mouen Architects
Munder Skiles
Michael Murphy
Murphy Design & Drafting
Robert Murphy Painting and
   Design, Inc.
Narmour Wright Creech,
   Architecture Planning Int
Adrienne Neff Design Services
Neumann Lewis & Buchanan
   Architects
The New Urban Guild
NHM Interiors
Nina's Nuances, Inc.
Amanda Nisbet Design, Inc.
Noble Interiors Inc.
Nottingham Builders and Cabinets
Oak Grove Restoration Company
Dan Ollis
Ruthann Olsson
Padgett Residential Design, Inc.
Arturo Palombo Architecture, LLC
Florian Papp Antiques and Art
   Galllery
F.H. Perry — Builder
Period Style Homes, Inc.
Kirk E. Peterson & Associates
   Architects
David Phoenix Interior Design
Pierce Architects
Plath & Company, Inc.
Pompei A.D.
Portera Antique Spanish Doors
Donald Powers Architects
Preservation Foundation of
   Palm Beach
Provenance Collections Ltd.
Anthony M. Pucillo
Bethany Puopolo
John Kenneth Pursley Architecture
Queen Charlotte Antiques
Bradford Radnor LP
T.N. Rajkovic Archtiect, Ltd.
Mary Randelman
RCI Company Architects
Real Illusions Inc.
Residential Design Solutions, Inc.
Reynolds, Smith & Hills, Inc.

Rhomboid Sax
Ricci Greene Associates
Georgina Rice & Co., Inc.
Donald Richardson, AIA
Randall A. Ridless, LLC
Robertson Interiors
Romero Cook Design Studio
E.M. Rose Builders Inc.
Rose Iron Works
Rossi Antiques
Penelope Rozis Interior Design
Don Ruth, FAIBD
Ryall Porter Architects
Ryan Associates
Robert Safran Architect
Alexandros C. Samaras &
   Associates SA
Samsel Architects
Scot P. Samuelson, AIA
Maureen Sanborn
The Sater Group, Inc.
James Schettino, Architect
Sean W. Scully
Sebastian & Associates, Inc.
Shears & Window
Charles Shipp/Architect
Bruce Shostak
Shumake & Williams, PC
Simpson & Brown Architects
Robert G. Sinclair Architecture, Inc.
Patti Skouras, Inc.
Sloan Architects, PC
SM Architects, Inc.
Thomas Gordon Smith Architects
Smith Architectural Group
T.V. Smith Design
Philip Hugh Smith Interior Design
E. Frank Smith Residential
   Design, Inc.
Edward H. Springs Interiors, Inc.
Sotheby's International Realty
K Spiegelman Design Studio Inc.
Spitzmiller & Norris, Inc.
John B. Springer
G. Morris Steinbraker & Son, Inc.
St. Clair Builders, Inc.
St. George Euro Designs Corp.
Stocker Hoesterey Montenegro
   Architects
Stonebridge @ 59th
Madeline Stuart & Associates
Studio Cooper
Studio for Civil Architecture, PLLC
Studio SPF, LLC
Sroka Design, Inc.
Steichen Interior Design
Sullivan Goulette
Super Enterprises
James Swan & Company Inc.
Hal Swanson
Ricardo Taborga Architect
Tall Grass Interiors
Tanglewood Conservatories
TC2 Design, Inc.
Andre Tchelistcheff Architect
Therien & Co.

Thistle & Rose
Timberlane Woodcrafters, Inc.
Timeless Architectural
   Reproductions, Inc.
Matthew Tirschwell
Tomasetti Architects
Don Tooley
Torti Gallas and Partners
Traditional Architecture, Inc.
Trafidlo Design
Tri-State Elevator Co., Inc.
Trust for Architectural Easements
Gary Turlington Design &
   Consulting
US Courts
Jessica Vaule Interiors
Russell Versaci Architecture
Visbeen Associates, Inc.
Vitoch Interiors Ltd.
Vogel Residential Design
Voila Gallery
Vollmer Associates LLP
Von Morris Corporation
Birgitta Von Zelowitz
R. Walsh Gate & Railing Co.
Doug Walter Architects
Wayner Construction Company,
   Inc.
Weaver Design Group
Dennis Wedlick LLC
Martin Eli Weil Restoration
   Architect
Michael Whaley Interiors, Inc.
Hubert Whitlock Builders, Inc.
Wickstead, Inc.
Wiemann Ironworks
Winterthur at Home
Wilfrid Wong Design Int'l.
Woodstone Architectural Doors
   and Windows
Worth Home Products
James R. Youngson
Linda Yowell Architect
Peter Zimmerman Architects Inc.
Paul Zink Architect
Zivkovic Connolly Architects PC

*Members between January 1, 2005 and
August 15, 2007*

Residence in Atherton, California

ANDREW SKURMAN, ARCHITECT

3654 SACRAMENTO STREET
SAN FRANCISCO CA 94118
415/440-4480

32 RUE FABERT
PARIS 75007
33 (0) 6 08 60 48 32

www.skurman.com

ARIEL

the art of building

FOR MORE INFORMATION ABOUT
THE ART OF BUILDING,
PLEASE CONTACT KELLY THOMPSON
AT 212-987-0666
OR INFO@ARIEL-LLC.COM

315 EAST 91 STREET, 5TH FLOOR
NEW YORK CITY 10128

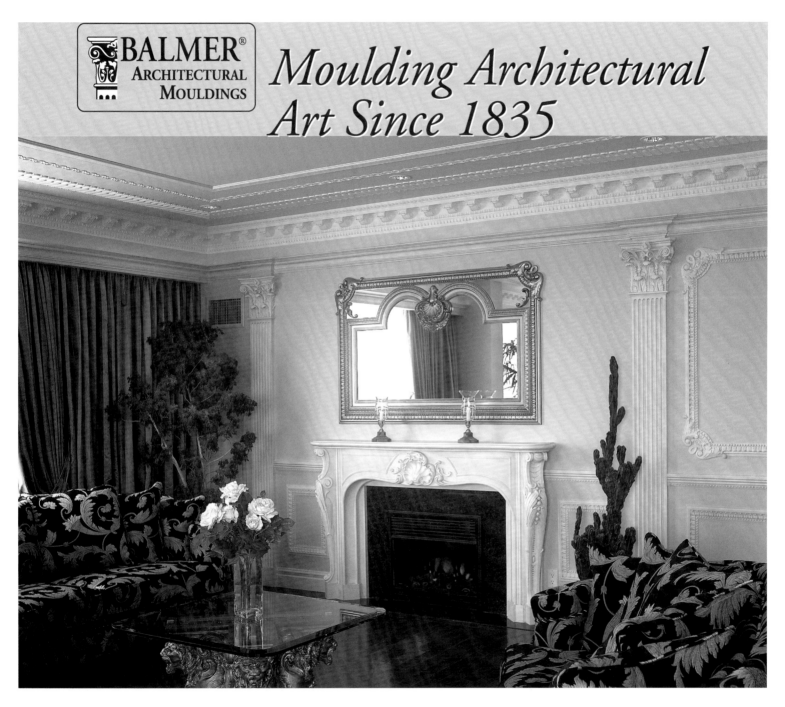

BALMER®
ARCHITECTURAL
MOULDINGS

Moulding Architectural Art Since 1835

FROM DESIGN INCEPTION TO INSTALLATION

CUSTOM – IN-STOCK – 3D CAD/CAM

www.balmer.com

BROCKSCHMIDT & COLEMAN DECORATION AND DESIGN
139 READE STREET NEW YORK CITY 10013 212.608.5065

CARNEGIE HILL BOOKS
Rare & Out-of-print Books and Monographs

Architecture - Interior Design - Decorative Arts
Gardens & Landscape Architecture

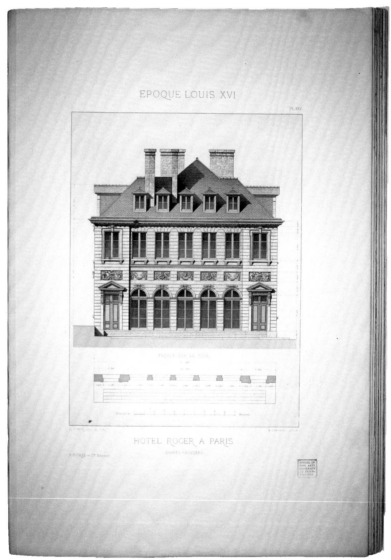

"Hotel Roger, Paris" from Architecture Epoque Louis XVI

Open By Appointment
206 East 90th Street #3W
New York, NY 10128

Tel - 212 410-9085   Web - www.carnegiehillbooks.com
Email - ann@carnegiehillbooks.com

CHADSWORTH'S 1.800.COLUMNS®

www.columns.com

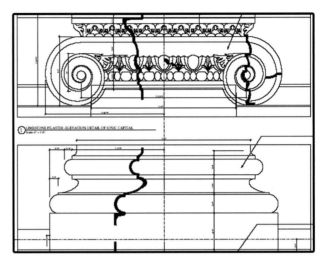

THE CLASSIC GROUP, INC.

ARCHITECTS AND BUILDERS

420 Bedford St., Lexington, MA 02420   781-761-1200

www.theclassicgroup.net

CURTIS & WINDHAM

Architects

3815 MONTROSE BLVD. SUITE 100

HOUSTON TEXAS 77006

713-942-7251

Since 1973

◄••►

Servicing the New York City Residential Community
with High-Quality Electrical Construction

DECORA ELECTRIC CO., INC.

135 LINCOLN AVENUE · BRONX, NY 10454 · TEL 718-585-3800 · FAX 718-402-2804

◄••►

DYAD COMMUNICATIONS *design office*

INTEGRATING AESTHETICS WITH REASON ~ IDENTITY, PRINT AND WEB
1429 Walnut Street, #700 / Philadelphia, PA 19102 / *dyadcom.com* / 215-636-0505

E.R. BUTLER & CO.

E.R. BUTLER & CO.

Enoch Robinson Co. Collection

FINE ARCHITECTURAL, BUILDERS' AND CABINETMAKERS' HARDWARE

ERIC J. SMITH ARCHITECTS

72 SPRING STREET, SEVENTH FLOOR, NEW YORK, N.Y. 10012

(212) 334-3993 PHONE   (212) 334-3339 FAX

THE PROPOSED CHARLESTON HOTEL ON MARION SQUARE, CHARLESTON, SOUTH CAROLINA

FAIRFAX & SAMMONS
TRADITIONAL ARCHITECTURE FOR THE MODERN WORLD
————CHARLESTON ~ NEW YORK ~ PALM BEACH————

FAIRFAXANDSAMMONS.COM

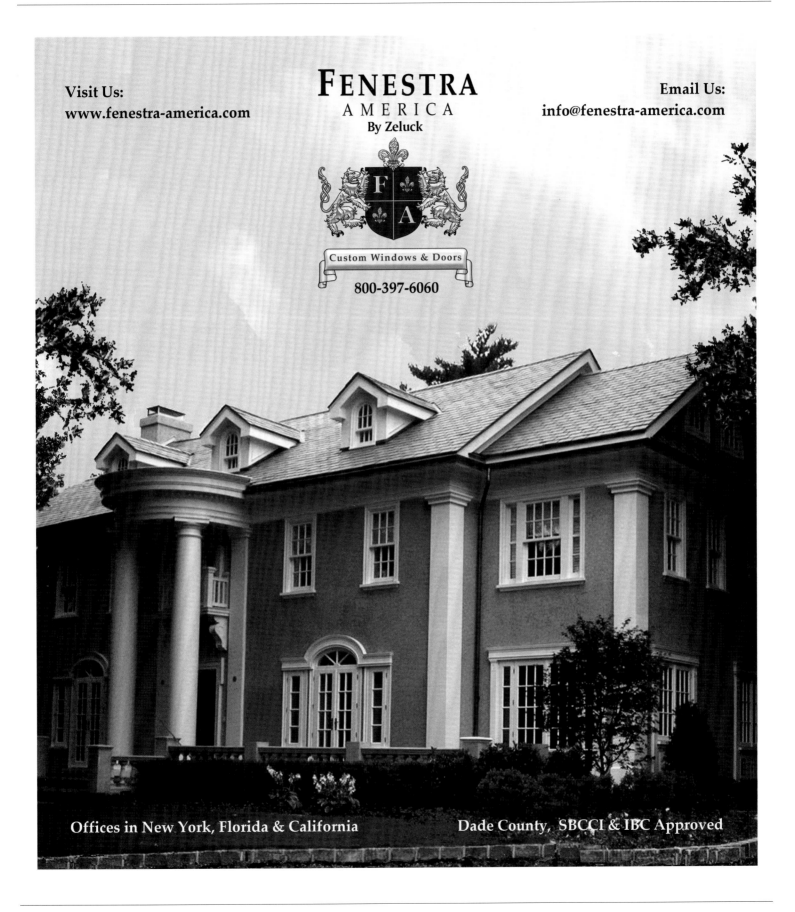

FERGUSON &
SHAMAMIAN
ARCHITECTS, LLP

270 LAFAYETTE STREET, NEW YORK, NEW YORK 10012
TELEPHONE: 212-941-8088   TELEFAX: 212-941-8089   www.fergusonshamamian.com

G. P. SCHAFER ARCHITECT, PLLC

——— ARCHITECTURE & DESIGN ———

270 LAFAYETTE STREET, SUITE 1302, NEW YORK CITY 10012, TELEPHONE (212) 965-1355

WWW.GPSCHAFER.COM

David D. Harlan
Architects, LLC

938 Chapel Street New Haven Connecticut 06510
TEL 203.495.8032 FAX 203.495.8034
WWW.DDHARCHITECTS.COM

"Casale"
Additions and Renovation
Outskirts of Rome
2005

© Peter Aaron/Esto.

IKE KLIGERMAN BARKLEY ARCHITECTS P.C.

330 WEST FORTY-SECOND STREET • NEW YORK NY 10036

TELEPHONE 212 268 0128 • ONLINE WWW.IKBA.COM

Jacob Froehlich
FINE ARCHITECTURAL MILLWORK
~ est. 1865 ~

560 BARRY STREET, BRONX, NEW YORK 10474 ⁎ TELEPHONE (718) 893-1300
JFROEHLICH.COM

JAMES BLEECKER

❧

ARCHITECTURAL PHOTOGRAPHY

ESTATE PORTFOLIOS

FINE ART PRINTS

❧

JOHN B. MURRAY ARCHITECT, LLC

48 West 37th Street, 10th Floor, New York, New York

212·242·8600

WWW.JBMARCHITECT.COM

Leonard Porter, *Wall Decoration in the 'Etruscan' Style*, 2002, Oil on canvas, 42 x 30 inches.
© Leonard Porter MMII · For more information, please visit: www.leonardporter.com

LEONARD · PORTER · STVDIO
PAINTINGS OF ANTIQVITY AND CLASSICAL MYTHOLOGY

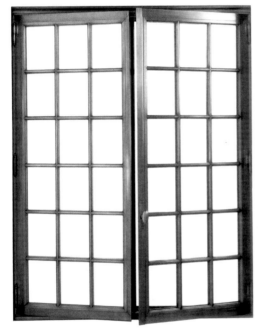

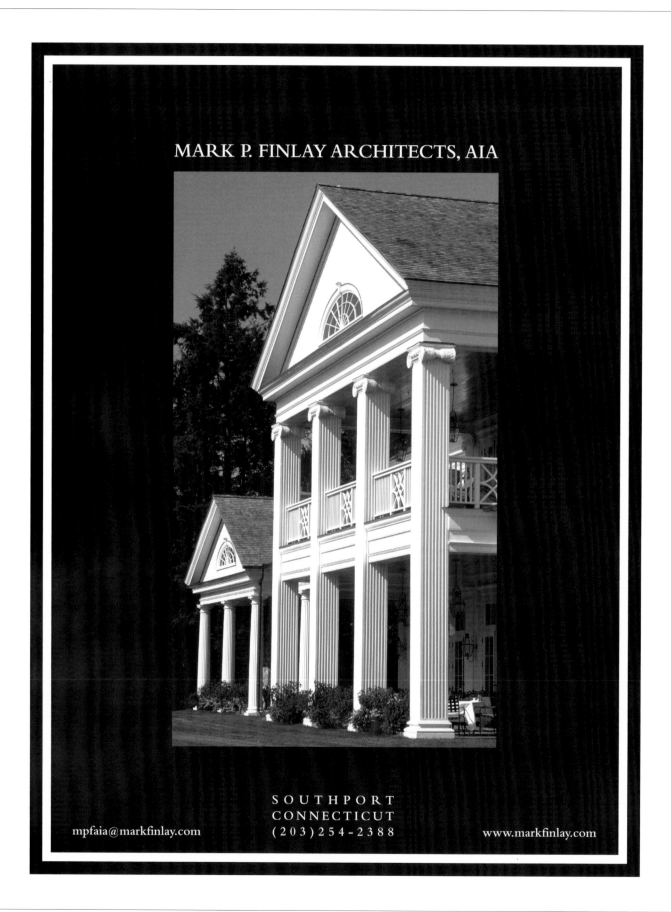

MARK P. FINLAY ARCHITECTS, AIA

SOUTHPORT
CONNECTICUT
(203) 254-2388

mpfaia@markfinlay.com   www.markfinlay.com

FACADE DETAIL OF HOUSE, 2004

PETER PENNOYER ARCHITECTS
432 Park Avenue South, 11th Floor, New York, New York 10016

PPAPC.COM

Watercolor by Anton Glikin

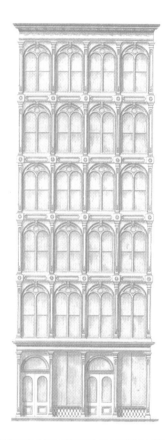

House at Seaside, Florida

ROBERT A.M.
STERN
ARCHITECTS

460 West 34th Street New York, New York 10001
Tel 212 967 5100   Fax 212 967 5588
www.ramsa.com

Interior by Robin Bell

ROBIN BELL DESIGN, INC.

155 East 56th Street New York, New York 10022 Telephone: 212.753.5600

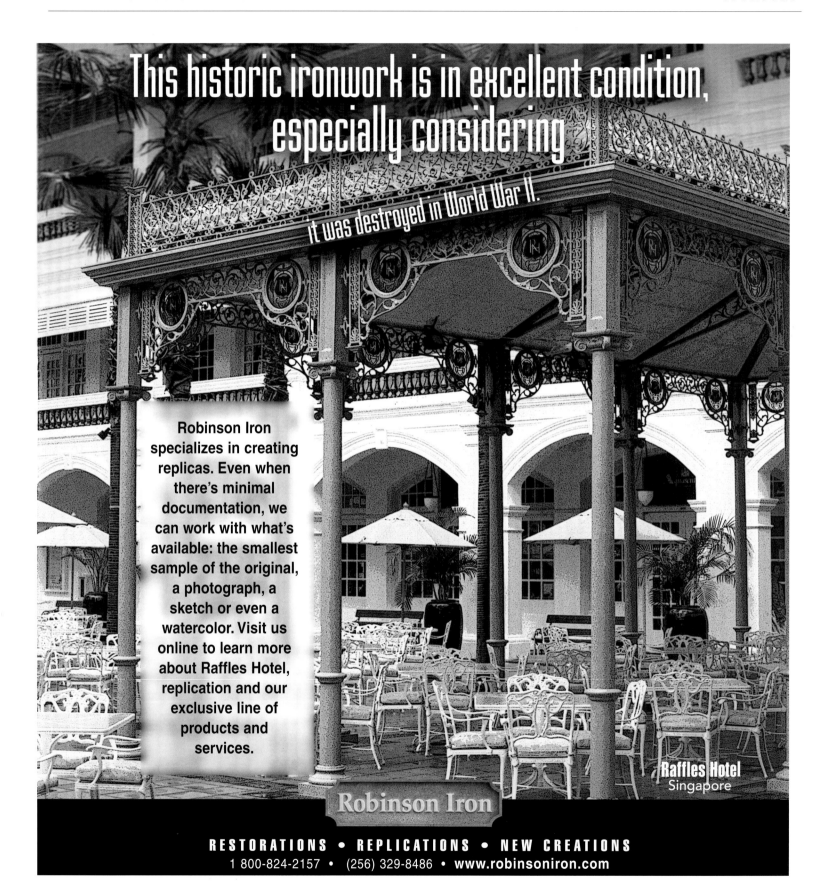

This historic ironwork is in excellent condition, especially considering

It was destroyed in World War II.

Robinson Iron specializes in creating replicas. Even when there's minimal documentation, we can work with what's available: the smallest sample of the original, a photograph, a sketch or even a watercolor. Visit us online to learn more about Raffles Hotel, replication and our exclusive line of products and services.

Raffles Hotel
Singapore

Robinson Iron

RESTORATIONS • REPLICATIONS • NEW CREATIONS
1 800-824-2157 • (256) 329-8486 • www.robinsoniron.com

ALEXANDRA PARK, ATLANTA, GEORGIA
Residence and monument to commemorate the visit of the Princess Royal

RODNEY M. COOK INTERESTS

3855 RANDALL MILL ROAD N.W.
ATLANTA, GEORGIA 30327
PHONE (404) 237-8970
FAX (404) 237-1707

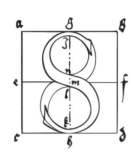

Architecture: Shope Reno Wharton Associates

Thoughtforms www.thoughtforms-corp.com

Custom Builder | West Acton, MA | Osterville, MA
978.263.6019 | 508.420.5700

urban ARCHAEOLOGY

INSPIRED BY A FRENCH
SCONCE DESIGNED IN
THE LATE 1920'S.
AVAILABLE IN VARIOUS
METAL FINISHES WITH
AN ALABASTER SHADE.
UL LISTED FOR DRY
LOCATIONS 60W.
ONE OF 54 INTERIOR
SCONCES BY URBAN
ARCHAEOLOGY.

URBANARCHAEOLOGY.COM

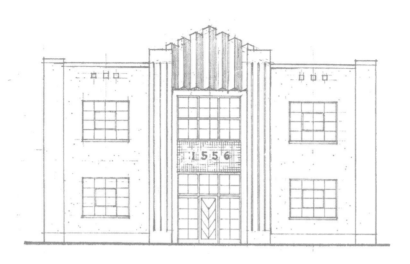

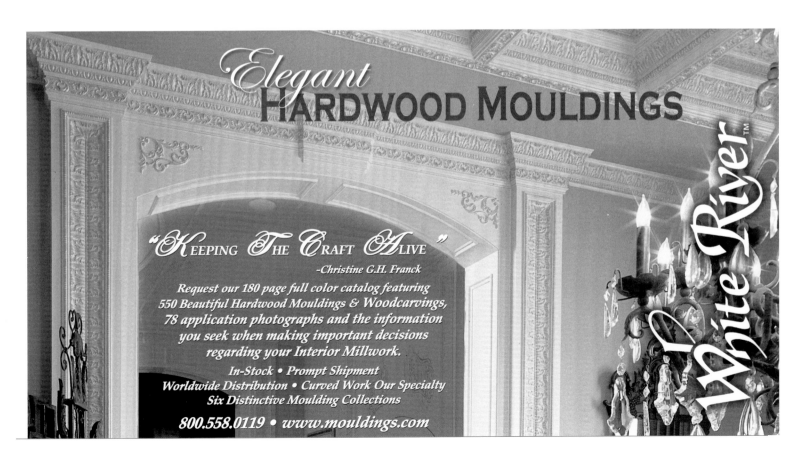

Index

Page numbers in italic refer to illustrations.
Page numbers followed by n. refer to numbered endnotes.
Locations of structures discussed in the text are indexed
by U.S. state or by country.

COLOPHON

Production:
Composed with Quark XPress 7.01 and Mac OS X

Text: Lustro Dull 100# Text
Cover: Lustro Dull 100# Cover
Separations: 300 line screen
Printing: Offset Lithography
Binding: Perfect Bound
Edition: 3,500

Typefaces:
Centaur, designed by Bruce Rogers
for the Metropolitan Museum in 1912–14,
based on the Roman type cut in Venice by Nicolas Jensen in 1469.

Trajan, designed by Carol Twombly in 1988,
based on the inscription carved on the pedestal of
Trajan's column Rome, 113 A.D.